TARNISHED LEGACY

A Reluctant Memoir

PATRICIA REID-MERRITT

outskirts
press

Dedication

To my ancestors:
Pattie Wright,
Jessie Mae Chapel,
Lester Chapel,
Rosa Hill Reid,
Lee Reid,
and
Curtis MacDonald Reid, Sr.

Table of Contents

July 30th, 2000 –
The Long Journey Home

"*When, do you think, is the best time to visit the dead?*"

It was a pestering thought, one I'd pondered for a very long time. I mean, "*Is there ever a good day to visit your dearly departed relatives in a poor Black cemetery on the edge of town?*" Probably not. Death, dying, funerals and burials: All part of a wretched human experience forced upon our very mortal existence. But dying is the natural ending to a wonderful life; or is it, "Life sucks and then you die?"

It was a brilliant summer morning. Crisp, clear, powdery blue skies with mysterious looking white puffy clouds greet me as I leave the driveway. The radio said to expect a high of 85°, with low humidity. The atmosphere smells clean, Clorox clean. It reminded me of the scent that permeated the air when Granny (my paternal grandmother) used to do the laundry for a house filled with six smelly kids. I purposefully waited for the right day, the right time, and the right moment. I wanted to make certain that my first visit to the graveyard would not be on a rain-soaked, weather-dreary Sunday afternoon when thoughts of the glory of God, religion and doing good deeds were still fresh in everyone's mind following the three hour morning service. It's a Tuesday morning, the middle of the week, and dead-smack in the midst of an uneventful summer. Today is perfect.

There's a part of me that feels ridiculous. Yes, totally stupid! After all, it's been more than forty years since Great Grandmother Pattie died; thirty-three since the death of her daughter, Grandmother Jessie; twenty-eight years since my Daddy died from alcoholism, cirrhosis of the liver and diabetes; and, twenty-seven since his mama, Granny, followed him to the grave nine months after he passed away. Still, with all those deaths, I had never gone to a cemetery, and I had never been a part of any kind of memorial or burial service. Throughout most of my life I have been morbidly frightened of death, dying and all the strange social customs and rituals that followed the dead to heaven – or to hell if you cut up too much before your departure. And in the larger scale of things, I somehow knew that my life was small, insignificant and inconsequential. Nothing I did really mattered. Yet, I wondered if anybody would truly miss me once I was gone. Losing family members was always emotionally unsettling to me. When death came a calling, time after time again, the family always felt it prudent to leave me at home for the final end of life send-off services. And, ever so appreciatively, I stayed put. However, at this point in my life a visit to the cemetery is an absolute must, a rite of passage necessitated by guilt, maturity and morbid curiosity.

Several years earlier I started to question all of my living relatives about the final resting place of our ancestors. I'm uncertain what put me on this path. I suspect some of it can be attributed to my discover-your-heritage-blacker-than-black-back-to your-roots Afrocentric lifestyle. But it's much deeper than that. After a series of brief question and answer sessions with resistant family members (many of whom are steeped in denial about our ancestral legacy), I discovered that all of these graves were unmarked. I found that to be extremely disturbing. It was downright sacrilegious. *"How does one live a good life, praise God, contribute productive offspring to the clan and then leave this Earth in an unmarked, pauper-style grave?"* It just didn't seem right.

Stranger still, no one in the family seemed to care very much at all about those who were dead and gone. This was true for the Chapels and the Reids – the progenitors of our fifth generation African American family. I couldn't help but question why. For more than three decades I had been reading about the intertwining nature of the living and the dead. How the dead are never really gone as long as the living spoke their names; and how the ancestors were always present, there to guide you in times of need. They were intercedents, temporarily filling in for God who was often too busy to take care of the little problems. Your ancestors handled all the small favors, like praying for food, money and good fortune when you simply didn't have enough. Yes, the celebration of one's life after death is a time-honored African tradition. But little of this appeared to be true for the Reids, for the Chapels, or for us. Once you were dead you were gone: *Dead and gone.* And how you remembered the dead were lessons that I learned early in childhood and carried with me throughout my adult life.

I do recall that on rare occasions family members talked about the dearly departed, but mostly to tell jokes about how they spent their time here on Earth. When the family gathered, someone would, inevitably, mention Heavyweight. That's the nickname we gave to our Daddy. He was a tall, burly, handsome man, six feet two, at least 280 pounds. He possessed perfectly flawless, copper-toned brown skin with a head full of jet-black wavy hair. He looked especially good when he slicked on the Murray's grease from the orange and black can that seemed to be on everyone's dresser long before the advent of the afro. His stomach was his most prominent feature; he always looked to be at least eight months pregnant. Daddy seemed to have trouble shifting his body from one side to the other, and sometimes he swayed as if he would lose his balance. Struggling to get out of his favorite greased stained, ratty-looking brown chair, he always seemed stuck, as if the force of gravity, with the assistance of a suction cup, had glued his butt to the bottom of the cushion. My brother, Wayman, the fourth child born into the fifth generation Reid clan, convincingly argued that his body was trapped by mounds of fat from lard, pork chops and fried chicken and preceded to call him Heavyweight. We all followed suit.

Daddy was Granny's baby. Lee, Varnell, Maggie and Susan were her children too, but Curtis, my daddy, was her baby. Daddy never got used to being away from his mama, and my Granny never cut him loose. No one was surprised when she died nine months after he passed.

"Lord, take me now," she probably shouted, just at the moment when she heard of his passing, when none were near to hear her wailing cries. And the Lord did.

I'm certain that she just willed herself to death. Long after their passing we often joked about the symbiotic relationship that existed between mother and son and wondered what life would have been like if Daddy had truly separated himself from Granny.

But we also told jokes about Momma's dead relatives too. They were the light-bright, nearly white people who wanted to be Black and embrace their culture long before it was fashionable. Great Grandmother Pattie was the love child of a white Irishman and a poor mulatta and Native American washerwoman. She could pass, but decided quite early in life that Black was the thing to be. Her daughter, Jessie, possessed a hint of color, what folks might describe today as vanilla, without the bean. She, too, could trick people into thinking that she was a white woman. However, Grandmother Jessie had a penchant for chiseled-faced, chocolate colored Black men. To her great pleasure, all six of her children - Savannah, Lester, Lucille, Dorethea, Edward and Nita - are different shades of coffee color brown, some with a little more cream than others. She wouldn't have had it any other way.

The Reids were southern poor folks who always bragged about their heritage being directly linked to a rich southern white man who was vice-president of the United States; the Chapels were uppity urban dwellers with a strong northern Black middle class heritage. The families lived in sharp contrast to one another. Yet, they were all laid to rest in the same Colored cemetery in unmarked graves in a place called Eden. And no one gave two hoots or a damn. Those living were still mad at the dead about some unknown slight, harshly spoken words or physical altercation. Years passed, but they hadn't gotten over it quite yet.

I was finally ready for my trip to Eden. Sharon, my dear undertaker friend of more than thirty-five years, tried to prepare me for the visit.

"Keep in mind that they're Black," she cautioned.

"What are you trying to say?" I snapped back in an instant. I was always quick to respond defensively when snide, derogatory remarks were made about my people. I sometimes viewed myself as the defender of the race: an ivy-league educated college professor who knew a thing or two about our cultural heritage.

"You know that our folks don't spend as much money on the upkeep of burial grounds," Sharon responded vigorously. "Half the time, there's barely enough money to take care of the body and provide a proper send-off. Maintaining the burial site is just not a high priority for folks, especially not the ones who have been buried in Eden."

The burial site - one's final resting place - not a high priority for Black folks? How could that be the case?

I had no real point of reference to fully comprehend what she was saying. I did, however, remember some controversy surrounding the gravesite of tennis legend Arthur Ashe somewhere in Virginia. The upkeep was so poor, the family actually threatened to remove his body and have it buried elsewhere.

"What?" I shouted distressingly. "Is this a ghetto site?" I questioned with an equal amount of guilt, anxiety and bitterness in my voice.

"Call before you go," she cautioned. "Make certain that you have all the right information regarding the deceased. And don't be surprised if they can't find the bodies."

"Can't find the bodies!" I shrieked. My sweat glands cut loose, sending heavy drops of moisture down the side of my face and ruining my perfectly good *Fashion Fair* make-up.

"You're joking...right?" I needed some reassurance.

"No. I'm not," she said in a sharp, clear voice, carefully articulating each word that rolled, like liquid, off her tongue. She was no longer speaking like my dear true friend, but just like an undertaker.

"It has happened before, you know."

No, I didn't know. My mind conjured up the worst possible scenario. Not only were my ancestors' graves unmarked, they had been placed in a poor Black cemetery more than a quarter century ago and, in all probability, the caretaker wouldn't be able to find their bodies. Perhaps, I had been negligent too long. I should've gone on this quest earlier in life. Instead of flying off to Disney World and buying timeshares, I should've taken that money and put tombstones on the graves.

Perish the thought. Even as an adult I lived to visit Mickey Mouse and the Magic Kingdom.

"Don't panic yet," Sharon gently reminded me. "If you need help, give me a call. And one other thing..."

My palms felt slick and sweaty as I pressed the phone closer to my right ear. I stammered, nervously, as I again tried to prepare myself for the worst.

"What's that?"

"Stop calling me an undertaker," she snapped. "I told you my title is Mortician or Funeral Director. An undertaker is what they used to call people way back in the day, you know, the old days."

As I left the driveway I started thinking about that. Yeah, the good 'ole days, when the sound of Motown, a cheap half dozen fried chicken wings, and a 12 ounce can of Frank's grape concord soda was all I needed to feel like every bit of life was worth living. Well... it still feels like the good old days to me.

2

All of Us

"Patricia."

It was my Daddy's sweet voice. His lyrical, melodic words floated through the air like an old, bluesy love song. Soft and mellow, he was calling out to me, only me, as he entered the house that cold winter evening.

I was always excited when my Daddy came home. He made me feel so special. It was hard being the middle child, never the oldest and never the youngest. Always stuck, like butter and applebutter to soft dough white bread, right in the middle. And sometimes I felt cheated. But everyone had a special role to play in our stair-step family of seven kids, including, of course, me.

Vernard was my oldest brother. At fifteen he was, without a doubt, the greatest big brother on Earth: God's gift to all Colored women. He was short, but tough and handsome, capable of ruling all the kids on the block. He was the gang leader, head of the Southern Coast, and he and his boys could whup anybody. On special occasions he came round to visit, which seemed to be less and less after we moved to our new wood and brick row home on Catherine Street in an area they called *West Philly*.

Vernard rarely lived with us, and I never understood why. He seemed more like Grandmother Jessie's child and not Momma's.

He called Grandmother Jessie Mother. He always referred to my Momma's baby sister, Aunt Nita, as his sister. And, unlike the rest of us, he called Momma Lucille. I guess only the oldest child got to do that, 'cause Momma threatened to slap us into the day after tomorrow if we ever tried it. It was so very confusing.

Curtis, Jr. was eleven and the oldest in the house, so he got to play the role of big brother far more often than Brother Vernard. He and Vernard were as different as a split green bean and a black-eye pea in the same washing pot. Vernard was chocolate, good and chocolate. We sometimes called him "Hershey" because he was several shades darker than all the rest of us. He had a full, thick head of nappy hair that curled up real tight when he got to sweating. Curtis Jr., on the other hand, was often referred to as the light brown Jesus. There was no doubt that he was good looking, too. He was four years younger, but already three inches taller than Vernard. His slightly nappy, sandy brown hair was only a tad darker than his creamy tan skin tone and every summer the heat from the sun would bleach his hair blonde. It gave him a holy look and Jesus was the only holy figure that we knew. I often wondered why Momma didn't name Vernard Curtis, Jr. I think that woulda made Hershey feel a whole lot better.

Darlene was the oldest girl and I thought she was terrific. She had smooth, unblemished, caramel taffy skin with a heavy, dark unibrow that connected at the top of her face as if it was one. Momma always said she had deep beauty. "She'll continue to look good long after your cuteness wears thin," Momma once warned me. Huh, I wasn't too sure about that.

Darlene was in charge when no other adult was in the house. Even though Curtis, Jr. was the oldest child living at home, the oldest girl was more powerful, and Darlene always got to do the good stuff first. She could leave the block before me, wore a bra and lipstick before me, and even got to wear Momma's clothes to school long before my skinny little butt could fit into Momma's hand-me-downs. Darlene often bossed us around and told us what to do. She would threaten to tell Momma (she rarely did) if we didn't act right.

Momma always said that Wayman, with his roly-poly belly and

chubby Santa-looking cheeks, was her baby boy. At nine, he was older than me and I just hated it when Momma gave him the title as baby boy. But Wayman, with his freckled face, shredded wheat color skin and reddish-brown nappy hair, was very special to my Momma.

A few years back, while we were still living on top of the bar in the four-room apartment at 4803 Woodland Avenue, Wayman dashed outside the house (Granny said like a bat out of hell), flying into the street without looking both ways. Momma always told us to look both ways before crossing the street, especially where the PTC had trolleys running every fifteen minutes. The moment he leaped his narrow behind off the curb, he was hit by a fast moving, newly-waxed, green Chevrolet.

Wayman laid perfectly still, in the middle of the street. He didn't cry and didn't wiggle. He was dead. I had heard about dead people before, but I never wanted to see one. I didn't want to see Wayman lying there, lifelessly, either. He had on a new pair of blue shorts with his yellow polo shirt trimmed in navy blue. Momma had warned him about tearing-up his new clothes. She'd just brought those pants from the John's Bargains store on 52nd Street between Walnut and Chestnut. I knew she'd be pissy mad.

Six Seconds Smitty, who could drink a whole can of Ballentine beer in six seconds, scooped up Wayman's body off the cement between the street and the trolley tracks and threw him into the back of his old scratched-up blue Buick. We ran in the house, with Curtis, Jr. in the lead, and told Granny. Granny didn't say anything. She ran downstairs to the bar underneath our apartment to ask the skinny, pimpled-face colored man if she could use the telephone to call Momma at her job.

We all followed suit. Kids were not supposed to be in the bar unless it was a holiday or special occasion, and there was nothing special about a Thursday, but nobody said a thing to us.

Momma said to never call her on the job unless it was an urgency. She worked in a big, tall, gray-stone building downtown on 12th and Filbert Streets at the Caldwell Dress Company. She must have been important because she often came home and bragged about her work with some rich white man called Mr. Caldwell. She knew his business by heart and always talked about what Mr. Caldwell did for us today. According to my Momma, Mr. Caldwell helped put food on the table, clothing on our backs, money in our pockets, and helped to pay the rent and the electricity bills, too. Mr. Caldwell must've been a powerful man with lots of money and Momma wasn't going to be happy that we had to call her for this urgency.

Granny had to wait a good long while before they could find Momma to bring her to the phone. Granny tried to be patient. Her hands were trembling, beady little sweat balls appeared on her forehead that she was trying to sop up with toilet paper, and she stuttered like she didn't know how to talk. Her face looked the same way that it did when she said that she'd put the fear of God in us. This time, I think the fear was on Granny's face.

"Lucille...Lucille," Granny blurted out. "Lucille, you gotta come home 'cause Wayman's been hit by a car!" Granny didn't say anything else. She just thanked the pimple-face man at the bar and rushed back upstairs, with all the kids in tow, to wait for Momma to come home.

We waited, too. And we cried for Wayman and prayed for Wayman. Granny was so upset that she forgot to fix my grilled cheese sandwich and powdered milk that I was supposed to have for lunch. And that cheese was the best part of the government's free food giveaway.

For several hours no one really knew where Wayman was. Momma was pretty upset (Daddy said hysterical) when she arrived home, weeping and crying like I've never seen before. She kept calling on the Lord and falling on her knees and praying.

"Oh my God, no," she shouted out.

"*Jesus*, (not my brother Curtis, Jr.) no," she screamed, repeatedly.

"Who took him away? What happened to my baby? Where's Wayman?"

None of us kids had ever experienced anything like this. We stood around the kitchen looking at each other with the fear of God on our faces, too.

Mrs. Carrie, a neighbor from 'round the bend' came to comfort Momma. Ms. Carrie said that she saw Wayman lying there in the street straddled across the trolley tracks with his head split wide open. Dark red blood was gushing out from the right side of his head, which had swollen to the size of a football. She thought he was dead, but she couldn't be certain. However, she was pretty sure that Six Seconds Smitty had taken him to the PGH - Philadelphia General Hospital - that's where most of the Colored people went for 'mergency treatment.

We didn't have a car. And Momma was too crazy-like to wait for the bus or the trolley right in front of the house on 48ᵗʰ Street. Ms. Carrie's husband, T.K. Bone (who according to my Daddy, was a good Christian man always getting into somebody's business and trying to save somebody's soul) carried Momma to the hospital to see my dead brother.

I stayed up late with the rest of the kids, eating peanut butter sandwiches on the living room floor which hadn't been swept clean in a week. Curtis, Jr. wanted to go outside and play, but Granny said no. She wasn't about to lose another grandchild. Darlene and I thought that we should start praying, but we didn't know how to do that.

Momma came home later that night, without Wayman. It turned out that he wasn't dead after all. His football-sized head was not split open and his brains were still inside his skull. He didn't even break any bones. The doctor said that he was not conscious and that something might be wrong with his innards. His hurtin' was bad enough that he had to stay in the hospital for several days.

All of a sudden, Wayman was super special. People would visit him in the hospital and bring him toys, cards and gifts. Some would bring stuffed animals. Others would bring Snickers, M & M's and jelly beans. Grandmother Jessie went and prayed over him. And Wayman got to eat vanilla, chocolate and strawberry ice cream every night. I never got any of that stuff at home.

Everyday Granny would praise the Lord for saving Wayman.

"*Jesus* (not my brother Curtis, Jr.) is my Lord and savior," she sang, repeatedly.

"Pray to the Lord and He will answer you," she kept saying. "He will see you through!"

Granny planned on cooking Wayman something delicious when he came home. She often bragged about her cooking skills. Granny knew how to prepare fancy meals for the white folks she sometimes worked for in the three-story, fairytale looking houses on 49th and Parkside Avenue near Fairmount Park. She was a baker, too. She would make crackling cornbread with pork rinds; bake blackberry muffins from the blackberries we picked from the bushes on the railroad tracks 'round the corner from the bar; and the very best biscuits with water, baking powder and the government's surplus flour that we picked up from the recreation department the first Friday of every month. Granny was thinking about baking a big butter pound cake just for Wayman soon as they turned him loose from the PGH.

The day after Wayman finally came home, the man in the green Chevrolet came round to see if he could help with my brother's bills. He was a short, fat, greasy-headed man with the coloring of a full-grown pecan. He was all dressed up in a blue pastel, one-button roll suit. He had on a Slim Jim tie with a thin stingy-brim hat. And he had a zillion razor bumps on his face and neck and was uglier than any man I'd ever known. He said that he was a big time numbers writer and covering the hospital bills would not be a problem for him.

Momma bragged that she had Blue Cross and Blue Shield and that she was a member of the union - THE INTERNATIONAL LADIES GARMENT WORKERS UNION. She had talked with the people on her job (probably that Mr. Caldwell) and they told her that she needed legal advice.

"I don't know what to do or what all the expenses will be," she kept telling that ugly, pecan-colored man.

"No need to worry," he said, "don't you worry about a thing."

Momma told him that the family didn't have a whole lot of money lying around. The ugly, pecan-colored man in the green Chevrolet promised that he would be able to handle everything.

"Don't you worry," he repeated. "Don't you worry about a thing."

I didn't understand what was happening, but there was excitement in the air 'cause Daddy was grinning like crazy, showing every single one of his perfectly matched pearly white teeth. Now, it seemed, Wayman's accident meant that he would be getting some money, too: One hundred dollars! That's what the man in the green Chevrolet gave to Momma and Daddy. Wayman was getting everything. He got a new set of clothes from the John's Bargains Store and a brand new red wagon, with *Radio Flyer* blazing on the sides, for his troubles.

We waited for the ugly, greasy-headed, pecan-colored, green Chevrolet man to come back. He never did. But soon after that, Wayman got to be Momma's baby boy, and he had to be treated real special for now, and ever more.

Jessica and Marie were the baby girls in the family. "Isn't that strange? How can you have two baby girls, who weren't even Tastycake twins, in the same family?" Marie was five and Jessica was seven. Momma thought, and even prayed, that these two would be the last, but this would not be the case.

Marie, who had the waviest hair of us all, was Momma's name-sake. She was the seventh child born and Momma had grown tired of naming babies. Way back in the day, mamas rarely named their daughters after themselves, but Momma thought that doing so might protect her from having another baby. Momma's real name was Etrulia Lucille. It was a long time before I realized that was her name because her friends called her Trudy and brother Vernard called her Lucille. She decided on Etrulia Maria for my baby sister. Everyone always said that they had never met a Colored girl with a name like Etrulia. In fact, white folks never used those kind of names either. Some folks even called Momma foolish to her face. It was bad enough that she carried such a strange name. Why did she want her little girl to suffer? Etrulia was too hard for us kids to pronounce so we called my little sister Marie.

Jessica was…well…she was super duper special as well. She was named after both of my grandmothers. Momma thought that Jessica was a much prettier sounding name than Jessie, and Granny's real name was Rosa. Jessica Rose was just right. More than any of the other girls, Jessica looked like both of my grandmothers. Darlene said it was because she was yellah. I thought, that, maybe, Jessica really didn't belong with the rest of the family because she was so much lighter than me. But that couldn't have been so because people often said that Jessica, Wayman and Curtis, Jr. were cut from the same cloth. Me, Marie and Darlene were the darker side of the family, and Vernard was just Vernard. There were so many different colors among us seven kids that the people in the neighborhood started to call us as the League of Nations. Momma said we should be proud. We represented every shade of the Colored peoples' rainbow.

As a young girl of eight, I was totally confused about the color thing. I told my white first grade teacher at the Wilson Elementary School that I had one white sister and two white brothers living with us in the apartment over the bar. She became real curious and decided to come to the house to see for herself.

We all lined up against the wall in the hallway right next to the bar, grinning, as Teacher Missy came by the apartment to look us over. Jessica, Wayman and Curtis, Jr. stood together as the white people, separate from Darlene, Marie and me. In a few mere seconds Teacher Missy had completed her review. She seemed amused. Before leaving our apartment, she pulled Momma to the side and quietly whispered, "Your child needs to be 'instructed,'" she said. "It's for her own good."

Momma sat me down in the worn-out, vinyl-covered blue chair next to the kitchen table. She tried to explain that Jessica, Wayman and Curtis, Jr. were not white. They were Negroes. In fact, we all were Negroes. But, I didn't understand that either. "What's a Negro?"

3

The First Sign of Trouble

"Patricia."

It was Daddy calling, again, and I could tell by the sound of his voice that he had a surprise for me. He often called my name first when he entered the house. Most times, he never called anyone else, not Donald, Darlene, Jessica, Wayman, or Marie…just me. I looked like my Momma and my Daddy, the spitting image of the two. No one ever doubted that I was their child, except for me on the days when I was feeling sorry for myself and pity was my only true friend.

I had grown up with stories about being stolen from the Women's Hospital of Philadelphia when I was an infant. Momma and Daddy always told us stories about the past, about the good times and the bad. But my story was the wildest of them all. It was straight from a place called weird city, and I was tired of listening to the tale that grew bigger with added exaggerations each and every time it was told. Darlene and Donald said that if Momma and Daddy told the story one more time, "we're going to stomp you like a cockroach. You'll hear the squishing from here to tomorrow!" they promised. I was just a little bit terrified. And when Momma told the story, she sometimes used big, colorful words to add more flair and excitement. She wanted to help us kids understand just what really happened and how deeply she felt about the traumatizing experience.

I was born on Halloween. Imagine that, a day set aside for raising the dead, haunting the living, and celebrating the gifts of witches and goblins. My birth should have been normal. It was Momma's fifth child and she knew all that she needed to know about the baby delivery routine.

Momma always looked at the baby as soon as it came out - all bloody and slimy, screaming and hollering at the top of its lungs. She wanted to be certain about what she was getting. She would count all the fingers and toes and check to see if her child had been marked. She would look at the color (which was always light) and check to see how much darker the ears were. That's how you could tell what color the baby would be at turning.

I was a healthy baby: seven pounds, five ounces with a head full of jet-black curly hair. My face was plump and round, probably similar to that of an African Kikuya child that I had read about in the *Weekly Reader*. Momma said that most babies are ugly, but I was remarkably cute for a newborn (but that's what all the mamas say).

Daddy overreacted. At first sight he declared that I was the most beautiful baby he had ever seen and decided, at that moment, to name me Prima Donna. Momma thought it was a disgusting choice.

"The child will never be able to go to school and have a normal life," she protested.

"Lucille," as he often called her when he was angry, "you just don't know nothing" he shouted using a much too harsh tone. "Prima Donna means beautiful woman."

"I don't care what it means," Momma yelled. "You're not going to name a child of mine Prima Donna. The kids will beat the stuffing out of the child every day of her life if you give her a name like that."

Momma was tired and needed some rest. Being in the hospital was a comforting treat. As a new mother she would be pampered and waited on hand and foot, almost like being in a motel, and Momma liked that part of the baby birthing business. Momma still had five days before filling out the necessary forms and leaving the hospital. The matter of finding a good name for the new baby would simply have to wait.

When feeding time came the next morning a bubbly young nurse carefully handed Momma a small, bundled, screaming blue package that she called "a little milk chocolate drop." She suggested that Momma begin breast-feeding the hungry baby.

Momma was startled. She looked down at the baby and in a high pitched, fearful voice screamed, "This is not my child!"

The nurse was stunned.

"What do you mean that this is not your child?"

"I saw my baby when she came out," Momma said. "She didn't look like this. And my baby was not this dark!"

"Shame on you, Mrs. Reid," the nurse responded with a disgusting look on her face. She was unable to conceal her true feelings. "This is the child you gave birth to last night. This is the child that God gave you. This is a perfectly healthy baby and you ought to be grateful. Just learn to accept it! Take this baby and feed it!"

Momma was furious. She was, for the most part, a calm person, always in control of her temper. She didn't have a nasty mouth and thought cussing was un-lady-like. But a few God-damn-its began to flow freely as she tried to explain that this was not her child. And at the same time, she realized that the baby before her was wrapped in a blue blanket.

"This is a boy!" she screamed. "I had a baby girl. This is not my baby!"

They called the nursing supervisor – who Momma always describes as a big white woman with short red hair and red rimmed oval glasses. A few other doctors and nurses began to gather as the conversation became heated and gained the attention of everyone in the Negro section of the Maternity Ward. And there were a lot of new mommies on the ward that day.

Momma told us about the skinny little crazy lady who had left all of her baby weight right there on the delivery table. She was with Momma in the delivery room, screaming and hollering the whole time, cussing like a sailor and calling some man named Richard a "son-of-a-bitch." Momma said she must have been "delirious" because she didn't seem like the same angry crazy woman who had given birth the night before.

There was the big, oversized, mature, long-haired yellow woman who Momma said reminded her of Mother. She had nine children already and wanted the tenth to be her last. She was over thirty, had two husbands (and a boyfriend) and was still having kids. And there was the seemingly terrified, wide-eyed young teenage looking girl who Momma said had just gotten out of diapers. But everybody's attention was focused on Momma.

And there was no calming her down. She lifted herself out of the bed and began whooping and hollering like a sister possessed. She was threatening to snatch off the heads of all those who crossed her path. Momma refused to feed the infant and wanted to know what had happened to her baby. A nurse's aide walked by and shouted, "You're just a Hellraiser!" Momma didn't give two hoots and a damn. This was not her child.

Nurse Anne, the soft-spoken, slow speaking, sun-kissed tan Colored woman who chose her words so carefully, arrived and tried to offer some assistance. She had, after all, assisted the evening before when Momma gave birth. She took one look at the child and declared, "That's not Mrs. Reid's baby! I remember the infant quite well. She has a head full of curly black hair, and she wasn't quite that dark."

"You know that these children can turn color overnight," the nursing supervisor retorted as she snatched her red rimmed glasses off her fat sweaty face. "I don't know why you're adding to this mess. White-looking babies mean everything to these Colored women."

"That's not Mrs. Reid's baby!" Nurse Anne shouted right back. And she stood her ground. She, too, had admired the newborn and was certain that this was not the same child whose birth she had witnessed the night before. "The woman knows her child when she sees it! And I'm telling you, that ain't it."

The infant boy was taken back to the nursery and the search began for the missing baby girl.

Momma was a lot calmer now, but she continued to cry. She knew that, sometimes, they mixed up babies in the hospital. She had heard many stories about kids being sent home with the wrong mommies and daddies. And she had seen a many a family where the child didn't look anything like the mommy or daddy that claimed it. But that coulda' been something else.

More than 24 hours passed before the mix-up was resolved. I had been placed in the arms of another new mother. She was preparing to take me home. She said that she honestly thought that the baby girl belonged to her. She had four boys at home and desperately wanted a little girl. God, she said, had answered her prayers.

Momma said the woman was delusional.

Momma finally got to see me early the next morning. She knew from the color of the pink blanket that Nurse Anne was handing her a baby girl. I had been nursed and fed already, so I wasn't screaming and hollering like a banshee. Momma took one look at me and confirmed that I was the one. She was relieved, but remained uneasy about what could have been...her child carried off by some other mother (f...ker).

Nurse Anne explained the mix-up. She apologized, more than ten times, on behalf of the hospital. She offered assurances that the mistaken mother would never have been able to leave the hospital with the wrong infant. Nurse Anne added that the other mother really thought that I was her baby.

"Liar!"

That's all Momma would say. She pulled me close to her breast and held me, tightly, in her arms, still cussing and using the vilest of words underneath her breath. Words that she hoped would never penetrate the innocence of the newborn's ears.

There were lots of papers to sign the next day. Momma was treated with a great deal of respect after the baby mix-up incident. She was even given an extra gift pack filled with baby formula, vitamins and cloth diapers to take home with the new baby. And everyone who spoke to Momma that day had a big grin glued on their face.

On the sixth day, Daddy and Granny boarded the PTC and went

to the hospital to take Momma and me home. They caught a yellow cab on the way back.

"This is a sign," Granny warned. And she was serious. Granny told Daddy that the temperature had soared to a record-setting 85 degrees the day after I was born. Nothing like that had ever happened in the City of Philadelphia. She looked out the window, looked up at the sky and checked around to see if anything else was different about this unusually hot, sunny fall day.

"You're gonna have to watch out for this child," she repeated. "She's gonna be special."

Granny was steeped in the folklore from the old south. She believed in God, the devil, roots, spirits and warnings from dead people. She worshiped at a strange church that Momma used to call "holy rollers." But Momma paid little attention to Granny's warning. She had been raised a Catholic, and she hadn't received a warning from Jesus, Mary or any of the Saints that she prayed to as a little girl.

"The girl was born on Halloween," Daddy chuckled. But Momma found no humor in that.

"Lucille," Granny wondered out loud, "whatcha gonna name this one?"

"Patricia…Patricia Anne."

4

Negroes, Whites and Jews.

"Patricia Anne!" Daddy shouted for the fourth and final time.

"Yes Daddy," I hollered out loud over the banisters in the second floor hallway, "I'm coming."

I scrambled down the stairs to see what my Daddy had brought me. It was always something good to eat. Some special treat he had taken from the restaurant that he had been working at for almost a year.

Daddy worked at Casa Conti on Old York Road in Glenside, Pennsylvania. Momma said that it was a good job. She hoped Daddy would be able to hold on to it for a long time. Daddy said he was a chef; Mama said he was a cook. White people would come to Casa Conti all during the day and night to sample my Daddy's cooking. He said he was an artist in the kitchen, but he rarely prepared special meals for us at home. Daddy said he didn't have the proper equipment, nor the money. And White peoples' food was expensive.

Momma said Daddy was creative. He could make a meal out of leftovers, feeding the multitudes just like Jesus did in the Bible. Momma was good at stretching dollars and Daddy was good at stretching meals. Most of the time we had food to eat, even when we didn't like it. But Daddy would tell us stories about the gourmet meals he enjoyed at the restaurant. He called it a fringe benefit. Daddy cooked exotic meals like London broil, pork loin, lamb chops and flounder. It was rich white peoples' food and we never had those meals at home. And I don't think other Negroes ate that kind of food either. We were never allowed to visit Casa Conti, so we never sampled any of the food that Daddy called "delicacies." But Daddy was the chef, and he was permitted to eat the leftovers after he prepared the meals for Mr. Conti's guests.

Daddy stood at the foot of the steps grinning. I could see all 32 of his white, pearly teeth that everybody always said were perfect. Daddy's big grin, pearly white teeth and Murray slick hair made him look like Fats Domino. And when he was in a good mood he would sing "Blueberry Hill" to us and pretend that he was a lounge singer.

"I found my thrill," Daddy would start to sing.
"On Blueberry Hill," and then he would cut his eyes at Momma.
"On Blueberry Hill...when I found you."

He would snap his fingers and wiggle his legs. He would point his shoe toward the splintered-rich worn-out wooden floor and start to do that old man jitterbug dance. Daddy would wave his arms in the air and glide up and down the little bit of space left on the hardwood floor in the center of the room. Then he would pause for a minute and wait for a response from Momma.

"Stop it Curtis," she would say without a smile.

We all would crack up.

Daddy wasn't singing tonight. He was waiting for me at the foot of the stairs.

I focused, quickly, on the shiny object he held in his hand. It was a small package wrapped in aluminum foil.

"This is for you, baby," Daddy said as he stretched his heavy arms out to give me the present.

"Thank you very much Daddy," I said, smiling generously and giving him back that big pearly white grin and flashing my 24 pearly white teeth. I quickly grabbed the package, gave him a big hug and ran into the kitchen.

I pushed the dirty dishes on the kitchen table aside and started to unpeel the three layers of aluminum foil wrapped around my present. I was excited because I knew it would be something to eat, and I loved good food more than anybody. I heard Momma coming down the steps.

"Stop it Curtis," she shouted at Daddy. "I've told you a thousand times not to do that. You're going to spoil that girl rotten, and then you won't be able to do a thing with her."

I hated being the object of my Daddy's affection. Most of the time, it brought me nothing but trouble. Momma and Daddy would fight when he brought me a special treat, and Wayman, Darlene, Jessica, Marie and Curtis, Jr. made it so hard for me to come back to the girls' room. Momma said she loved us equal and didn't have any favorites. That was not true for my Daddy. My Daddy loved me and I loved my Daddy.

It was red and brown and I could see blood dripping out of the aluminum foil and onto the gray speckled table that stood in the middle of the kitchen floor. It was meat, raw meat. I burst into tears.

"Why did Daddy bring me raw meat?" I cried out loud to Momma. "I'm not a dog!"

"It's not raw meat, sweetheart. It's half cooked," Momma responded. Seeing that I was visibly upset, she moved quickly to the other side of the room to comfort me, 'cause Momma loved all of her children equal, and I loved my Momma.

"It's what they call rare," Momma continued to explain. "White people like to eat it that way. Not Jewish people, the white people. Jewish people boil their meat for hours and you never see blood on their plates." Momma took the aluminum foil package and moved toward the hot plate on top of the wood shelf near the extension cord in the corner of the kitchen. "I'll finish cooking this meat and we can use it for dinner tomorrow."

I always thought Jewish people were white people. Now here Momma was telling me that I had to learn the difference between the two. They all looked the same to me. How was I supposed to tell?

"Let her have some now, Lucille," Daddy pleaded. He was never happy when Momma took away my presents. But this was not a gift that I wanted. We had already eaten our dinner – neck bones with soup, beans and rice, white bread and grape Kool-Aid - and I really wasn't hungry. I especially didn't have a taste for raw meat.

Momma paid him no mind. She heated up the black cast iron skillet, which she always used for frying chicken backs and necks, and threw the meat in the pan. I didn't stay to hear the argument, 'cause Momma and Daddy fussed a lot when he didn't treat all of us as equal.

I went back upstairs to the girls' room and found the choir assembled and singing:

"Here she comes," they all crooned, "Miss Special K.
You think, you're cute. You think, you're cute.
But you're just a nappy-headed booga,
With neck-grabbing cooties to boot."

Everyone knew the drill. I bet it was Wayman who organized the punishment this time. He was the biggest teaser of them all. I wasn't gonna break down and cry like I used to, 'cause nobody really cared.

We all had nicknames, sometimes more than one. We called Marie "spook" because she couldn't stay out in the sun for very long. She would leave the house looking like a cute, clean, caramel-colored doll and come back blacker than burnt fish. All you could see were her fully expressive eyes that popped out of her head when she talked so fast that you couldn't understand what she was saying even if you wanted to.

Jessica was "yellah" every time we got mad at her. She cried when we called her that and Momma told us that we were cruel. Jessica was sensitive to everybody's needs. No matter what illness one of us kids had captured, Jessica would make certain that she came down with it too.

Wayman was "Mommy Boy." Whatever he wanted, Momma never deprived him of a single solitary thing. Even though it had been two years since Wayman was knocked unconscious and got all his innards smacked down in the car accident, Momma was still grateful that he was alive.

When Curtis, Jr. wasn't Jesus we called him Donald. His middle name was MacDonald, just like the nursery rhyme, and Momma said one Curtis in the house was more than enough. We called him "Fart Butt," too. In the middle of his lying, storytelling routines, he would always fart to make his point. We never knew when the fart was coming. No sooner than he had captured our attention with one of his wild stories about his adventures running around the streets of North, West and South Philadelphia, he would squeeze his butt hard. We could smell fart gas everywhere. And you could always hear him singing:

Beans, beans, they're good for your heart,
The more you eat 'em, the more you fart,
The more you fart, the better you feel,
So eat those beans for every meal!

So disgusting! We always jetted out the room in a huff, but usually there was nowhere else to go.

Momma was cloaked in silence. She kept some things from us and we were never certain what was going on. Sometimes she would stop talking when we came into the room. When we got too close to her conversation she would shoo us away, reminding us to "stay out of adult business." When she got all dressed up in her red satin dress with the big diamond hole cut open on her chest, so everybody could see her brown fleshy bosoms, we always asked her where she was going. She responded, "None of your business." Darlene called Momma "Secret Squirrel."

No one dared give Darlene a nickname. She stood between us and Momma, Granny and Daddy. When Momma was too busy, we went to Darlene to get the things that we wanted. She knew when trouble was lurking and always managed to get us out of harm's way. She took us to the candy store so we could buy *Squirrel Nuts* and *Mary*

Janes after we got our ten cent allowance on Friday nights. And she would break up the fights between me and Jessica and Marie. Darlene was tough as nails and would kick your ass if you messed with her, or any one of us.

They called me Piggy because eating was my favorite activity. I adored food. However, I was terribly skinny and underweight and no one understood why my excessive eating never led to weight gain. I begged Momma to buy me some *"Weight-On,"* a new medicine that I saw advertised on TV, but Momma refused. She said one day I would pay the price for eating everything in sight and that I would end up being as big as a house. Fat chance!

I was "Miss Special K" every time Daddy did something incredibly stupid like bringing me all the cookies, all of the cakes or all the leftover sandwiches that he would take from the restaurant. He couldn't bring something every day or the boss might think that he was stealing. He only brought home the food that was about to go to waste. Daddy said that they would feed it to the hogs if he didn't take it home. He wrapped the food carefully and put it in his inside coat pocket. I think the rich white people were pretty damn greedy during the summer time because they never left enough good food for Daddy or the hogs. But we got plenty of leftovers in the fall and winter.

The teasing never lasted very long, but they never let me forget that I was my Daddy's pet. And for that, I would have to pay the price, 'cause one day, Daddy would fuck-up everything and it would change my life forever.

5

5828

Spook, Jesus, Hershey, Yellah, Mommy Boy, Darlene, Momma, Daddy and me were all looking forward to a better life on Catherine Street. We hadn't been there for long, only about eight months. Our new number was 5828. Momma was so proud of this new house. She was the first one in the family to own property (except for the stories that Daddy told us about all the land his family owned in Clemson, South Carolina, but left behind when Pop Pop chased some heifer up north to Philadelphia and Granny and the children soon followed). She borrowed $500.00 from the credit union to make the down payment. When Daddy found out that Momma had that much money, he borrowed $200.00 dollars from the secret drawer of her old brown jewelry box to take care of his business. It was hidden at the bottom of the bedroom closet and stuffed with a few cherished memories.

We could hear the fighting in the living room. Daddy said he needed the money. Momma kept screaming about the kids. Daddy kept talking about goldfish. Darlene said that we were too young to understand what was happening, but told us that Momma would never be happy again - something about "never trusting him again with a damn dime!"

Momma went right back to the credit union and got $200.00 more. The credit man was not too happy to see Momma's face again.

"Mrs. Reid," he said, "you'll be the one responsible for paying the money back."

"I've always paid my bills on time, and I won't be making any exception for this one," she snapped.

The stumpy white credit man who was sitting behind the desk at the credit union office on the corner of 16th and Pine was beet red in the face. But Momma didn't care. She didn't like people telling her what she already knew. She was really proud of being a member of the credit union.

"Never mess up your credit," she often reminded us. "Always pay your bills first; then pay yourself. You'll be able to make it in this world. If you mess up your credit, you'll mess up your whole life."

Momma was mad as hell at the credit union man and madder still at my Daddy. When she was in her furious state she called it steaming. She said that the credit union man had brought out the Indian in her. I never thought much about the Indian in Momma. I knew my Great Grandmother Pattie was part Cherokee, but we didn't talk about it too much. And at first, I thought she was a white woman until Momma told us stories about what happened a long time ago down in Danville, VA. And we weren't too proud of the Indian part of our background. When we used to watch TV on Saturdays, the Indians were always the bad guys. We rooted for all the white cowboys on white horses to catch and kill the bad Indians, scalp them if you could. Dumb, stupid us! We didn't know any better. Momma was a short, small-framed woman with sunny brown skin. Everyone always said that she was a special kind of beauty. I guess that was the Colored mixed with the Indian part. I was happy about that.

Momma marched right down to the bank to get her mortgage. But she was disappointed. The bank man said that Momma couldn't get a mortgage with the FHA without my Daddy's signature because she was a woman. Momma explained that she had been working at the same job for ten years. She was a member of the union and pulled out her card, THE INTERNATIONAL LADIES GARMENT WORKERS UNION, shoving it in the face of the bank man. No matter. Daddy had to sign the papers if Momma wanted that house.

Momma wanted us to move into our new house before the start of the school year. In August 1958, we packed all our personal belongings into dingy white pillowcases that were so thin you could see through the treads and moved to Catherine Street. Six Second Smitty helped out, too. He carried the kitchen table and beat-up chairs in the back of his old Buick to the new house. *"I wonder if Wayman left any blood stains on the back seat of his car."*

5828 Catherine Street was so much different from Woodland Avenue. On Woodland Avenue we had a four-room apartment right on top of the bar. You could hear music all day long, except for Sunday mornings. During the summer, when we opened all the windows in the apartment because it was pissy hot, we could hear the bar people talking loud and roaring with laughter.

The girls' room was at the front of the apartment, right next to the kitchen. Granny called it the living room during the day, but it was the girls' when we were sleeping in there at night. Every night we would pull out the couch and climb into bed. Me and Darlene would sleep at the bottom; Jessica and Marie at the top. Momma said that Jessica and Marie had to be protected from falling out of the bed by the arms on the couch. The girls'/living room was also the location of our first Magnavox black and white TV set that Daddy bought on time. That's how Black folks bought stuff they couldn't afford - pay five dollars a week, every week, for what seemed like the rest of your life. The purchase price said $89.95, but Momma said it would cost three times that much before Daddy finished paying for it. He had to pay "Colored interest rates." Daddy put it in the doorway, right between the girls' room and the kitchen. This made it harder for us to go to sleep because Daddy liked to watch TV late at night when white people told funny stories about how they lived their lives. We almost never saw Black folks on TV, but Daddy always gathered us around when a slick-headed man named Nat King Cole was on the set.

There was a white porcelain gas stove in the kitchen next to the refrigerator. The dirty brown linoleum on the floor had been there much too long and Daddy was always asking the bar man about when it would be replaced. Never. We had a light gray speckled table with four unmatched chairs. The stuffing was coming out of the backs and seats, but Granny said that the chairs were sturdy enough to hold our little butts.

We never sat at the table together. We ate in shifts. First the girls, then the boys and Granny (who showed up first thing every morning to take care of us), and Momma and Daddy were last.

The boys' room was in the back along with Momma and Daddy. We stayed out of Momma and Daddy's room because it was private. Sometimes Darlene and Donald would sneak in the room to see if Momma had hidden our Christmas presents in the closet. For a piece of our Friday night candy they would tell us ahead of time about the gifts that we were going to get. Granny didn't need a room because she went home every night to the basement on 50th and Chancellor Street where she and Pop Pop lived.

There were two sets of stairs and a hallway right in the middle of our second floor apartment. We went from the sidewalk through the front door, down a little hall, then upstairs into the big hallway of our apartment. We were told never to use the second set of stairs that led to the apartment on the third floor. No relations lived upstairs. It was a pretty, dark woman and a thin, yellow man that we would see at all different times of the day. They were free to walk through our apartment at any time because it was the only way that they could get home. Granny taught us to be polite, because sometimes they were ignorant.

Holidays were the best. Daddy would take me downstairs to the bar and let me dance for a nickel, dime and sometimes a quarter. The men would pick me up by the bottom and put me on top of the bar. They would stick money in the jukebox and select a song for me to dance. "Shake, Rattle and Roll" was my favorite. I would twist, turn and shake for three minutes before stopping. Then I would get my nickel, dime or quarter. One man would lift me off the bar by my bottom and another would pick me up. My Daddy was real proud.

Nobody liked it when the men had too much of the drink. Sometimes when we came home from school we would find a foul-smelling man sleeping in our hallway. Others would walk in, stand up against the wall and pee. Darlene said they were drunken bastards and we were never to go near them.

There were all kinds of stores up and down the Avenue. We would buy day old bread and donuts from the bakery, *Mary Janes* and *Squirrel Nuts* from the penny candy store, neck bones from the butcher shop, and fish from Mr. Gene. Momma would never buy fish on Mondays. It wasn't fresh because it had been sitting there all week-end. Daddy said a good sniff could tell you if you had good fish. But Mr. Gene didn't like Daddy sniffing around his place.

Catherine Street was just not the same. It was a row house with twenty-five fully attached, identical looking houses with little porches lined up on the left side of the street and twenty-one on the right. There was a tiny yard in the front and in the back of the house as well. Daddy planned on growing some fresh vegetables like collard greens, tomatoes, cucumbers and peppers. We had an upstairs with three bedrooms and a downstairs with a living room, dining room and kitchen. We were going to live like the rich white folks.

There were only a few stores at the end of the block. The drug store was on the south corner, the same side of the street as our house. Sharon Baptist Church stood across the street on the north corner and took up enough space for three houses. A dry cleaners and steak and hoagie shop rounded out the four points. Crest Bar, owned by a man named Mr. Kelly, stood at the other end of the street. Momma didn't want us kids, or Daddy, to hang out at that end of the block. She had hoped that we left that troublesome lifestyle back on Woodland Avenue. And she feared that Daddy would spend time there if he wasn't careful.

White people lived on Catherine Street, too. Momma said it was because this was a good neighborhood and that meant that we had finally moved up in the world. Jennifer was a skinny eight year old girl like me, except she was white. She had long flowing blonde hair and looked like the people on television. Momma let me play with Jennifer even though she lived across the street from the bar. We played twice before she moved to a new house in Northeast Philly. Most of the white people were gone before the first summer. But Miss Sadie and Mr. Jeffrey, they stayed until they died. I don't think they had anywhere else to go.

White people didn't like the Colored, but I didn't know why. Momma and Daddy didn't talk much about white people. Daddy said there was trouble down south and, that someday soon, a change was gonna come. Momma taught us to be proud and always "stay with your own kind." Our future survival, she said, would depend on it. Of course, all of us kids thought things were just about perfect. We were all together. We were joyful. We had a new house, and both Momma and Daddy had jobs. There was food on the table and plenty of extras with the government surplus. The push for something they called civil rights was gonna to change our lives. We were a few short months away from a new decade – the 1960s. It was a great life for Colored people. We just had no idea how bad things were gonna be.

6

Living with Jesus, Spook, Mommy Boy, Yellah and Darlene

That first summer on Catherine Street was great. Granny didn't want me, Jessica and Marie to play in the street (still skittish about Wayman), but she did allow us to walk around the block from Catherine to 58th to Webster to 59th and back to Catherine again. We would circle the whole area without ever hitting the asphalt. There was a lot to see and do. Houses were lined up on every single stretch of the sidewalk and kids with their mommies and daddies were all over the place. We would stop at the corner on 58th to look and see if we recognized anyone coming out of Mr. Kelly's bar. It was open all the time, and some of the men, and the women, who lived on our new block were in and out of the bar on a regular basis, hugging and kissing each other like dogs in heat.

The 5800 block of Webster was smaller than Catherine Street. There were just as many houses, but you could tell by the tiny little cramped up porches that their houses weren't as big as ours. Most had pink, beige and green aluminum sliders that were much too big for the small porches. When they moved back and forth, the big slider would bump against the matching chair and an awful, clanking screech of a sound would follow. It seemed pretty dumb to me, but folks kept buying them anyway, stuffing their little porches with too much furniture. I think white folks could sell Colored folks just about anything.

We didn't always make it to the corner of 59ᵗʰ. Before we got to the end of the block we would cut through the back alley that connected Webster and Catherine Streets. It was best if we didn't go walking around the block on Wednesdays; that was garbage day and the alley was always stinking. Even after the trash men took away the garbage, you could still see the white maggots crawling around in the bottom of the trashcans and on top of the lids. The smell of the garbage and the sight of the live maggots killed my appetite and it was difficult to search for the honeysuckle flowers that we plucked from the bushes, pinched off the bottom and sucked out all the sweet juices. The alley was a shortcut back to Catherine Street, but, mainly, I was in there searching for honeysuckle. It was free and it was good.

On our journeys around the block, we saw lots of people and they saw us. But nobody ever said anything, so we kept on walking. We did that a lot in those first two years. It would take a while before we got used to living on Catherine Street. This was a real neighborhood, with real families, that lived in real houses right next door to each other. We had to watch our manners, and practice not acting like roughnecks who had lived in a tiny apartment, on the tracks, on top of the bar in another part of town.

After the second summer was over, I was ready to go back to my new school. We all went to the Harrity Elementary School at 56ᵗʰ and Christian Streets. We were the only family on the block to attend Harrity - all six of us. Everybody else went to Bryant at 59ᵗʰ and Cedar Avenue. Momma said we moved on the block in the wrong year. I think that there were just too many of us to put in Bryant at the same time.

Everybody at Harrity seemed to know that we were coming. Our clan was large, real large. There was a Reid child in every grade. During the holidays they would call one of us down to the office and give us a gift basket. It was filled with everything that you needed for a festive holiday meal. Sometimes they would give us bags filled with clothing, too. I thought it was wonderful. Darlene said that it was disgusting.

We would walk to school every morning, huddled together, holding hands in twos to make certain that nobody got lost. In the first few weeks we saw a little old white lady in a Black Oldsmobile spying us. Donald saw her first, and then Darlene. They were sure that she had her eye on us, so we guarded each other as we walked because we didn't want to be kidnapped. It turned out to be Mrs. Goldberg, the sixth grade teacher at the new school. Before it was over, she would have everyone one of us in her class and she would teach us some new things about white people and about being Jewish. (I still couldn't tell the difference.) Mrs. Goldberg said that she was concerned about us because there were no safe-crossing guards at the corner of 58th and Catherine. I guess not, we were the only kids headed in that direction. But Mrs. Goldberg had a solution to the problem. She recruited Donald into the Safety Patrol - gave him a badge and everything. We would all walk to the corner of 58th and Catherine and wait for Donald to stretch his arms out wide to stop us from crossing the street. Once he was certain that no cars were coming, he would give us permission to cross. He thought he was something, standing there with that white strap with a silver badge on it wrapped around his chest. It was the only corner he had to protect. There were plenty other safeties as we got closer to Harrity. But that thin little silver badge sure made a difference with him. And he wore it every single day, except for Saturdays and Sundays when Momma made him take it off in the house.

Mrs. Goldberg was so proud of Donald. She followed his progress throughout the school year. And then she had Darlene, Wayman, me, Jessica and Marie. In a strange way, she knew us and we knew her and we were certain that she cared about us. She got to be the model for a good Jewish woman. The others, up there on 60th Street that owned the hosiery store, the shoe store and the children's clothing store, we weren't so certain about them. They were friendly enough, but always in the position of taking our money.

School was okay, but I always preferred the weekends. Good stuff happened on Saturday and sometimes Sunday. That was when we let the good times roll. There was food, music, dancing and plenty of boys. I had my eyes on a few, but Momma had already warned me about being fresh.

It was a Saturday afternoon. The weather was still nice because it was September and the green leaves on the trees had not yet turned to red, yellow or golden brown. I saw the small stick figure walking in the middle of the pavement two blocks away on 57th Street. I could barely see his special features, but I knew it was Brother Vernard.

I could recognize Vernard a mile away. I thought about how easy he was to detect with his Hershey colored skin. I wouldn't call him Hershey to his face. It's not that I thought that Hershey was a bad color, and I loved chocolate Hershey candy bars with almonds. I just didn't know if Vernard knew how special he was because he was Hershey.

He was still on 57th street when I caught a glimpse of him. It wasn't his Hershey color that first caught my attention. It was the walk, his syn-co-pa-ted stroll. Vernard's weight fell heavily to his right foot and with perfect rhythm he dragged his left foot as he carried it forward. His shoulders were synchronized, like a song in perfect harmony. His right fist was clenched tight as he swung it hard behind his back, just like he did on the dance floor. Vernard was one of the baddest strollers and the baddest dancer around. He had time, rhythm and soul.

I started to move in his direction. If Vernard had any sweets, I would be the first in line to receive them. The last time I begged him for candy he took me to the drug store and brought me a two-cent cherry favored Tootsie Roll Pop. It was still daylight and I knew the drug store was open.

Wayman was in the middle of the street playing a new game called Skully with a boy named Richie. He was the one who had been hit by the greasy-headed man in the newly-waxed green Chevrolet, but it was still Jessica, Marie and me that Granny wouldn't let go in the middle of the street. Granny was strange like that. She let the boys do things that she wouldn't let the girls do. When the boys gave her trouble or sassed her in disrespect she would holler, "Wait till you Daddy gets home."

Granny handled the girls differently. She never hesitated to whip out her belt, take off her old worn out brown shoes, or grab a switch from the green bush in the front of the yard and wear our asses out. Once when she made us one of those nasty butter and applebutter sandwiches for lunch, I scraped the butter off the soft dough white bread and threw it on the linoleum floor under the table. When Granny saw that, she grabbed her belt and asked, "Which one of you wasted that good butter and messed up that clean floor?"

"It wasn't me," I shouted, first proclaiming my innocence with my lying-ass self.

"I wasn't in here," Darlene said, "so you know I didn't do it."

Marie sat there looking like a spook and said nothing. Granny knew that it couldn't have been her.

Jessica started crying when she saw the belt.

"It wasn't me Granny," she cried. "I think Patricia did it."

"I did not!" I shouted a little louder. "It must have been you!" I pointed to Jessica, emboldened by my loud brash tone and deep commitment to the lie being told.

Granny knew that it was one of us who threw that applebutter stained butter on the floor. She beat us both.

I pretended that I didn't see Wayman playing Skully as I skipped, hastily, down Catherine Street. I wanted to make certain that I was first to greet Brother Vernard. I saw those two pretty girls, Michelle and Paula, on the porch at 5820, but I didn't bother to stop and say hello.

"Hi Vernard," I giggled.

"How you doing, Piggy," he said without the slightest sign of emotion. I didn't like him calling me Piggy, but it was better than Miss Special K. I knew Brother Vernard loved me much more than my other knuckleheaded brothers and sisters. I was special. In fact, it was he that made all of us feel extra special. Whenever he was around, Vernard offered his protection. His mere presence was enough to scare anybody. I would never do anything to upset him or make him angry with me.

I grabbed his left arm and squeezed tight. I was hoping that he would pick me up and spin me around, but he didn't.

"Got any candy today?"

"Nope. Nothing."

There was something strange about him. He wasn't right. He didn't seem happy to see me at all. That was so unlike my brother. He was always so happy to be home. Vernard wanted to stay with us all the time, but Daddy wouldn't let him. When we first moved to Catherine Street he moved in with us and stayed for two whole months. But he and Daddy didn't seem to get along. Brother Vernard was sent back to live with my Grandmother Jessie. That wasn't such a bad thing because Grandmother Jessie had everything. I often asked him why he and Daddy didn't get along, but he said it was none of my business. I think he must've done something wrong before I was born because, except for that brief moment in time when he stayed with us, I never remembered my Daddy being mad at Vernard.

We continued to walk in silence. Maybe he was mad at me because I asked him for some candy. Brother Vernard said nothing. But the closer we got to the house, the more certain I was that he had the fear on his face. Somebody had died, but I didn't have a clue. Who?

7

Death Comes a Calling

I stayed on the stoop outside and let Vernard go into the house by himself. I didn't want to hear talk about dead people. Our relations kept dropping dead all the time and Daddy said it meant that he would never see the autumn leaves fall. First, it was Uncle George; drowned. Uncle Herman was next - hit by a car - then Aunt Ida, Uncle Ed, Uncle Bill and Aunt Nellie. Momma didn't know what killed them but they were all dead. But it was Granny's brother, Uncle Andrew, which scared me the most.

Just a few months earlier, Daddy came home and told us that Uncle Andrew was dead. He died poor and penniless, like everyone else in the family, and nobody had any money to bury him. The family (that damn Pop Pop and my Daddy) decided that the funeral would be at our house. They would dress up Uncle Andrew in his best suit, put him in a coffin and bring his dead body in the house and lay it out to rest in the living room. That's the way they did it back home in the South. Daddy said that we were the only ones in the family to have a parlor large enough for the funeral. We would have to play the role of the Reid Family Funeral Home.

I was absolutely terrified. A dead body was coming to stay in our living room. Fear surrounded my being and snatched every bit of my breath away. I couldn't talk. My heart was beating so fast I was certain that it would leap out of my chest and hit the scratched-up wooden floor in the dining room. I was unable to eat my scrambled meat dinner. I thought I was going to die.

I went upstairs to my chair, which also doubled for my bed at night, and cried myself to sleep.

I was caught in the grips of a nightmare. I felt the embrace of Uncle Andrew's dead arms. I could smell his dead, garlic breath right in my face. I began screaming in the middle of the night as my conscious voice attempted to awaken me from my nightmarish state. Uncle Andrew grabbed me and started to shake me with tremendous force. He was trying to choke me, smother me, strangle me, or something like that, just so he could take me to Deadland with him. As his grip tightened, I screamed louder and louder, my throat dry, my voice hoarse. It wouldn't be long before his strange embrace smothered me to death. Suddenly, my eyes flew open and it was Momma kneeling at the foot of the chair holding me in her arms.

"Patricia... sweetheart... wake-up," she said gently, but with a powerful voice. "You're having a bad dream."

I burst into tears, weeping uncontrollably as I confided in Momma my deepest fears about having Uncle Andrew's dead body in the living room.

"Who told you that?" Momma asked.

"Daddy," I sobbed. My face was drenched, my undershirt soaking wet, and I had peed all over the chair.

"Honey, your Daddy is only teasing you. I would never let them bring a coffin in this house and take over the living room. Go back to sleep and try to forget about it," Momma pleaded. I never did. *"Was my Daddy just teasing me? That son-of a ..."*

Momma was furious at Daddy for scaring me half to death. He cracked up. Daddy always laughed about people dying. Momma didn't, although she was never hysterical again like the time when we thought our brother Wayman was dead after he was hit by the pecan-colored, greasy-headed man in the newly-waxed green Chevrolet. The hysterical stuff was left to me.

The world seemed to pause and take a breath every time they announced that somebody had died. We wasted so much time talking about the dying. I was only nine, but just the thought of dead people was starting to get on my nerves. And after what happened to Grandmother Pattie...well....

Great Grandmother Pattie was the first dead person that I knew really well. On Sundays, Momma used to dress us up and take us to South Philly to see Grandmother Jessie and Great Grandmother Pattie. Sundays were the only day that we could visit because the PTC let all children under the age of twelve ride the trolley and buses for free. Sometimes the driver of the 36 trolley didn't want to let us on because there were too many of us. Momma, standing there with all six of her raggedy-muffin-looking children under the age of twelve, trying to get on the trolley with only a quarter in her hand must have been a horrifying sight.

"They all belong to me!" Momma would say over and over again.

We had to wear our very best clothes when we visited Grandmother Jessie. We didn't have many dresses and all the girls' clothing was identical. Momma would take the leftover scraps from the dress factory at Caldwell Dress Company and piece them together until she had enough to make a whole dress. Sometimes we would see the same print material advertised in the Causal Dress Section for the John Wanamaker Department Stores in the Sunday *Philadelphia Inquirer*. I wanted to cut the pictures out and show it to my teacher, but Momma said that it wasn't a good idea.

Grandmother Jessie lived in a fancy, grand three-story brick house near 22nd and Reed. Her front steps were made of white marble and sometimes when we visited her in the summer, she would make us wash them down with ammonia and Comet cleanser.

Everything about Grandmother Jessie was beautiful, grand and elegant. She was a classy lady, just like some fairy-tale white woman that you would see on TV. She would come to the door dressed in chiffon robes and dresses that flowed in the moist summer breeze. She sprinkled her body with lavender-scented talcum powder and no matter how hot it got, she refused to sweat. Grandmother Jessie wore white pearls on her neck with a matching pearl bracelet. Most often she would have matching pearl earrings that were bigger than quarters. Her face was covered with creamy white powder, red rouge and red lipstick. I don't ever recall seeing her without make-up. She was whiter than Jessica, and Great Grandmother Pattie was whiter still. I asked Momma how come our grandmothers were white. She said that they just looked white but they were really Colored and that they were Negroes like all the rest of us.

There was furniture in every single room of Grandmother Jessie's house. The living room had a soft green couch with three different kinds of Victorian chairs. There were matching lamps and dark walnut wood tables with doilies on each one. She had shiny hardwood floors but covered most of the room with a rug that had too many colors. It was like a kaleidoscope had spilled onto the floor. Grandmother Jessie had a sitting room downstairs decorated with ivory colored lace and satin. There was a small beige couch with lots of fancy little pillows right behind the double glass doors with glass crystal door knobs that you could see straight through. Sometimes when we came to visit she would be sitting in that room talking to a blue-black man named Mr. Carter.

A large, oval mahogany table stood in the center of the dining room surrounded by eight chairs. They all matched too. Against the wall was a china cabinet where she kept her prized dishes and silver. We never got to eat off of anything from the china cabinet. She had pictures of Aunt Nita and Brother Vernard and lots of pictures of her when she was a fine young woman. A framed picture of Jessica and me stood next to the crystal bowl on top of the cardenzia. None of the other kids had pictures in Grandmother Jessie's house, just Jessica and me.

The kitchen was like none that I had ever seen before. She had a big refrigerator with a white porcelain double sink. There was a real stove, not like the hot plate that we used at home, and she could cook on top of the stove and inside the oven. Unlike my Daddy, she had all of the equipment that she needed to make us a special meal.

There were seven bedrooms and all of them were furnished with the most beautiful things that I had ever seen. You entered each room through a white wood door that had a thick glass panel on the top with the crystal glass doorknobs. There was a set of dresser drawers in every room. And the second floor bedrooms even had hardwood vanity dressing tables. The bedrooms had big mirrors with huge double beds, white bedspreads and giant pillows. The rooms were picture-perfect 24 hours a day. Everything was simply beautiful. We traveled on the PTC all day to get to Grandmother Jessie's house, but it was worth it. I always felt important whenever I visited.

"Hello Mother," Momma would say in a voice that best could be described as a monotone.

"Lucille," would be Grandmother Jessie's standard response.

"Hi Grandmother Jessie," we all would say in unison.

There was such formality in Grandmother Jessie's house. Momma never called her mother mom, mommy or mama. Just Mother. We were never allowed to use a fancy title like granny, grandma, nana or mom mom. We were required to address Jessie Chapel as Grandmother Jessie. And although Grandmother Pattie was our great grandmother, we were permitted to call her Grandmother Pattie just like Momma did.

Grandmother Pattie stayed in the bedroom in the back of the house on the second floor. I was frightened to go in to see her because she looked like a ghost to me and she was never able to call my name (although she knew that I was one of Lucille's kids). Her face was pale and powdery like cornstarch and her beady little eyes looked like they were falling out of the sockets. She was a short, frail woman, but I could never be certain how tall she was because I never saw her standing up. Momma said she weighed less than 100 pounds and every time I greeted her with a hug and a kiss I thought that she was going to break. Great Grandmother Pattie had long, thick black hair that fell around her waist. Momma said that it was good hair that she got from the Indian side of her family. Grandmother Jessie had good hair, too and, when Momma was a little girl, her hair was so long that she could sit on it. Everybody in Momma's family had good hair, except us.

There was an awful smell in Great Grandmother Pattie's room and I didn't want to stay in there for too long. Darlene said it was the old people's smell; Donald said it was fart gas. When I asked Momma about it she told me it was Old Grand Dad.

Momma wasn't very close to Grandmother Pattie, and much of what she knew about her past was told to her over and over again by her mother, Jessie Chapel.

Pattie Wright led a colorful life. She was born in Danville, Virginia, sometime in the 1880s, but no one knows for sure. Slavery was fresh in the memory of most. Even though the law ended slavery, white folks and Black folks had difficulty terminating relationships. Pattie's mother, Maria Mae, was free, but she continued to sleep with the same white man. Why? I don't know, but that's the way it was back in those days. Maria Mae's old master claimed that he loved her, but certainly not enough to marry her. White men just didn't marry their Colored mistresses back then. For as long as it lasted, Marie Mae was the mistress of a powerful white man and Pattie, and her sisters, were the daughters of a concubine.

Maria Mae loved her freedom but hated the poverty that was forced upon her. Taking in white women's laundry and darning the family's wardrobe was the only way to make a living that was available to her. But she was a proud woman and always hoped that Pattie's life would be different.

There was reason for optimism. Even though Danville was a rural rebel town in the heart of the south, Pattie was born a good twenty years after they stopped slaving folks. Promises were made and expectations for opportunity to achieve the good life ran high. Colored children could do well, even those like Pattie, whose thinly-chiseled white features were a constant reminder of the power of the white man.

Pattie was barely ten when she started to take notice of the excessive attention that she received from everyone—Black and white. She was blossoming into a beautiful young girl with uncommon poise and beauty. Her mixed racial heritage gave her an exotic look that most people noticed.

Far too often, Pattie had to assist her mother in her laundry chores, scrubbing dirty draws, long johns, shirts, dresses and skirts, but she knew early on it was not the life for her. She hated doing laundry - cleaning, pressing, mending - all of it was disgusting ("And that's why," Grandmother Jessie would always say, "I'm not going to be anybody's domestic!"). She hated acting like a servant when she was free. And she was fully resentful of her second-class status. She dreamed of catching a train and heading north like so many of the menfolk to places like Chicago, New York and Philadelphia.

Maria Mae was always proud of her heritage. She was a Colored woman and she would make do. Pattie, with her creamy vanilla skin, knew she was a Colored woman too. And as she got older, she could distinguish the difference between how she was treated by the white men - a disrespected, disposable plaything - and how she was treated by the Colored. She decided to cast her lot with the Colored men.

They adored her. She never lacked attention. If she had chosen to do so, a different beau was available to her every night of the week. She had the ability to pick and choose. Beauty was her most valuable asset and she was determined that it would take her miles away from the plantation style life of Danville, Virginia.

She was only seventeen when she married Eston, the first of five husbands. I don't know if they were looking for a match, but he too was a fair-skinned, mixed-up race child. They were an ambitious couple. They left the south before the turn of the century traveling north to Upper Darby, Pennsylvania, right outside of Philadelphia. He worked hard as a day laborer. She stayed home and bore his children.

The children were born in rapid succession. First John, Nellie, George, Me, Basil, Eston, Jr. and Ida Mae. I remembered being quite terrified when I was a child because my younger brothers and sister started to be taken away by the creeping death. Basil, Eston Jr. and Ida Mae were dead before I turned seven, and my Daddy died before mother was thirty. She was out in the world again, looking for a way to make it, fairly determined that she wasn't going to do laundry.

She used her good looks, small but firm and shapely body and fair skin to capture men. And Colored men were absolutely foolish about fair-skinned women. She took on a new husband and a new lifestyle. There was no old time religion to keep her on a righteous path, just booze and parties. I don't know how, but husband number two dropped dead too; then three, four and five. That was one of the interesting things about Pattie. She never divorced a man. She didn't have to. Pattie put all of her husbands six feet under. She had a white liver, and it was the killer of men.

The older she got the less desirable she became. Booze and parties continued to be a major part of her life. She would go where the men were...in saloons, bars and juke joints. She would flirt with them all, creating jealousy among them. A fight would ensue and Pattie would go home with the winner. She was living the low life.

Pattie was damn near sixty when she came home with husband to be number six. That's when people started to raise questions. "How could a woman be so lucky or unlucky in marriage? Weren't five husbands enough? How did they all die? Did she help them to their graves, or what?" There was even talk of an investigation. That's when I put my foot down. There would be no husband number six. Pattie protested, but I stuck to my guns and ran Mr. Greyson away from here. I know I did the right thing. And I no longer fret over it.

Pattie remained a feisty old woman, wanted to be in charge of her own destiny. Nobody could tell her what to do. The older she got the more she got to be a pain in the ass. Oh, she had her good days. She loved my children and doted on them whenever she had a chance to see them, which was not often. Remember how she would give you all sweets and always asked how everybody was doing? Once, when I ran into difficulty, I sent your sister, Dorethea, to live with her down there on South Street. It was a good arrangement for both of us. She was helping me out and Dorethea could keep an eye on her. Sorta like supervise her. I guess she wasn't totally insensitive to family needs. Pattie was a sweet woman in her own way. But she would return to Old Grand Dad every night. She was difficult to control, although I'm uncertain if it did her any harm. Pattie's still going strong. And she refuses to die.

I've taken my mother in on two separate occasions before she finally came to stay. We tried living together before, but she got on my nerves. She never understood how hard I worked to better myself. I'm just as good as anybody else out there and nobody's going to tell me different. We never did get along. Mother would run her mouth too much and she was always talking about my business. She was too critical of my life, and I was just *as critical of hers. "How did she think she could tell me how to live?" She lived a low-class, scandalous lifestyle. She had good looks going to bed, and she never did figure out how to use it. Just wasted away all of her feminine wiles.*

Pattie was eighty-three when she came here to live with me in this house, for what I suspect is the last time. It has really cramped my lifestyle. With all those men she buried and put in the ground, nobody left her a damn thing. There's no real money, certainly not even enough to bury her when the time comes. And you know how her sisters feel about her. Now I'm responsible for her care. She drinks, then leaks all over her bed. There's a foul odor seething from every pore in her body that I can't get rid of. She continues to mourn the loss of her mother who was buried more than thirty years ago, someone I hadn't seen since I left Danville in a hurry with Lester, and she talks about a Daddy she never knew. It's been somewhat disruptive. I guess it's not all her fault. I think God put Pattie here before her time. She wanted to live a good life before Colored people had a chance. She was a wild woman, a pistol. Even in her fifties and sixties she would dress up, paint her face - and she needed to have her eyeglasses glued to her face just to see where she should put the eye shadow - and sport around town always looking for somebody to take care of her. It was her fair skin and good looks that made Colored men stupid. I guess she just played the hand that she was dealt.

Lucille... I always want you to remember that aging is real hard on a beautiful woman.

Momma never told me much about Grandmother Pattie. I would learn the truth much later. When I asked her to tell me about Old Grand Dad, she told me never mind. I knew Pattie sounded an awful lot like Patricia and some white people used to call me Pattie before I corrected them and said that my name was Patricia Anne.

"Am I named after my Great Grandmother Pattie?" I asked Momma one Sunday when we were leaving Grandmother Jessie's house.

"No," Momma said. "I named you after someone else. You're nothing like your Grandmother Pattie."

Just after we celebrated our first anniversary year on Catherine Street, Great Grandmother Pattie died. I remember it quite well because Momma came home from work on Tuesday night with the same fear of God death look on her face as I just saw on Brother Vernard's.

"Your Grandmother Pattie has passed," she announced to all of us kids sitting on the living room floor watching the Magnavox.

"Where did she go?" Marie asked curiously.

"She's dead, dummy," Wayman shouted.

"She's gone to Heaven," Momma told us in a soft voice.

I knew about Heaven. It was way up in the sky, right above the large white puffy clouds. You couldn't see Heaven, but it was up there. If people did good deeds during their life, when they died they would go to Heaven. When you floated up to Heaven, your face could touch the clouds and you'd be in the presence of God. People walked around Heaven all day having a good time. Mrs. Williams, our Sunday school teacher at Sharon Baptist Church, said that dead people who had gone to Heaven "praised the glory of the Lord all day, every day until eternity." I started to wonder about that. *"Did people stay in church all day long?"*

The next day Momma took the PTC downtown to Grant's five and dime store on 11th and Market Streets. She needed some material to make a dress for Great Grandmother Pattie's funeral. Momma said Grant's material was cheaper and they were running special sales all the time. Sometimes you could get a good buy – two yards for a dollar. You could make a whole dress for two or three bucks.

Momma spent $2.76 on the black cotton material from Grant's. There were no specials that day and she had to pay 69 cents a yard. She made a long blouse and an A-line skirt, with a two inch matching belt that Momma turned inside out with a pencil. It wasn't fancy like the red satin dress with the big diamond hole cut out at the chest that showed her fleshy brown bosoms. This new outfit was for mourning.

On Saturday morning Momma got dressed in her new black clothes and boarded the PTC to go to Mr. Chew's Funeral Home, at 2125 Christian Street, to say one last good-bye to Great Grandmother

Pattie. We all got to stay home. Momma said that it would cost too much money to take us on the trolley and none of us had proper funeral clothes.

It was a strange funeral. Not too many people gathered, but the family from Virginia, who hadn't seen Pattie in a hundred years, decided to be present at the send-off services. The atmosphere in Mr. Chew's funeral parlor was chilly. Momma said that Sister Surana disliked Pattie the most and she was determined that her transition to the afterlife would not go uninterrupted. Surana knelt by the coffin to say her final goodbyes and faked sadness and sorrow over the passing of Pattie. She stared at the body for a good long time. She stood up and reached into the coffin, pretending to tuck her in as a final tribute to the passing of her soul. It was at that moment that Grandmother Jessie detected the shinny object in her hand that Surana slipped under Pattie's burial pillow. She knew it was a curse of some kind and she rushed forward to confront Surana and to remove the object from the coffin.

Grandmother Jessie cussed Surana to her face and demanded that she leave the funeral home. It was a terrible ruckus. Most folks thought that both Jessie and Surana were overwhelmed by grief, but Grandmother Jessie was prepared to fight. (Fighting is something that we always do at funerals.) Everybody started to run for cover 'cause they were afraid that Jessie and Surana would knock Pattie out of her coffin. Talk about disrespecting the dead!

Momma came home late that night looking mighty strange. The newly-made, stiff black outfit, now wilted and wrinkled from the stress of the day, hung loosely on her body like an old burlap sack. She had a blank look on her face and seemed to stare right through us as she entered the house and walked into the dining room. In the glow of the bright light (which, as Daddy said, must have been connected to the moon, because every light in the house was on) you could clearly see how bad she looked. Her eyes and cheeks had receded closer to the back of her head and she looked extremely sad. We circled around her, jumping up and down with excitement.

"Momma, what happened at Great Grandmother Pattie's funeral?" we asked, each one of us competing to see who could get the closest to Momma.

"They placed her body in a white coffin, prayed and fought over her at Mr. Chew's, then laid her to rest in a place called Eden."

Great Grandmother Pattie was the first in the family to go to Eden. She would be there all by herself in an unmarked grave 'cause wherever they put husbands number one, two, three, four and five, nobody ever thought about joining her bones with one of theirs for her trip into eternity.

My Great Aunt Surana was still mad at Grandmother Pattie when she died. Nobody knows why, for sure, and we never heard from her again.

Grandmother Jessie was a little mad, too, but at least for now, she no longer had to worry about caring for my Great Grandmother Pattie. She could clean up the room and get out that awful smell. Then it would be just as beautiful as the rest of the house.

Momma thought, but never talked about, how she didn't want any of her daughter's lives to be anything like Great Grandmother Pattie's. She was ashamed of how she lived and how she died and wanted the secret stories about her past to remain hidden.

And my Great Grandmother Pattie...well...she was just dead and gone. And nobody talked much about her after that. I wondered if the newly departed would experience the same fate.

8

The Strangers We Call Family

Brother Vernard hadn't been in the house long and I still wasn't ready to hear the death announcement. Who was it this time? My Grandmother Jessie? Momma's baby sister, Aunt Nita? Or maybe it was her big sister, my Aunt Savannah? I didn't even want to know. But thoughts about dead people continued to rush through my mind. Why were my people dropping dead like big black flies in summer heat?

Wayman was still in the street playing Skully's with Richie. Richie's family was much like ours. They lived two doors down at 5832 and had been living there for less than a year. There were as many kids in their house as ours, but you couldn't be certain how many. When Richie's mommy and daddy moved in, they didn't bring all the kids with them. Every few months or so a different kid would show up and be introduced to the block as another sister or brother. Momma said the State had those children and that none of her kids would ever be foster. There were eight, nine or ten kids when they finally stopped coming. Yet, we were always waiting and wondering to see if there would be more. At thirteen, skinny little Richie was the oldest and he got along pretty good with Wayman.

Before we moved to Catherine Street we had never heard of this game they called Skully's. The boys would use orange, red and yellow chalk to draw nine Cheerio sized boxes within the boundaries of two row houses. They would number each box from one to eight, crisscrossing on different sides of the board. On the box in the center they drew a big skull and cross bone. That was the Skully box.

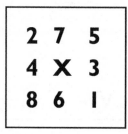

Smashed soda bottle tops were used as shooters. A good pluck like a kick with a finger would send your bottle cap flying from one side of the street board to the other. Each player had to put his shooter in the correct box while avoiding the center (Skully) box. You were dead and out of the game if you landed in the Skully box. All the boys on the block - Putt Putt, Butchy, Bucky, Lump, Musk, Lewis, Denny, Dougie and Champ - got to play Skully's. Butchy and Musk were pretty good at it. They didn't want the girls to play, but I knew that I could be just as good at Skully's as any of the boys. It pissed me off that the boys got to do more things than the girls. Girls had to play Hopscotch on the sidewalk or jump Double Dutch between the parked cars. Once, Momma brought Wayman a big colorful bag of marbles. They were green, blue, yellow, beige and tiger-eye. The boys laughed and told him marbles were for sissies. Skully's was a man's game.

I walked up and down the street looking for someone to play with. Since Jennifer left, the little white girl at the end of the block, there were no other girls on the block my age. I was nearly ten now and there were no other ten or eleven year old girls on Catherine Street. Sheila Frazier and Debbie Quillen were both twelve and they were Darlene's friends. Darlene wouldn't let me play with her or her friends. She thought I was a pest and wouldn't have anything to do with me. Michelle and Alma were all about to be nine, like Jessica.

Paula, Cookie, Theresa and Donna were about the same age as Marie. They all played with each other and the younger children. I had to play with the boys because they were the only ones left.

At first, the boys resisted my efforts to hang out with the Crew. That's what they had taken to calling themselves, the Crew. They didn't want to be seen as a club, only white kids did that. The Crew wanted to be like a street gang, where loyalty to one another meant everything. They weren't thinking about stabbing or beating up anybody, but Catherine Street was their territory and they weren't about to let kids from another block violate it. Wayman would fit right into the Crew; I couldn't because I was a girl. But Wayman was my best friend. During our first year on the block we hung tough together and nothing, especially not these knotty-head boys, could come between us.

Me and Wayman, we made every day an adventure. We were used to hustling-up small change from our experience on Woodland Avenue. We would collect old rags and clothing from people in the neighborhood and sell them to the junkyard up the street and around the corner from our apartment on top of the bar. The junkman brought old newspapers, scrap metal and cans too. We collected soda bottles from the trash and returned them to the store for the 2 cent deposit. We were environmentalists, into recycling before we even knew what the word meant. In the summertime we picked blackberries from the railroad tracks around the bend and sold them for a quarter a pot. Wayman and I were always finding ways to raise money so that we could have enough for the 15 cent movie matinee on Saturdays. We had to be real creative on Catherine Street 'cause Momma told us not to go begging the new neighbors for clothes. A lot of times, we went looking for trashy treasures at the old supermarket.

There was a Pantry Pride on 57th and Baltimore Avenue, only five blocks away from our house. Well, it was only five blocks, but it still took a long time to get there. There were one or two small streets in between each one of the big blocks and that made the walk even longer. We had to pass Webster, Norfolk, Montrose, Alter and

Ellsworth before you could see Cobbs Creek Parkway which collided with Baltimore at 58th.

One hot and muggy Saturday morning, Wayman and I walked up to the Pantry Pride. We wanted to search the trash to see what we could find. The early morning dew caused the boxes to feel wet and sticky, but we continued to plow our way through mounds of trash in search of a bargain.

In the back of the store right next to the brown trash bins were stacks of wooden bushel baskets that were used to ship the fruits and vegetables from far away places like *Mary Land* and *New Jersey*. There were little black gnats and fruit flies circling the bottom in search of a good meal. We just blew them out of the way. We knew these bushel baskets were good for something. Granny used to use them to take our dirty clothes to the laundry. The fish man had them piled up in the back of his truck. And when he came down the street hollering, "fish man, fish man," you could see how he separated the Whitings, Porgies, Croakers, and Blue Fish into different baskets. We separated the stinky, broken baskets from the clean, sturdy ones and grabbed as many as we could as we started toward home.

We walked down South 58th Street knocking on people's doors trying to sell our bushel baskets for ten cents apiece. They sold like hot cakes and we were empty-handed before we hit Catherine Street. So, we went back for more.

We came home with eighty cents apiece and flashed our coins in front of all the boys on the block. Putt-Putt (who had a square face, a broad nose, and was smarter than all the rest of the boys) wanted to say something smart to me and Wayman. But he didn't. We went to the drug store and brought 2 cent Tootsie Roll Pops and handed them out to everybody. That's when the Crew decided to let us in. First, they just wanted Wayman, but Wayman said he wasn't joining without me. (That was my older brother, Momma's baby boy, sticking up for me.) They agreed, as long as I didn't expect any special treatment because I was a girl. I had to be treated just like one of the boys.

The Crew had never heard of the name Wayman and joked that our Momma was high on pot when she gave birth and didn't know how to spell his name. I didn't know what the pot was, but I pretended I knew exactly what they were talking about.

"Isn't it supposed to be Raymond?" Champ inquired.

"No. It's Wayman. W.A.Y.M.A.N.," my brother protested.

"What about his skinny sister," quipped Bucky.

"We call her Piggy," Wayman volunteered, much to my utter dismay. They roared with laughter.

"Piggy," Butchy hollered, "I think we should call her stick!"

"No. Let's leave it at Piggy," Putt-Putt argued. "Nobody would ever want a girl named Piggy." They screamed and hollered, patting each other on the back in the process. Lewis, who was much older than me and all the other boys, stepped forward and attempted to shield me from the poking and teasing that they all seemed to relish. He warned them about the cruelty of their verbal insults.

"One day you're going to be sorry you treated that girl like that!"

"Oh shut up four eyes," Musk shouted. "You're not even a member of the Crew!"

It was settled. For years to come I would answer to the name Piggy. It was used in a variety of ways - to poke fun at, tease and to humiliate. Eventually, it would be used as a term of endearment. But for the most part, Piggy was used to remind me of my undesirability as a girl. And none of that really mattered. What was far more important was that the Crew had, finally, accepted us.

I couldn't find the Crew anywhere. I looked over the porches at 5834 and 5836 for Butchy, Bucky and Putt-Putt. They lived three and four doors down, but nobody was out on the porch. I jumped over the banisters and peered in the front doors of both houses, hoping to catch a glimpse of what was going on inside. I saw nothing. I walked down the street toward the drug store, stopped in to buy a Hershey chocolate bar with almonds, and then crossed over to the other side of the street. I saw a couple of new boys playing handball against he brick wall outside of the drugstore. I dared not approach them. I was looking for Champ, Lump, Musk, Dougie or Denny. Anybody would do. But they were all missing in action. I knew they were somewhere doing something good and deviant without me. I started to roam around the corner to see if they were on Webster Street, but I didn't want to leave the block by myself. It wasn't safe. There was nothing else to do but to go into the house and face the music. *"Who was it that had died this time?"*

I was scared and nervous as I stepped through the front door. The room was always dimly lit. Not much lighting came through the front windows in the living room that were covered with the heavy white aluminum blinds. And the one lamp that sat on top of the dark wood table next to the plastic covered green sofa did not provide sufficient light for the entire room. There was a little pen light on top of the colored picture of the white Jesus which hung on the wall in a heavy black wrought iron frame with little shelves on the side for knick knacks. But that light brightened Jesus' face and nothing else.

Momma was on the couch (right under the picture of Jesus) and Brother Vernard was sitting on the plastic, slip-covered gold chair. Much to my surprise, Momma didn't look too bad. Not sad. And certainly not hysterical! Brother Vernard had come all the way from South Philly to tell her that her Papa - Lester Chapel - was dead. I was happy that he was the dead one because I never knew my grandfather. Momma hadn't seen him for years and she never talked about him. This was not a big person dying and I didn't think that anybody would have to go to the funeral. For what? I was practically giddy, knowing that this dead kin wouldn't touch my life.

Brother Vernard stared at Momma. "Lucille," he shouted, "are you going to be okay?"

Momma smiled back. Her mouth was turned up at both corners and her cheeks worked hard to keep her lips pressed tightly together.

"I'm fine," she assured him in a calm pleasing voice. "I can't say that my heart is overwhelmed with grief and sadness." She chuckled, a bit, as she stared in my direction. Brother Vernard jumped up from the chair and began pacing the floor.

"How can you talk like that, Lucille?" he demanded to know. "The man was your father."

"Frankly, I can't even say that I knew him that well." And Momma was about to tell Brother Vernard why.

My daddy, Lester Chapel, was born in 1902 in Danville, Virginia. He was the descendent of former slaves. Like everybody else, he started out as a farmer and then ended up as a laborer. Farming had become the tradition for the Chapel family. His parents, August and Margaret Chapel, had eight other children. Lester, the oldest boy, was the family's pride and joy. He was a tall, thin, muscularly built young man with deep chocolate colored dark brown skin. I remember him as a very imposing figure, always bigger than life.

It's difficult for me to recall my earliest memories. And sometimes it's too painful. It's easier for me to forget. I remember being shot in the head when I was two years old by a buck shot gun. Nobody believes that I remember when it happened, but I do. Mother will tell you that the story is true. She and Mrs. Boxwood were fighting over me. Mrs. Boxwood didn't have any children of her own and told Mother that she could take better care of me. Mother refused to turn me loose. I remember Mrs. Boxwood saying, "If I can't have her, nobody will!" That's when the gun went off and the bullet hit my forehead. There was blood on my blouse and all over Mother's white dress. I don't know what happened after that. It's strange. I can't recall a thing. Mother always said that Mrs. Boxwood was only fooling around and never intended to hurt me. But we never saw or heard from her again.

I had just turned four when Daddy took Savannah, Junior and me away from Mother. We moved in with Uncle Fletcher and Aunt Fannie. They lived in Harlem, in a giant apartment building right next to the Hudson River. Uncle Fletcher already had plenty of mouths to feed. Before they were finished, Uncle Fletcher and Aunt Fannie would have 14 kids. All single births. There were too many children in the house, but Daddy insisted that we stay. Aunt Fannie was his sister and, I guess, she felt compelled to take us in.

Daddy rarely paid us a visit and Savannah, Junior and me clung together like sticky saltwater taffy. Savannah was six and Junior was three. We were inseparable. We lived in a small, cramped apartment and all three of us slept together on a cloth mat, filled with bed bugs and other pests, on the hardwood floor. Red bite marks were all over our bodies. Mother would try to visit us often, but Uncle Fletcher and Aunt Fannie didn't want her around. On Savannah's seventh birthday Mother brought her a big box of chocolate candy and a square vanilla coconut cake that she baked from scratch. As soon as Mother left, Aunt Fannie threw the chocolates and the coconut cake out the back door into the Hudson River. Savannah ran out back and jumped into the river trying to save her presents. Some boys, we never knew their names, saved her life. After that, Uncle Fletcher and Aunt Fannie sent for Daddy.

"Get them chillum out of here!" Uncle Fletcher shouted at Daddy when he arrived one cold winter day in late January. They fought, argued and exchanged harsh words. Daddy gathered our meager belongings, took us outside and put us in a big Black Ford and drove us away. We were gone, never to see Uncle Fletcher and Aunt Fannie again.

We took a forever long ride all the way down south to Danville, Virginia. Daddy said he was taking us back home to his peoples. Everywhere we went we saw miserable people, on the roads, in the streets, sitting on front porches and hanging around back alleys. Daddy said the country was suffering from a deep depression and that we should be grateful that family would take us in. And Daddy told us that things were real bad for Negroes like us. There were more sisters and brothers in Danville and plenty of room for us to run around in the country.

I don't think that this Uncle and Auntie (I can't even remember their real names) knew that we were coming. They screamed when they saw him, not screams of joy but screams of pain and sorrow. They kept hollering, "I told you so," over and over again. We knew that they didn't like Mother, but we didn't know why. Something she did down there in Danville. All Daddy's people were real dark and they didn't seem to like light skinned Black people, and Mother was certainly one of them.

I was six when I arrived, but by the time I was seven I was convinced that we had been taken to Danville to die. I heard about Hell on Earth, and this was Hell…without the fire!

We barely had enough to eat and Uncle and Auntie were angry every time they put food on the table. We stayed filthy dirty, barely clothed and never had any shoes to wear. We didn't go to school and we had to walk barefoot for miles to get to the church Sunday school service. There were no other children on the farm, just Savannah, Junior and me. We were assigned chores to do on the farm and I remember working from sun up to sun down.

One day Mother pulled up in a big black car with a blue-black man in the driver's seat. He was just as big as Daddy, but much darker, so we knew that it wasn't him. Daddy had not been back to Danville since he left us at Uncle and Auntie's for about a year or so. He abandoned us and went back to New York, moving way up there to Albany. We wept and cried when we saw Mother, jumping up and down, filled with joy and happiness. We were certain that Mother was there to take us back home, away from this hell house. But Uncle and Auntie refused to let us go. "Them chillum belong to Les, even the court say so. Take your white blood butt back up North where you belong." Like I said, I don't think that Uncle and Auntie cared too much for the white looking Colored folks. Mother stayed with us for a while, showering us with hugs and kisses. She brought us food—fried chicken, potato salad, green beans and sweets. Mother wanted to bring us some good clothing but she didn't know our sizes any longer. Before she left, she said she loved us and kissed us goodbye.

We watched the car pull away from the house out onto the rocky gravel dirt road. We cried alligator sized tears as we waved goodbye to Mother and the blue-black man. He was actually blacker than sin. At that time, I thought to myself that I would never see Mother again.

After Mother was long gone I stayed in the yard and played with Chicka, my pet chicken. Chicka was the only friend that I had other than Savannah and Junior and I often wondered what my life would be like if all I had to do was to walk around the yard and eat feed all day like Chicka. I tried to eat feed once when the hunger pain took hold of my stomach, but I couldn't develop a taste for it.

Months passed and nothing changed. The chickens, hog and cat always ate better than Savannah, Junior and me. I used to go sit on the front porch after dinner to see how much food I could steal from the gray and white cat. One night Auntie gave the cat a big plate of red kidney beans. Cat started to eat those beans before I got to them. I just pushed her aside and finished the plate myself. I went to bed on a full stomach.

Auntie's screaming and hollering woke me up. The cat was dead. She found it stiff as a board stretched out in front of the screened door on the front porch. The beans had gone bad and poisoned the cat. I screamed and hollered too.

"I'm going to die. I'm going to die, too. I ate Kitty cat's beans last night." The excitement caused me to wet my pants, I had the runs, and a foul-smelling, dirty brown pee ran down my legs. Auntie poured a bottle of castor oil down my throat and sent me to the outhouse. I shitted for three days, but I survived. I'll never forget that either.

Uncle blamed Auntie for forcing me to eat cat food. On the fourth day, we sat down to dinner to a full plate of fried chicken, mashed potatoes, sweet peas, collard greens and corn cakes. I ate everything in sight. I was stuffed like a pig, full and happy to be alive when I left the kitchen table to go outside and sit on the front porch. I wanted to play with Chicka.

"Chicka, Chicka," I cried out.
"Too late," Auntie hollered out the screen door.
"Chicka is what you ate for dinner."

Mother made another visit in the spring. Savannah told Mother I almost died when I ate the cat's food and Mother was furious. For the first time I saw tears running down Mother's face. We cried, too. She promised that she would do something real soon.

We continued a miserable existence. The summer was hot and sticky. The extreme heat and humidity sucked the life right out of us and we all began to whither away. We looked like ratty-tatty walking skeletons. Mosquitoes and flies were everywhere and they used our unprotected bodies for breakfast, lunch and supper.

One day in early October Uncle and Auntie rushed to get the house in order. We overheard them talking about the court coming to check on us kids. They tried to straighten a few things out around the farm and even washed some old clothes and put them on the three of us. The white lady who came to the house covered her face with a handkerchief and shook her head repeatedly. She was a very forceful woman and seemed to strike fear in Uncle and Auntie. We could tell that Auntie was real angry, but little conversation passed between her and the white lady.

Once she was gone, Uncle and Auntie walked around the house hollering and screaming at each other. They didn't say a word to us. Junior finally asked for supper and that's when Auntie went in the back, picked and cleaned a switch, and then wore our asses out. As she whipped us she screamed that it was all our fault that the law had come to her house.

In the dead of winter Daddy showed up in a bright car with a cinnamon brown woman sitting in the front seat.

"Hallelujah Jesus," is what Auntie shouted when Daddy pulled up.

"Thank the Lord," added Uncle. "I'd done seen that you found ya' way back home," Uncle chuckled as he looked over the cinnamon brown woman.

Savannah was all over Daddy, hugging and kissing him like her long lost Papa. But not me. I held Junior close to my side and stared at Daddy from afar. I had to tell Junior who the big man was because he couldn't remember what Daddy looked like. It was the first time that I remember being so angry at my father. Somehow I knew that he was responsible for keeping us down South in Danville, living out this hellish existence, and for taking us away from Mother. I didn't want to have anything to do with him.

Daddy and his lady friend stayed at the farm all evening talking to Uncle and Auntie. Before the sun rose and the rooster crowed, Daddy told us to get our things and get into the car. We were going back North to Albany, New York to live with Daddy and his girlfriend, Dana. It was 1934 and things continued to be bad all over. Work was hard to find, especially for Colored folks. But Daddy had a good job in the warehouse making good money.

Aunt Dana was much nicer than Uncle, Auntie, Uncle Fletcher and Aunt Fannie. She cooked our meals, bought us clothes and enrolled us in Catholic school. I was afraid to get too close because I didn't know how long we were going to stay. There were too many mamas and papas in our lives; none of them particularly comforting or caring. I expected the worst out of life and, most times, that's just what I got.

It was a whole year before we saw Mother again. I started to feel like I didn't know her either. Then one day out of the clear blue she showed up on Daddy's doorstep.

She was so beautiful. So glamorous. Gorgeous! Mother was all dolled up. She wore a pale yellow dress with a matching hat. She wore white gloves and carried a white bag to match her white patent leather shoes. Mother was always dressed to the nines, although I could see that she was starting to change. She was much bigger now than she had ever been before, but still beautiful. We sat down and talked with Mother - polite talk. She didn't talk to Daddy or Aunt Dana, just Savannah, Junior and me. I don't think that we knew what to say. We didn't talk about going home. We no longer knew where home was. She brought us treats and a few items of clothing and said that everything was going to be alright. And then she left.

For a brief moment I thought that things were going to be okay. We studied Catechism and were preparing for our first holy communion at the Catholic Church. There was always food on the table and we never suffered like we did in Danville. Daddy didn't spend much time with us but Aunt Dana was there. Then one day Daddy was arrested in what they called a Jewish Insurance case. The warehouse where Daddy worked had burned down. Daddy's boss said that he was an arsonist. Daddy said it was his boss that started the fire. They sent Daddy to jail.

Mother came back to see us a few months after they sent Daddy to jail. She and Aunt Dana didn't get along and Savannah, Junior and I had no idea what was suppose to happen to us now. Aunt Dana and Mother fought and Aunt Dana told Mother to leave her house. Mother said nothing, not even goodbye. She stormed out of the house, slamming the door in Aunt Dana's face. I thought I would never see Mother again.

I was ten years old and pretty good at keeping time. Daddy had been in jail five months and in three weeks school would be out for the summer. Then one day when we were walking home from the Catholic school, Mother drove up in the huge car with the blue-black man behind the wheel. She opened the door and motioned for us to come forward.

"Get in," she shouted. We were too shocked to move.

"Where are we going, Mother?" Savannah asked.

"Just get in the car!" Mother screamed back. We raced toward the door and jumped in the back seat. I was afraid; Junior wasn't. Savannah appeared to be dumbfounded.

The blue-black man zoomed down the street, barely stopping to check the traffic signs. Mother took us back to Philadelphia and moved us into a big house in South Philly. That's when we met Dorethea and Edward. She was three and he was four. Mother said they were our sister and brother. I guess she had these children, without anybody knowing, while we were roaming from the North to the South and back up North again.

Daddy stayed in Albany, New York, until he got out of jail in 1939. He came back and forth to visit a few times, but he and Mother never could get along. It lasted for a few years. Then, we stopped seeing him after that. Eventually, we heard that he got a good job at the Brooklyn Shipyard during the War. They were hiring Colored men and women because they needed help for the war effort. It's not like we didn't have to fight to get good jobs because white people really didn't want to work next to Colored people. The unions didn't want us either. We fought hard to get into the union. That's why I pay my dues and keep up my membership in THE INTERNATIONAL LADIES GARMENT WORKERS UNION. It's protection for us Colored people.

Daddy was always good at making money and I knew that he had a good position as a foreman in the shipyard. Now that you've told me a large steel beam slipped from the crane, rolled forward and crushed him to death, well...I guess it was just his time.

I could tell by the look on his face that Brother Vernard was truly disturbed by Momma's story. He rose abruptly and headed toward the front door.

"See ya!" he hollered back at us. And he was gone in a split second.

I stayed in the house to comfort Momma, but she went about her business like nothing had happened. Momma was still mad at her daddy for all the things that happened in her childhood and she hadn't gotten over it just yet. His dying didn't change a thing.

Aunt Savannah and Grandmother Jessie gathered their belongings to go to New York to take care of my Grandfather Lester's business. Uncle Junior was already there. He had settled in the City after his marriage of one year to Aunt Blanche went sour. She was a high yel-lah woman with long, flowing sandy brown hair. She expected to be cared for in the proper fashion. Uncle Lester, who had grown up to be a gorgeous, five foot ten, wavy hair yellow man, said that whatever she wanted or needed, he was certain that he was unable to provide it. He struggled with it for a year before he stopped dealing with it - left her, and the baby, behind.

Momma and Daddy didn't go to the funeral. Momma didn't both-er to explain why and laughed every time somebody mentioned her dead father's name. Daddy said he never met the man and wasn't go-ing to New York to bury him. He said that all preachers do at funerals is to stand up and tell some lies about the deceased—that's what he called dead people. He called Grandmother Jessie a hypocrite for act-ing like she was grieving the loss of the no good bastard. And he said that insurance money was the real reason she needed to get to New York as soon as possible.

They funeralized Grandfather Lester in a hurry, dropped his body in an unmarked grave and met with the people from the Brooklyn Shipyard to see about the money. They almost came back empty-handed. There were many questions raised about Grandmother Jessie's rights to widow benefits. Another woman, Miss Geneva, who everyone thought was Lester's wife, was the one screaming and cry-ing all over the coffin at Lester's funeral. And she had seven kids, claiming that they all belonged to Lester. People said that she was common law. But my Grandmother Jessie was prepared for this fool-ishness. She pulled her official marriage license with the raised seal out of a white envelope and argued that she was the legal wife of Lester Chapel. They were never divorced. Miss Geneva, she said, didn't have a foot to stand on. Then she pulled out another official piece of paper and put forth some arguments about the need to pro-vide for Lester's young child. Grandmother Jessie produced my Aunt Nita's birth certificate, and it had Lester Chapel's name on it.

She must have won something because when Grandmother Jessie came back home to South Philly, she fixed a big fancy dinner and invited us all to her house to celebrate, and it wasn't even a holiday.

We all got to go. Donald, Darlene, Wayman, Jessica, Marie and me. Aunt Doretha and Uncle Edward were there with a bunch of kids they called our cousins. Aunt Savannah came too, with my cousin Romaine and a cute curly headed man named Joe.

Money was set aside so that Aunt Nita could attend college and Grandmother Jessie seemed real happy.

But that was the last time we heard mention of Lester Chapel. It was a "don't ask and we won't tell" approach to family history that we learned, rather quickly, not to violate. My granddaddy, Lester Chapel, he was dead and gone...and nobody even thought to ask where they buried the body. I guess it was the fate that awaited us all.

9

Reality Check
_____

I made a sharp right turn to avoid the dead gray squirrel in the middle of the road. I hate trampling road kill. You see all kinds of wildlife out here in this suburbanized country area that they call South Jersey. I don't know if I'll ever get used to it. I've been out of Philly for more than twenty-five years, but I'm still a city girl at heart.

I needed to remain focused. I had been on the road for more than forty-five minutes, yet I couldn't remember the trip from my driveway in Hamilton Township to the Benjamin Franklin Bridge.

I'd traveled from my home near Bordentown to the route 130 highway by rote. I saw signs, I think, that said Florence, Willingboro, Pennsauken and Camden, but I'm not sure. I was on the right track, and I knew where I was going, sort of. Although it's a trip that I've made less frequently in the past few years, you never seem to forget your way back home. I've been living in Jersey since 1973, but you'll never hear me refer to myself as a Jersey Girl. I'm from Philly.

For a brief moment, I stopped thinking about the past and concentrated on safely crossing the Benjamin Franklin Bridge from Camden into Philly. The Ben Franklin takes all prisoners. This is the same bridge that almost claimed my first husband's life in a car accident early in our marriage. I wasn't about to let it claim mine. I wasn't interested in a trip to Our Lady of Lourdes Hospital in Camden, or

Thomas Jefferson in the City of Philadelphia.

My childhood memories tumbled rapidly through my mind and I couldn't concentrate on the directions that Sharon had given me to get to the graveyard. She told me exactly which way to go. Cross over the bridge and take the Schuylkill Expressway to the University City exit. Take it all the way out to Baltimore Avenue until it turns into Philadelphia Pike. Stay straight on that road until you enter Collingsdale, PA. I'd find Eden on the left.

A wave of nostalgia washed over me as I hit the Schuylkill. I felt the lure of Catherine Street, strengthened by fond memories which were forever etched in my mind and soul. I jumped off the express-way at the South Street exit. It was the quickest way to get over to Southwest Philly.

I drove slowly up Spruce Street, passing through University City where the University of Penn and Drexel University had managed to gobble up the entire neighborhood. The streets were familiar, but different. I turned right onto 48th and headed toward Walnut. I wanted to take a quick cruise by West Philadelphia High where my close friends Sharon, Anita and Debbie had attended. Crossing over the strip at 52nd Street and seeing the black steel tracks of the El, stretching all the way up Market Street as far as you could see, carried me back to a comfortable place. I drove past 54th, 55th and 56th before making a left turn to travel down 57th Street. This was my neighborhood - small, warm, friendly, greasy, grimy and Black. There was a new generation of kids, but the vacuous expressions on the faces of struggling working and non working class Black folks was prevalent at every corner. Kids of all ages were sitting on front porches and steps, gossiping, hanging on the street corners and, generally, racing up and down the street looking for something to do. Some of the moms and dads were at work, but others hung out the front doors keeping a careful eye on their young brood.

I stopped at the corner of 58th & Catherine, took several deep breaths and giggled nervously as I wondered why I had returned to see this place. My hands tingled as I gripped the steering wheel. I started to feel tightness in my chest. Maybe I was having a heart attack! Probably not. I concluded, rather quickly, that the beige-colored Lycra leotard that served as my only foundation was too tight for my expanding chest. Next time, I'll order a large instead of the medium.

My palms were sweaty and, as I grabbed the wheel even tighter, I guided the car to the right. It was all there in front of me, in full panoramic view - the block, the houses, the people and the past. The flood gates opened, and memories of my childhood flowed effortlessly, seamlessly and uncontrollably to a time gone by.

10

Our Southern Roots

Momma was getting fatter by the day, and Daddy kept talking about goldfish.

"Sing'um goldfish. You got a fresh bowl of water coming!"

That's what Daddy always used to say when he and Momma got to arguing. I didn't understand. We didn't have any goldfish and there certainly wasn't a need to change any water. Still, Momma would start steaming every time Daddy said it.

I started to feel sorry for Momma. She was having a difficult time. She worked every single day without taking a break. Momma was the first one up in the morning shouting for everybody to get out of the bed. Daddy, who no longer worked at Casa Conti and didn't have a job at all, would grudgingly drag himself out of the bed to assist.

Getting to the bathroom ahead of everybody else was the tricky part. Whoever got there first got to use the washcloth and toothbrush, first. I hated using the washcloth after someone else had washed their dirty behind. I would search around the house for some scraps from Mr. Caldwell's (looking for a good substitute rather than use the same funky washcloth). The material from Mr. Caldwell's was a flimsy, lightweight quality. Momma said it was used to make Sunday dresses for white women with a few bucks to spend. Rayon is what Momma called it. And Rayon didn't hold water very well. Sometimes,

I found a big enough piece of Rayon to pretend that it was a wash-cloth. Sometimes not. But any piece of cloth was better than the wet one that somebody had just used a few moments before, especially one of the boys.

The water out of the spigot was icy cold; that usually meant that we were out of oil. When there was no oil, the furnace wouldn't click. Sometimes we would run downstairs into the basement and try to "prime it" by wiggling the cardboard-like substance on top of the oil tank that Momma used to call the wick. If a little oil was left in the bottom of the tank, Momma said that the constant friction of wig-gling that wick back and forth would ignite the burner and make that furnace click. Most of the time, the tank was empty, but if we prayed real hard, Jesus would click the furnace and allow it to burn on fumes. (Granny told us that.)

If we wanted to wash in comfortable warm water, we had to fill the thin green pot with the two black handles on the side with water, boil it for ten minutes on the hot plate on the shelf in the corner of the kitchen near the extension cord, and run back to the bath-room while it was still your turn. And none of that meant that you would get to use the sink when your water was ready. Most days we just didn't have the time. The icy cold water would have to do. We washed in Ivory soap and all shared the same, sticky roll-on deodor-ant in a white, pink and blue bottle called Tussy. I thought that was pretty unsanitary too.

Picking up a wet toothbrush was even more disgusting. And trying to brush your teeth without Pepsodent toothpaste was unbearable. Daddy said baking soda would do. We didn't have any baking soda, so we used baking powder instead, because it was the only other thing that we did have in the house that had the word baking in it.

We all ironed our own clothes on top of the long brown wood dresser in Momma's room, and fighting over the use of the iron was a daily occurrence. When Darlene, Donald and Wayman wanted to be mean to Jessica, Marie and me, they would heat up a nickel and leave it on the top of the dresser. The first one to grab it got their hands burned. The burn wasn't hot enough to put butter on it, but the sting would last for hours. They tricked us a few times before we finally caught on. Sometimes I hated my brothers and sister.

It was Wayman who first told me that Momma was pregnant. It was only the second time that I heard that word and really didn't know what it meant. One day while we were all listening to Mr. Lloyd Price's, *Personality*, and practicing the bop in the basement, Wayman and Donald got to fighting. Donald said, "If you come at me one more time, I'm going to give you a pregnant lip." Darlene ran upstairs and told Momma. Momma came flying down the steps and grabbed Donald by his scrawny little creamy tan neck.

"I better not hear you using that language around here again," she shouted as she threatened him with bodily harm. That was the end of that, and all of us kids knew not to use the word pregnant again. Later that week, I went outside to play with Butchy, Putt-Putt, Champ, Musk, Lump, Denny and Dougie. They teased me and asked me if I wanted to get knocked-up like my Momma.

"Hey Piggy," Champ snickered. "How about letting me bust that cherry?"

"Don't think you can," I snapped back, "Your bone ain't big enough."

The Crew roared with laughter.

"Busted. Busted," Butchy shouted. "She scored big time. Shame, shame on you! You gonna let that stick get away with that?"

I didn't really know anything about the bone or a cherry, but it had something to do with doing it. One night, when I was pretending like I had fallen asleep in the worn-out old sofa chair on the front porch, I overheard Sheila, Darlene and Debbie talking dirty on the steps in front of the porch two doors down. They were talking about some girl in junior high school, "Suzie with the big lips, the sucker of all D.I.C.K.S." I knew what a dick was and was fairly certain that a bone was the same thing. I wasn't sure about what I said to Champ, but I thought it would be funny.

"Let me show just how deep this bone can go," Champ asserted aggressively, pulling on the zipper of his denim shorts like he was going to do something. He moved toward me like he meant business, and all the boys were egging him on.

"Go on and do it to her," Musk shouted.

"Yea!" Denny added. "Make her pregnant like her momma."

I ran flying to the front door as Champ continued invading my personal space. I flipped the door handle and jumped inside the living room in a split second. I slammed the door in his face. I was safe, until the next time.

I asked Darlene about Momma being pregnant. Darlene said that pregnant meant she was having another baby. I finally understood why Momma was getting fat and why she was unhappy. Momma had always told us that Marie would be her last child.

My little brother, Alfred Butler Reid, was born on May 13, 1961. Alfred was named after A.B. Reid the first who, supposedly, was the illegitimate descendant of John C. Calhoun, vice-president of the United States from 1825-1832 under John Quincy Adams. My Daddy used to brag about being Calhoun's great, great grandson. Calhoun was a famous plantation-owning white man from Clemson, South Carolina, and our great-great-great grandparents were part of that crew. Daddy was from Clemson and Pop Pop was born in Clemson, too. Momma said he should be ashamed because the Calhouns were nothing more than a bunch of stinking white masters taking advantage of a poor slave woman. And Donald got in trouble that time he went to school and told Mrs. Goldberg that we all were Calhoun's descendants. She told him it was a big lie and he should never repeat it. The same thing happened to Darlene when she completed the family tree that was her homework assignment in Mr. Adkins' class in the seventh grade at Sayre Junior High. Momma and Daddy were so mad that Mr. Adkins gave Darlene an F on her assignment (and told her that she was a liar) that they went up to school to meet with him and the principal. Daddy threatened to slap the piss out of him. Mr. Adkins removed the F, but he still thought that Darlene, Momma and Daddy were big liars. But it didn't matter much to Daddy because he loved to tell us stories about his heritage, swearing that he was "not all nigger." And the birth of his newest son, who he had given the name of Alfred Butler Reid, made him as proud as ever. And when Daddy told us his story, he always included the tale of the Calhouns as if it were a glorious part of his past.

I was born on September 27, 1927 in Clemson, South Carolina. That's where I spent the happiest days of my life. We lived on a big farm, more than 100 acres. We inherited land and money 'cause we were related to Calhoun, and everybody knew it. It wasn't no accident that so many of my grandparents looked like Calhoun's folks. We were never more than a stone's throw from the Calhoun plantation. Before we got the land, it was all owned by the Calhouns. We were one of the best Colored families in all of Clemson.

My great grandmama was named Easter. She was born free, half white and half Black, or what they call mulatto. Great Granddaddy, A. B., had a white daddy, too. He was a fine, good-looking man, almost white. Women were on him like flies on shit and stink on swampwater. He dropped kids like maggots all over the place. And he was the Granddaddy of them all. He had two wives, and they both had children about the same time. About twenty in all; that's twenty that he knew about. Your Pop Pop, Lee Reid, was one of them. The women chased him like crazy too. Everybody wanted a piece of him, and there was nothing that he couldn't handle. Short, tall, fat, thin, redbone or chocolate, it didn't matter. He loved them all. He and Grandmama had four kids together.

They all had land and lots of it: Uncles George, Robert and Erskine; Aunts Cindy, Pauline and Helen. We grew cotton, tobacco, greens, corn and everything else and sold it to the folks all around us. My daddy was not a sharecropper. We owned our house. Sure life was hard, but we had it made in the shade. Mom and Pop had a large three-bedroom ranch-style brick house with a piano in it. That's when I learned how to play. I played and sang for the church. I was the best thing they had going for them in Clemson.

Your Granny was from Six Mile. Her roots were real good. When she and your Pop Pop got married, people came from miles around for the ceremony. They got married in 1919. Granny was seventeen and your

Pop Pop was eighteen. Thought they knew what they were doing. Had all us kids right down there in Clemson: Lee, Margaret, your aunt Susan and me. Varnell was born when your Granny was only a kid. Nana Ellen kept Varnell with her, but we all knew that she was our sister. We were all happy in Clemson, except for the time when my sister Margaret, we called her Maggie when she was alive, died.

Maggie was only fourteen years old. She was trying to have a baby but it wouldn't come. Breeched and wouldn't turn around. They treated the Colored real bad back then. Mama and Pop Pop couldn't get a doctor for her because she was Colored. And we couldn't take her to the hospital where all the white folks could go. Momma sent for the midwife. They tried to do their best, but she couldn't be saved. She died before the baby was born. The baby died, too. I thought Momma was going to die because she grieved so hard. We laid Maggie out in the parlor before we buried her over at Abel. Everybody was buried behind that church. They wrapped the baby up in a blanket right next to her and cuddled it in her arms. Maggie looked real good. The baby didn't. We were all sad and unhappy. Maggie was only three years older than me and I never thought that we would lose her. But a lot of people didn't make it to autumn back then. That's just the way it was.

Colored people did have problems with the white man living in the South, but that's not how we got here up North. Pop Pop met some hussy named Miss Lucy Rae and he couldn't turn her loose. He was sniffing those draws day, noon and night. Church folk got whiff of what was going on and decided to tar and feather her butt. Drove her right out of town...before the tar was hot and ready. She jumped the hound and headed north to Philadelphia. Pop Pop started looking like a runt ready to die. Before Mama could get him back, he was gone. Your Granny said the hussy worked a root on him. He was powerless, unable to control what was going on in his life. Pop Pop packed one little bag soon after that and he jumped the hound too. Nobody thought that he was gone for good, but he didn't come back. Your Granny got hot and fired up and said that she wouldn't stand for it. Before I realized what was happening, Mama took us all down to the Colored section of the Greyhound station and headed for Philadelphia. We left everything behind...the house, the land, and my piano.

It was 1939, the first time I left South Carolina and traveled up North to Philadelphia. We couldn't find Pops when we arrived so we went to his sister's house, Aunt Ida. There were five of us then. Maggie had passed on to glory. That's what your Granny said, over and over again, soon after Maggie died.

It took your Granny about a month to find your Pop Pop. He was living in a basement on 50th and Chancellor Street. Pop had been hired as the janitor and general handyman for the apartment building. He knew nothing about city life and we never could understand what possessed someone to hire him to care for city apartments. But he was a janitor in South Carolina and he continued to be a janitor in the big city. The basement apartment was a fringe benefit, free of charge, as long as he kept the job. He's been there more than twenty damn years.

That apartment is the same as it was when we first got to Philly. There are three tiny little rooms in the basement and three side windows just above ground level. Most of the light comes in through the front door. It takes little of nothing to get inside of that apartment. You walk down four steps from the street level and you're standing in the living room. The bedroom is right next door. There's an itsy bitsy bathroom between the bedroom and the kitchen that's way in the back. There's a big hallway on the side with all the guts of the building. You kids have been there long enough to know. Once you learned the secret pathways, you could get into that apartment, and everyone else's, from the side doors that connect the basement to the other side of the building on Walnut Street. After living there for only a few months in the cold of winter, Mama promised that we would go back to Clemson, soon. We never did. Your Pop Pop ruined all of our lives over a piece of tail. I made a promise to myself... pussy will never take hold of me.

We were all excited when Momma brought Alfred home, although things really started to go downhill after that. I was ten and a lot more capable to help around the house...not that I ever wanted to do anything closely related to housework, cooking or cleaning. I had a better sense of who I was and started to understand the situation we found ourselves in as Negroes in America. I was real clear about who the Negroes were now. Mrs. Jeffries, my 5th grade teacher at Harrity, spent an awful lot of time trying to make certain that all the kids in her class understood the importance of being a good Negro. And by the time I got to 5th grade, there were nothing but Negroes attending Harrity.

"I want you to grow up to be a big N," Mrs. Jeffries told us. "Never use a little n to write the word Negro," she would stress over and over again. And then she would take the time to show us who the big Negroes were. In the fifth grade, I learned about dead people like George Washington Carver, Harriet Tubman, Frederick Douglass and Nat Turner. But I also learned about Jackie Robinson, Marion Anderson, Mary McLeod Bethune and Katherine Dunham, and they were all still living. "Do great things for yourself and the race," she reminded us. "Make your people proud."

Mrs. Jeffries taught me a lot of things about the world and was one of the first people to help me understand that my family was poor. It was a surprise to me. I thought all the poor people lived in the country, way deep down in the backward area called the South. I thought poor people didn't work. I thought poor people didn't have jobs. I didn't know you could have all those things and still be considered poor. As the summer approached, I paid more attention to the differences between our lives and the other people in the neighborhood. My world was never larger than twelve city blocks, and I compared my life to all the other Negroes who were in walking distance.

Darlene and I had to get the house ready for the new baby. We took the biggest drawer out of Momma's dresser to make a crib for the baby to sleep. We stuffed the drawer with a pillow from Momma's bed. I got to boil the water in the thin green pot to clean and help sanitize the pillowcase so that the baby wouldn't catch any germs from the old pillow or the drawer. The clean scent of Clorox would help keep the bugs away. Before Daddy went to the hospital to pick up Momma, I snuck into the bedroom and took two quarters out of his pocket. I went to the drugstore on the corner of 59th street and bought some Johnson & Johnson's baby powder for 49 cents. Darlene let me generously sprinkle the powder over the pillow and the drawer. It smelt like a new baby and Darlene never asked me where I got the money to buy baby powder.

Momma came home on a Saturday morning, just when the whole neighborhood was up and about. Mr. Quillen, Mr. Jenkins and Mr. Sarge (we called him that because he was a sergeant in the army) were outside supervising the street clean-up. Mr. Quillen had the big metal key to turn on the fire hydrant, so he really was the one in charge of everything. He was the man. In the summertime, when it was hot and sticky, he would use that key to turn on the hydrant so that we could get soaking wet. It was the next best thing to having a swimming pool. Mr. Adams, the local neighborhood committeeman and politician who lived in the next to the last house on our side of the block, also walked around greeting and talking to everybody. He had been doing that since he became involved in the Kennedy campaign and got all the people on Catherine Street to go to the polls and vote for Jack Kennedy on Election Day. Mr. Adams said that Kennedy would do some good for Colored folks. He won and we're still waiting.

Mr. Frazier was sitting on his front porch in a white undershirt with a can of Ballantine beer (he didn't drink his in six seconds) resting in his hand. Mr. Frazier always came outside to listen to his radio broadcast the Phillies game. He talked sports all the time and didn't bother to spend much time on the neighborhood clean-ups.

All the daddies on my block had good jobs. Mr. Quillen worked at a paint factory and, Momma said, that's why their house always looked so good. Mr. Jenkins slaughtered dead animals in a meat factory and Mr. Frazier had a job at the Westinghouse plant. Mr. Sarge wore a suit to work because he had a job in an office building, and Mr. Lyons had the best job of all. He wore a uniform and worked for the United States Post Office.

Lots of the women worked too. Mrs. Quillen worked as a seamstress at the Quartermasters, Mrs. Pitman cleaned offices at night and Mrs. Lyons was an elevator operator at City Hall. Momma worked in a dress factory and so did Mrs. Marshall. Mrs. Brown stayed home all day and watched Jean, Michael and Diane, but everybody else did something.

Saturday was everybody's free day and most folks were outside hanging around enjoying the good spring weather when Daddy pulled up in the cab with Momma. Daddy, who was sitting up front with the driver, jumped out of the yellow cab first and went to the back to help Momma and the new baby. He grabbed the baby and Momma grabbed the bags. Momma walked straight into the house, but Daddy, he stayed outside a little longer, proudly showing off his new son all over the neighborhood. By now, everyone knew that Daddy didn't have a job. *"I wondered what they were thinking."*

All the girls thought Alfred was such a pretty baby. He was brown like the rest of us and had lots of curly black hair. He was wrapped in new blue clothes – a layette is what Momma called it – that Grandmother Jessie brought to the hospital. He was the tiniest living thing I'd ever seen. Jessica and Marie still played with dolls then, but all four of us girls would be giving up our playtime to help take care of our new baby brother.

Granny was so happy that Daddy named Alfred after Pop Pop's daddy that she didn't know what to do. Pop Pop said that baby Alfred would be taken care of because he was the family namesake. And he told the same stories about his daddy, his grandma and all the Colored cousins who had been produced by the Calhoun family. He gave Daddy a silver dollar for the baby and told him that more silver dollars would be coming. They never did.

Grandmother Jessie wasn't happy at all. She came all the way from South Philly to visit Momma the day after she came home from the hospital. She arrived in a car, 'cause Grandmother Jessie didn't ride on the PTC. She wore a pale blue dress with lace and embroidery on the bottom. You could also see through the dress if you looked real hard. She had on white patent leather shoes and a bag to match. And even though it wasn't Sunday, she wore a pretty box-like blue hat that matched her dress pretty well.

"Haven't you had enough children, Lucille?" I heard her tell Momma when she came to visit the new baby in the drawer.

"What kind of life do you expect to have with all of these mouths to feed and not enough to feed them with?" she asked Momma, who was resting on the small bed in her bedroom. We were standing outside of the door, pretending not to listen, but we could hear everything that was going on.

"I'm raising one," she stated matter of factly, "do you need me to help you with the others? What about Jessica and Patricia?"

"No, Mother," is what I heard Momma say. "I'm keeping all of my children with me. I will never let them be raised by anyone else." I think Momma got to steaming right then and there, 'cause I never ever remembered her speaking so harshly to my Grandmother Jessie.

"Vernard is with you only because you felt that it would strain my marriage to Curtis if we started out with somebody else's child. I don't think you were right about that, just like you were not right about Curtis. A lot of peoples are raising somebody else's child and they're making it.

I still remember when Curtis and I first met. I was sitting at the table in the house on Carpenter eating a jelly sandwich. My head was all over my head and I wasn't studding nobody. Curtis walked in with Beady who was there to see Savannah. Savannah was one of the most beautiful women in the neighborhood and everybody wondered about who would be the lucky one to catch her. She was like a Colored movie star; a tall, shapely, caramel-colored queen. She had that beautiful long, wavy hair and that tiny waist and big legs that were unreal. When Beady started courting her, you thought they were the most adorable couple that you had ever seen. You always talked about how wonderful it was that Savannah and Beady had gotten together. That night when they told you that they were getting married, you were thrilled beyond belief. And I remember all of that well 'cause you never felt that way about me and Curtis.

Curtis was Beady's baby brother but you felt that he would never 'mount to much. Other women were always chasing him, but that wasn't his fault. Curtis was a singer and the women would fall out and scream all over him every time he sang a song. Yes, I felt a little jealous about what was going on, that's natural. But Curtis always said that he wanted to be with me. He understood me and what I was feeling when no one else did. He knew how hard it was for me to go to high school every day with all those bulldaggers

over there at William Penn. You know they wanted me. I came home everyday complaining and you kept telling me to stay in school. I couldn't take
it anymore. Curtis understood when I quit and went to work in the dress
factory. I couldn't sew a lick at the time, but I was willing to learn. And he
never said too much about what happened with Vernard. That's why we
ran off and got married the way we did. Once we realized that Curtis, Jr.
was on the way, we weren't going to let anybody stand in our way. Not you
and not Granny. I went down to Jonathan Logan's and brought a beautiful
white dress with white and silver beads. Mr. Logan gave me a pair of white
gloves 'cause he knew that I was going to use that dress as my wedding
gown. We left early in the morning and headed toward Maryland where we
knew we could be married the same day. We stopped at a service station
restroom to change our clothes. We both looked so good. We went to a
preacher's house in Elkton, Maryland, on April the 15th and had him marry
us. When we got back to Philly, Curtis went home, back to the basement,
and I went home, too, because we didn't want you or Granny to know what
we were doing.

We knew Granny wouldn't be happy about the marriage, either. Curtis
is Granny's baby and she has never been able to leave his side. Yes, Mother,
that's been a problem, 'cause I think that Curtis is a momma's boy, but
I thought that I could work it out. We knew we couldn't stay with you or
Granny so we waited, keeping the marriage a secret, until we'd found a
place to live.

We had to wait two weeks before we moved into that third floor apartment at 303 North June Street. It wasn't much, but it was our first home. I
should have taken Vernard with me back then, but I didn't. You know I love
Vernard. He's my firstborn. You know what happened and how difficult all
of this has been for me. I never wanted to leave him behind, and probably
shouldn't have never left him with you in the first place. But you insisted.
You wanted to keep him. I know he lives with you, but I take care of him.
I stop by every Friday on payday and bring you money to take care of him.
It's been tough on all of us. I don't want any of my children growing up
thinking that I don't love them all the same 'cause I do. I've worked hard to
keep all of my kids together, Mother. I worked hard to get and keep us in
this house. I'm the first one in the family to really own property you know.

I'm the first one in the union. I got a union job and I got good credit. I've done pretty well so far and I want all of my kids to have the opportunity to move up in this world. I want them to graduate from high school and get a good job. I don't want them to have to take factory jobs. I want my girls to work in an office or something like that. The boys will make it, but I have to make certain that the girls know how to take care of themselves."

Daddy was coming up the stairs so we had to scramble down the steps like we were busy doing something. I wanted to stay and listen to Momma steam at Grandmother Jessie, but when Daddy walked into the room, Grandmother Jessie gathered her belongings and left. Daddy told Momma that Granny was on her way…and Granny and Grandmother Jessie could barely tolerate each other. Grandmother Jessie was too refined, and Granny was just too country.

11

Grandmother Jessie

It was the last week in May and I couldn't wait until summer. It was absolutely the best time of the year. Summers were magical, filled with so much hope and promise, and plenty of talk about what everybody was going to do.

The summer of 1964 was going to be spectacular. Grandmother Jessie invited me and Jessica to come stay at her house for six weeks in South Philly. This was like a dream come true. I was going back, I hoped, for an overnight stay at Grandmother Jessie's house for the second time in my life. I would sleep in one of those big beds with the giant stuffed pillows and the white bedspreads that she had in every single bedroom. Since there were so many bedrooms, she'll probably give me a room all to myself. I was much older now - a teenager - and knew how to conduct myself like a proper young lady. There would be more lessons in social graces, something that I didn't quite understand the first go round.

Just two summers ago, Grandmother Jessie invited Jessica and me to visit for a week. She sweetened the pot considerably when she told us that we could bring a girlfriend along with us. I didn't have a best girlfriend. I was too busy hanging with the boys. I borrowed Darlene's friend, Sheila, and took her along with me. Jessica took Michelle.

Mr. Lyons, Michelle's father, volunteered to drive us to South Philly. He had a big green car with the words Impala on the rump side. We piled into the car, three in the back and one in the front, bursting with excitement and anticipating all the fun we would have in the upcoming week. We all smelled Clorox clean and wore freshly pressed short sets. Momma made Jessica and me new outfits from the scraps at Mr. Caldwell's factory. The print was all the same, but the colors were different. Jessica's was green and mine was a bluish-gray. Momma did some fancy, creative work to make each outfit look real special and unique.

Shelia's mother bought her two new outfits: a red, white and blue sundress that reminded me of the American flag, and a printed short set with yellow daises staring at you from her behind. *"This was going to be the best vacation in my life,"* I thought to myself. Just thinking about the food that I was going to get at Grandmother Jessie's made my mouth water and I tried not to drool in the car. I thought about the hot buttered biscuits, fried scrapple and real scrambled eggs with cheese. Grandmother Jessie would probably fry chicken for dinner and it wouldn't be the backs and necks. Grandmother Jessie would see to it that we got the chicken wings.

Lots of people were watching as Mr. Lyons pulled out of the parking space in front of his house at 5820. Mrs. Quillen, Mrs. Putman and Mrs. Frazier were all standing on their porches waving goodbye. Mr. Sarge told us to have a good time and gave us 50 cents apiece for spending money. Paula, Donna and Marie were outside playing on the front steps. Darlene stayed inside. Butchy, Bucky, Musk, Lump, Putt-Putt, Champ, Dennie, and Richie were playing stick-ball in the middle of the street. They tried to ignore us, but they knew that we were on our way to a fabulous vacation in another part of town. I didn't bother to say a word to nobody. I just wanted to go.

Mr. Lyons turned right at the end of Catherine Street and headed toward Baltimore Avenue. We cruised down Baltimore Avenue looking over all the bars, churches and grease joints before heading over to Greys Ferry Avenue. It was summertime and kids were all over the place; on the steps, on the pavements, in the streets and hanging out on the corners. It was hot and sticky, but no one had turned on the fire hydrant because it wasn't Saturday morning.

I think we were getting close to 4803 Woodland Avenue, but I was too afraid to say anything. I wanted to see the old apartment on top of the bar, and my old friend Monica Stone. I hadn't thought much about Monica since I left Wilson School after the 2nd grade. She was such a pretty little light brown skinned girl with bright eyes and an adorable smile. She was always happy. Her laugh made me laugh and I had such fond memories of playing with her during recess and after school. And I'd never forget that time we both got dressed up like little princesses (Momma bought my dress from Gimbels because I was going to be on television) and were taken to the WHYY Studio on Market Street for the filming of a children's educational program. My big moment came when they asked me to show the children who were viewing from home how to skip. I circled the stage three times before they told me to sit down. I felt like a star.

I peeped out the window to see if I could see Monica's house on the street behind the bar. *"I wonder if she'd recognize me."*

We hardly ever had the opportunity to get a ride in a car. I thought about being polite like Granny taught me. I didn't want to say anything that might offend a grownup. Mostly, I kept my mouth shut, hiding my excitement. I enjoyed being chauffeured around in the big green Impala. I looked out the window, staring at the rows of houses that we passed on our way to South Philly. I always wondered how other people lived and imagined that every house represented a joyful home - mommies and daddies who were happy to be together and loved having all their eight or nine children hanging around them. It was taking so long to get there and I want to yell, *"Are we there yet?"* But instead, I sat patiently until the car stopped in front of the enormous three story, red brick house with the polished white marble steps.

Jessica and I jumped out of the car first. It was our Grandmother and we knew where we were going. Michelle and Sheila followed and Mr. Lyons lagged far behind, engulfed, as always, in an air of confidence. He was a tall, honey-colored man, some would say gorgeous, with natural wavy hair. He didn't need any Murray's grease. He was strict and demanding. Sometimes he would stick his head out the door and whistle to summon his children. Michelle, Paula, Donna and Charles, Jr. would come, flying down the street from different sections of the block. The "Canine Brigade," that's what we called them. I was glad he wasn't my daddy because I didn't like getting whistled at.

"Hello Grandmother Jessie." My voice carefully articulated each word properly as I entered the front door taking in the smells of homemade foods, both baked and fried.

"Young ladies," she responded in a very refined and dignified manner.

We were a bit more assertive as we marched in the front door pushing the dry, stale air aside. Grandmother Jessie's invitation to Jessica and me and our two friends made us special. Grandmother Jessie's gift of choice - the selection of our two friends - gave us our first taste of power. We got to pick which girls on the block would make this special trip with us. On that particular Friday evening in July, we entered the house as if it we owned the property.

"This is my friend Sheila," I said, "and this is Jessica's friend Michelle." I was older, so I did all the talking.

"This is my Grandmother Jessie," I motioned to Michelle and Sheila, as if they didn't already know that.

Grandmother Jessie stood there for a brief moment, looking as beautiful as ever. She wore a soft, peach-colored dress with see-through sleeves and a sheer overcoat that landed gently around her calves. It was not Rayon. This time she wore large multi-colored beads with matching earrings. They weren't pearls, but looked pretty expensive. And she smelt real good.

"Welcome to my home young ladies," she said.

"Thank you, uh...Mrs. ..." It was an awkward moment. We forgot to tell Sheila and Michelle Grandmother Jessie's last name.

"Just call me Grandmother Jessie," she said in a hurry and with a pleasant little smile.

We stood there for a few moments in the vestibule leading to the long center hallway and waited for Mr. Lyons to enter the house.

He was taking too damn long. As he crept toward the front door Grandmother Jessie got her first glimpse of the tall imposing man. She brushed past us with a perky smile glued on her face as she greeted Mr. Lyons at the edge of the marble steps.

"How do, Sir," she whispered in a soft, sweet voice. "I'm Mrs. Jessie Chapel, Jessica and Patricia's grandmother."

"Charles Lyons," he said in a gruff, formal tone. His voice was ice cold and he didn't even crack a smile. I guess he didn't quite realize whom he was talking to.

"Come in, let me fix you something," Grandmother Jessie offered warmly as she quickly looked him over and sized him up in a spilt second.

"No thank you Ma'am. I must be on my way."

"How rude," I thought to myself. Granny taught us that no matter how limited the offerings, one should always be gracious enough to stop and sit still long enough to have a taste of something if offered.

Mr. Lyons grabbed the brass handle on the front door and swung it wide open. He turned around slowly like an alley cat sneaking down the backyard fence and glanced at Michelle.

"Behave."

Grandmother Jessie showed us to our rooms upstairs on the second floor. She pointed to the dresser drawer and told us to put our things away. There was an empty drawer for each one of us. At the bottom of each drawer laid a floral print sheet and a sweet-smelling pouch filled with talcum powder.

"After you bathe yourself you can get ready for bed," she said. That caught me by surprise. We were already clean and I didn't think that another bath was necessary, but I didn't want to disobey my Grandmother Jessie. I was real disappointed. She was sending me to bed without anything extra special to eat. Momma had fixed some hot Spam for dinner, but I didn't bother to eat it. I knew that there would be much better fixins at Grandmother Jessie's house. In fact, I never ate the surplus food at our house if I knew I could go to someone else's house to get a better meal.

She must have read the look of utter disappointment on my face.

"Are you children hungry?" she asked rather suddenly. Of course I was hungry. When did Grandmother Jessie ever see me when I wasn't hungry?

"Yes, Grandmother Jessie." Jessica was the first to respond this time. That was a good thing because it made me appear less greedy. Shelia and Michelle just nodded their heads.

"Didn't you all have dinner?"

"Yes, Grandmother Jessie."

Dinner didn't matter that much. We always ate food at Grandmother Jessie's. *"Wasn't she gonna fix us dessert or something?"*

"Come down after you settle in," she finally said. "I have a little something in the kitchen."

It didn't take me long. I stuffed a week's worth of freshly ironed clothes into the bottom of the dresser drawer and flew like greased lightning down the stairs to meet Grandmother Jessie in the kitchen.

"I was saving this cake for tomorrow night," she told me, "but if you're hungry, you can have some now."

"I'm hungry," I blurted out loud and clear. There was never any doubt. I always ate as much as I could at Grandmother Jessie's. She always had tremendously delicious food and I never refused a good meal.

I was already finishing my first piece of homemade, pineapple up-side down cake when Jessica, Michelle and Sheila got to the table. I was reaching for piece number two when I noticed a strange look on Grandmother Jessie's face as she stared in my direction. "Don't be greedy," she was thinking to herself as she peered over the round black glasses that framed her vanilla face, looking me dead in the eye. But she didn't say a word and I wasn't pretending to be a mind reader. I reached over and cut me another piece of cake and drank a glass of milk along with the rest of the girls.

After that special treat we changed into our pajamas and got ready for bed. Me and Jessica had new ones because we didn't wear pajamas at home. We slept in our underwear. Momma bought us pajamas for Grandmother Jessie's so we wouldn't be embarrassed. Michelle called them PJs. We acted like we knew what she was talking about, but we didn't.

Sleep was the furthest thing from our minds. We ran from room to room, played games, jumped on the beds and talked all night. We told lies about all the boys who wanted us to be their girlfriends, how smart we were in school, and about all the things we would do once we were grown-ups. It was three in the morning before my body gave way to exhaustion and the need for sleep snatched me away from the best night of my life.

I was totally exhausted in the morning but awakened to the sweet-smelling scent of fried pastries. Grandmother Jessie was making one of her specialties - fried apple turnovers. I jumped out of bed and ran down the flight of steps that connected the kitchen to the back of the house as fast as I could. My brand new PJs were wrinkled and sweaty from a good night's sleep.

I stood there with a wide-eyed expression on my face as I watched Grandmother Jessie, humming some religious song, moving back and forth from the kitchen table to the gas stove. She filled the pastry with fresh cut apples and sealed them in a quarter-moon shaped pocket dough that she made from scratch with flour, baking powder, sugar and eggs. She pressed the edge of the turnovers with a fork to make the outside trim look fancy, and then rolled them in white flour before dropping them in the hot lard in the frying pan.

"Is it time for breakfast?" I questioned. By this time I wasn't standing there alone. Jessica, Michelle and Sheila were resting comfortably on my heels as we watched Grandmother Jessie flip the apple turnovers.

She looked disgruntled. "Good morning," she said rather sternly as she looked over the four of us out the corner of her eye.

"Good morning Grandmother Jessie," we all said in unison.

"Did you wash your face?"

No, we had not, and Grandmother Jessie wasn't happy about it. We raced back upstairs and waited our turn to get into the bathroom.

That was another thing that made me so happy to be at Grandmother Jessie's. I had my own washcloth and toothbrush at her house. We didn't even have to bring them with us, 'cause Grandmother Jessie supplied everything that we needed.

Grandmother Jessie had more than one bathroom in her house. I got to use the biggest one on the second floor. There was a tub, a sink and a shower all in the same room. Big fluffy towels (which my Grandmother Jessie told me not to use) were hanging from the doors and the walls. Hot water came from the spigot and matching pink rugs were on the floor and the toilet seat. There was a sign pinned to the wall right in front of the toilet that you could read while sitting there peeing: *Flush as soon as you go so the stink don't travel downstairs.* I wondered if she put that sign there just for us.

I took my time in the bathroom. I wasn't in a hurry to get back downstairs because I felt a little embarrassed that Grandmother Jessie had to tell me to wash my face. I always wanted to do extra well in front of my grandmother. I admired her a great deal and thought that someday I would be as well off as she appeared to be. She was the smartest and richest Colored person that I knew, and Grandmother Jessie always told us that we had to learn to be better if we wanted to be somebody in this world. This was especially true for Colored girls, 'cause it was hard being Colored in America.

Everybody had to wait until I arrived at the breakfast table. It's not that I was special; Grandmother Jessie didn't let you eat until everyone was seated. She said it was the proper way to do things, not like we did, eating in shifts. I sat down quickly, but I didn't reach for the food because she had not prayed over it yet. Grandmother had religion. She went to the First African Baptist Church every Sunday and had made plans to tithe her way into Heaven. I was hoping that she didn't pray too long. I never did like hot food that turned cold.

"Dear Heavenly Father," she started, "we gather this morning to thank you for all the blessings that thou have seen fit to bestow upon us." It was already too long for me. "We come at this time," she continued, "to ask your blessings on the food that has been prepared for our daily consumption. Thank you for the hands that prepared it and the mouths that are about to receive it."

"Shut up, shut up," I kept thinking to myself. The cheese eggs are

getting colder by the minute.

"Dear Lord, bless these fine young ladies who have come to spend time with me and please watch over them as they enjoy this great day that you have prepared for them. And Jesus Lord..." My mind was completely gone by then. I squinted my eyes a little bit to see if anyone else had their eyes on the food. Everybody's head was down and eyes shut tight, waiting for Grandmother Jessie to finish. As soon as I heard "Amen" I lifted my head. Michelle was making the sign of the cross, just like all those Catholic girls do.

There was a lot of food on the platters before us. We got to pass around each plate and take what we wanted from each dish. This was the proper way to serve it. I loaded my plate with scrambled eggs and cheese, bacon, and apple turnovers. We had real juice, not Kool-Aid or Tang, but real orange juice with little bits of flesh floating around the top of the glass. I gobbled it all down in ten minutes. As soon as I finished, and I didn't ask for seconds, I asked Grandmother Jessie if we could go out to play.

"No," she said.

I had eaten much too fast. I embarrassed myself and my Grandmother. She turned to look at me and began to open her mouth. I knew I was about to be blasted. When she spoke, it was worse than I anticipated.

"You need to stay and help clean up the kitchen."

Clean the kitchen! I thought we were on vacation. I didn't think that we would be doing any sweeping, scrubbing, cleaning or anything like that. But Grandmother Jessie said that had we been trained properly, we would have known to clean up after ourselves. And my Grandmother Jessie knew all about proper training, good manners and all the stuff that went along with being a high class Colored woman.

It didn't take long. The four of us had the dishes washed and dried in no time. We collected all the garbage, wiped off the kitchen table and swept the floor. The kitchen looked real proper again. I was ready to hit the streets and I asked Grandmother Jessie if it were okay if I went outside to play.

She stared at me for two whole seconds before she opened her mouth and slowly articulated each single word:

"What are you going to do with that hair?" she asked.

"Nothing," I thought to myself as I looked back at her in disbelief. Momma had given me three fat plaits the night before. It was a hairdo that was good for at least two or three days. Most all of the Colored girls wore plaits to help keep their nappy hair together.

Grandmother Jessie went to the drawer and started to pull out her hair pressing equipment. She had a special hot iron device that you could stick the hot comb in. When we were at home, Momma would put the straightening comb right on the hot plate. Not Grandmother Jessie. She plugged in the heating iron, grabbed the Dixie Peach, an old towel, and then pulled one of the kitchen chairs right up to the stove.

I could tell that Grandmother Jessie really liked Michelle's hair. It was long, black and wavy and didn't need a hot comb. Shelia's mother had pressed her hair the day before because she was thirteen and on her way to junior high school. Me and Jessica had nappy hair, and Grandmother Jessie didn't like to see her grandchildren with nappy heads. All the poor struggling Black folks seemed to have nappy hair; the up and coming rich folks did not.

"Jessica," she called out first. "Let's see what I can do."

She unbraided Jessica's three plaits and started to struggle with her nappy head. She began to press it from the back and you could hear the grease sizzle each time she pulled the hot comb from the iron and placed it on Jessica's head. The kitchen no longer had that sweet smell of fried apple turnovers. Rather, some combination of sweet-smelling pastry, dirt, and fried hair wafted through the air. No sooner than she got Jessica's hair straight as a thread, she pulled out the curling iron and proceeded to plant Shirley Temple curls, one by one, all over Jessica's sandy brown hair. She looked real cute when she was finished.

I was next. My hair was short and nappy and didn't want to co-operate. I sat there pressing my ears forward trying to make certain that they didn't get burnt with the hot iron. Every Monday morning at school I would check to see whose mama had burned them with the hot iron, 'cause most girls got their hair hot pressed on Saturday night or Sunday morning so they would look good in church. A hot comb burn was hard to hide. And once it started to heal, it had a scabby nasty look about it. Vaseline would help with the healing, but it couldn't hide the dark sores or the embarrassment.

Grandmother Jessie had just finished turning me into a colored Shirley Temple when my Aunt Nita walked in.

"Hi, Aunt Nita," I said.

"Good Morning, Trisha," she responded.

My Aunt Nita never called me Patricia, Piggy or Miss Special K, she called me "Trisha" and that made me feel extra special 'cause Trisha was a fancy name. Aunt Nita was the person that I admired the most. I wanted to be just like her when I grew up. She was tall and beautiful with taffy-color brown skin, the same as Darlene's. She had jet black, long pretty wavy hair and, according to all the men, the best pair of legs in South Philly. Aunt Nita had already graduated from Saint Maria Goretti Catholic High School for Girls in South Philly and worked full time as a cashier for the PTC. She got to ride anywhere she wanted for free and sometimes she would take me along to see the shops and the restaurants downtown.

Aunt Nita dressed in the best of taste, just like Grandmother Jessie. Everything was the top of the line with Aunt Nita. She brought her clothes from John Wanamaker's, Gimbels and Strawbridge and Clothier department stores. I'm certain that she's never seen the insides of a John's Bargains Store. She was all dressed up in a matching red and white suit with a silk scarf around her neck. It was Saturday morning, but she still had to go to work for the PTC.

"Good morning, Mother," my Aunt Nita said to Grandmother Jessie.

Aunt Nita was in a rush and didn't have time to play chit chat with me. As she approached the door, I asked Grandmother Jessie if it was all right for me to go out and play. My hair was done, I had dressed myself in one of the newly made short outfits from Mr. Caldwell's scraps, and I had eaten my breakfast and cleaned up the kitchen.

"Don't go far...and watch yourself out there."

How far was far? I knew I couldn't walk all over South Philly because some neighborhoods were for the Colored, and others for the whites, mainly Italians, I think. Nevertheless, those were the magic words. Jessica and I rushed out the front door and joined Michelle and Shelia who were already outside because they didn't have to get their hair fried.

Sheila was a couple of doors down, sitting on the right side of the stoop talking to some dark chocolate-looking boys. I rushed over to join them. I didn't see Michelle.

"This is my friend...Piggy," she said.

I wanted to slap her. Sheila knew better to introduce me to some boys as Piggy. I think she was showing her butt off.

"You from West Philly, too?" one of the boys asked before I had time to defend myself.

"My name's Patricia and yes, I'm from West Philly. This is **my** Grandmother Jessie's house that we're staying at." I thought I would show Sheila and these boys who really was important and in charge. After all, Sheila wouldn't be here talking to these boys if it weren't for me.

"Mrs. Chapel is *your* grandmother?" one said in bewilderment.

"Yes, she is and Sheila is not a relation!"

I knew what they were thinking. They wondered about me and my relationship with this rich woman. I was more important than Sheila.

Before long, we were all trading stories about whose part of town was the best and whose block was the baddest. I, especially, bragged about the Crew and dared them to try and visit me on my block. I showed these boys how to play Skullys and raced them around the block to show them just how fast I was. I was fast, but I couldn't beat these boys. By the time I got back from the last race around the block Sheila looked like she had gotten into an argument with one of the boys. I think she was about to fight the freckled faced one with red hair.

"Piggy," Sheila hollered.

"What?" I yelled back as irritated as I could be. She was trying to be a smart ass again and I wasn't about to jump in and fight these boys for her.

"Grandmother Jessie!"

Sheila saw Grandmother Jessie before me. She was halfway up the street, huffing and puffing her way down the middle before I got a glimpse of her. She was dressed up like she was going somewhere. She had on one of those pink and blue Rayon dresses like the ones Momma made at Caldwell's Dress Company. She was moving fast and hollering something.

"Patricia," she shouted before taking a quick breath.

"Jessica," she yelled shortly thereafter.

"Come!" she shouted. "All of you come right now."

I didn't think we were gone that long. When Grandmother Jessie finally found us around the corner playing with the neighborhood kids, she looked like she was steaming. None of us paid any attention to the passing time. We didn't have a watch. We ran back and forth in and out the house to go to the bathroom on the first floor to pee a couple of times, but outside of that, everything seemed normal.

"Come," she repeated. "All of you, come."

"Fresh," she mumbled under her breath, "too darn fresh. Got me running 'round the world looking for you."

We all followed Grandmother Jessie around the corner. We didn't say a word, just looked at each other a few times. Michelle had dirt all over her face and hands and her clothes looked like they had never been to the laundry. Jessica's hair, which had converted back to its natural, happy but nappy state, was all over her head. I no longer had Shirley Temple curls, plaits or a part to separate my bushy, nappy hair. It stood straight up on my head like the bride of Frankenstein. I had been in the sun too long and was at least three shades blacker than when I left the house in the morning. I was dirty, sweaty and stinking by then because I couldn't bring the Tussy that we all used for deodorant. Sheila looked pretty clean because she never left the boys on the steps.

"You're filthy!" Grandmother Jessie shouted at us just after the front door had slammed shut. "And what were you doing with all those boys? You're worst than a bunch of little pickaninnies. Look at you. Is that what you think I want you to look like? Go. Clean yourself up! And pack your things while you're up there."

What was she so mad about? We didn't do anything wrong, and being fresh was the furthest thing from my mind. Grandmother Jessie had never fussed and hollered at me like that.

Before we came back downstairs Grandmother Jessie had called Momma, Momma had called Mr. Lyons and Mr. Lyons was on his way to pick us up and take us back home to Catherine Street. I didn't want to go. I didn't want to face Momma, Daddy, Granny or Darlene. I didn't want the boys to know what happened. I didn't want to be teased by the Crew. I didn't want my Aunt Nita to come home and not find me there. And from what I could understand from Grandmother Jessie's rantings and raving, we were a wild bunch of untrained, un-couth, nappy-headed girls that spent too much time playing in the sun getting dirty and thinking about being fresh. We weren't acting like proper, decent young ladies. We had put ourselves and our futures at risk. We could never reach the top of the social ladder with such a display of unruly behavior that was best left to the poor people run-ning wild in the streets.

When Mr. Lyons pulled up in the big green Chevrolet with the words Impala on the rump, I thought about the very last thing that he had said to Michelle before he left us there the night before.

"Behave."

We were back at home in no time. And I mourned the loss of my special opportunity for the rest of the summer.

12

I Wanna…Just let me go!

I had two whole years to think about how stupid I was and what I had done wrong the first time. This time around I would not disappoint my grandmother. I wanted desperately to be close to Grandmother Jessie and wasn't about to mess up.

I was happy that Grandmother Jessie picked Jessica and me to stay with her for the summer, but Momma wasn't so certain. In fact, she didn't say yes and she didn't say no. She hadn't made up her mind yet. Momma said that she didn't want any of her kids to be treated more special than the others. Grandmother Jessie hadn't asked for any of the boys, and she didn't ask for Darlene and Marie, just Jessica and me. As we cuddled tightly in our seats on the PTC trolley early Sunday afternoon, I kept wondering about what Momma was going to say.

All of the PTC's trolleys, buses and trains were crowded today. It was Mother's Day Sunday and everybody was taking advantage of kids ride for free. It was taking such a long time. We were trying to be patient, but the seven of us couldn't keep our butts still. We were all dressed in our Easter Sunday clothes and everything still fit. Me, Jessica, and Marie all had on the same outfits: white dresses with lime green capes and matching cummerbunds. Darlene's was lavender and white 'cause as Momma's firstborn girl, she was too old to be dressed like the three of us. We looked real pretty, everybody said. Momma was so proud of us when we walked outside on Easter Sunday. The whole block waited to see what we were wearing. Momma was a seamstress and she knew how to make us some real fine clothes; she just didn't make enough.

The boys wore new suits, but they weren't from the John's Bargains Store. Momma had to take Donald and Wayman downtown to buy their Easter outfits because John's Bargains no longer carried their sizes. Each one had on a striped blue seersucker jacket with dark pants and white shirt. They were real expensive suits and set Momma back a pretty penny. But my baby brother Alfred, who wore a size 4T, was able to get his royal blue suit with the pastel yellow shirt and matching tie from the John's Bargains Store for a good, cheap price.

People stared at us as we paraded down the street to Grandmother Jessie's big new house on 19th and Christian Street: four girls, three boys and a mommy and a daddy. We looked like brightly colored Easter eggs that had escaped from the basket. We kept looking around, checking all the addresses, trying to locate the new house. None of us had ever been there before. Which one was it?

The new house on Christian Street was just as big and grand as the one on Carpenter: three stories, six bedrooms, marble stairs, glass doorknobs...the complete works. Grandmother Jessie was loaded, but she didn't share too much of her money with us. Momma said because so much of her money went to the church.

We were the last ones to arrive and I could tell that Grandmother Jessie wasn't happy about it. Aunt Nita and Brother Vernard were already there, of course. Uncle Junior was there with a dark woman named Marge. My pregnant Aunt Doretha and two baby cousins were sitting in the corner talking to my Uncle Edward. He and Aunt Doris had four boys under the age of six. Aunt Savannah was there with my cousin Romaine, and she also brought along the curly-haired man named Joe. The house was ready for a big dinner party.

The dining room table was set with the special china. There were two forks and two glasses at each place setting and each plate had a cloth napkin with a silver napkin ring in the middle. The grown people got to eat on the mahogany table in the dining room. The kids got to eat in the kitchen.

Food was everywhere. A fat roasted brown turkey sat in the middle of the table on a silver platter. Roast beef was to the right and a honey-cured, Virginia baked ham to the left. They rested on silver platters, too. Sweet potatoes, macaroni and cheese, brown rice, and collard and kale greens were in various sized bowls surrounding the meats. Pig's feet and vinegar was on the table, along with giant yeast rolls that scented the entire house. It was the smell of fresh baked bread that first hit you and made your stomach ache for the feast that was laid before you. We had to wait a little while longer before we could grab our plates and dig in. First, Grandmother Jessie had to pray, and I knew that would take a very long time.

"Lucille, I can't take care of all of your children," I overheard Grandmother Jessie tell Momma. Grandmother Jessie, Momma, Aunt Savannah, Aunt Nita and the new lady named Marge were all in the kitchen cleaning plates. Aunt Doretha's belly was too fat to be in there. Me, Darlene, Romaine, Jessica and Marie escaped kitchen duty because they were in there talking like adults. All the kids knew to stay out of the kitchen and mind their own business.

"It's not that, Mother," Momma responded. "I just don't think it's fair to treat Patricia and Jessica like they're special."

"I'm not treating them special," Grandmother Jessie said sounding ever so indignant. "I am the grandmother, you know. I think it would be good for both of them to stay with me so they can get some experience, learn things about the world. I'll have them working with me during the day, and then they can enjoy themselves the rest of the evening. Besides, they'll be able to earn a few dollars in tips."

Grandmother Jessie had just opened a new restaurant called Chapel's Luncheonette. It was right off the corner of 16th and Bainbridge Street. Soul food was the entire menu. Fried Perch, Porgies, Whiting and Shad were the specialties of the house, but you could also get large plates filled with neck bones, ham hocks, chitlins and pig's feet. Grandmother Jessie could cook anything, and everything she made tasted real good. She was a smart businesswoman, what they called an entrepreneur.

"Maybe so," Momma nodded. But she still didn't say yes, and she didn't say no.

I was anxious as hell. Grandmother Jessie wanted me to stay with her and Momma had to think about it. *"What was she thinking?"* I was gonna be real mad at Momma if she messed up this opportunity for me to get away from Catherine Street for the summer. Working with Grandmother Jessie would be great. Me and Jessica would have the best of everything, day and night, and we wouldn't even have to pay for it.

"I'll talk it over with Curtis," is the last thing I heard Momma say as we were preparing to leave.

"Why?" I thought to myself. *"Why ask Daddy anything?"*

Daddy had nothing to say about whether me and Jessica should stay with Grandmother Jessie. Everybody was mad at Daddy. Me too. Daddy hadn't worked in more than three years and everyone seemed to know that our family was in trouble. Momma said he got fired from Casa Conti's because of his drinking. He never got to work on time. Daddy said he was a Colored man, and Colored men always had problems keeping their jobs. And, to add insult to injury, he had transportation problems. The buses weren't reliable and he didn't have a car. I wasn't sure which of the two stories held the most water. But Momma was right about one thing. Daddy drank lots of wine, cheap Swiss Colony and Thunderbird wines. They were only $1.99 a bottle and he managed to get a hold of a $1.99 almost every single day of his life.

Daddy was doing okay getting himself the things that he wanted. He fixed special meals for himself and wouldn't share it with the rest of us. I remember the day that we were scrambling to fix ourselves something to eat for lunch. There was plenty of surplus peanut butter, but no bread and no jelly. Daddy gave me fifteen cents and told me to go to the 57th street corner store and buy him three round hard rolls.

"But Daddy," I protested, "we don't have any bread."

"Use that meal and baking powder up there on the shelf in the kitchen and make you some cornbread," he snapped back.

"But we're trying to make peanut butter sandwiches," I cried out loudly. "You can't put peanut butter on cornbread."

"You can put peanut butter on anything," Daddy shouted. "You oughta be glad that you ain't starving and got some'in to eat. You know, people in China are starving."

"But we ain't in China," Wayman shouted back.

Daddy jumped up from his chair, hand raised high in the air, and went after Wayman. You could see the sweat popping out from under his arms, hitting the hardwood floor instead of his perspiration-stained t-shirt that barely stretched over his fat stomach.

"Don't you dare sass me, boy," he hollered as he moved toward him struggling to snatch his leather belt out of the loops of his brown pants. "I'll whup your ass!" he threatened. But Wayman was too fast, and Daddy was too slow. He raced out the back door and ran up the alley before Daddy could catch him. He wouldn't come back until he was sure that Daddy was gone.

"Can't I buy a loaf of bread with this here fifteen cents? We want bread!" I shouted at Daddy as he huffed and puffed his way back to the chair in the living room. He was so fat and out of shape that I thought he might drop dead before he got there. *"How could Daddy say no?"* I wondered silently to myself. Fifteen cents was all that you needed to buy a fresh loaf of Bond Bread and it had twenty slices in each loaf.

"Don't you start telling me what to do," he shouted. "Your name ain't Lucille. I don't care what you want. People in Hell want ice water! I told you to go down to the store and buy me three hard rolls. Now git!"

It was a scene that played out over and over again. Daddy would come home in the middle of the day. A skinny brown bag with the top twisted tightly around the neck of a bottle was clutched under his arm. Sometimes he carried a second brown bag with a special treat for him to eat. Sardines with mustard sauce, hot sausage, or fried chicken breasts were his favorites, but just enough for one. Nothing for us kids. We watched while Daddy prepared himself a good lunch, or early dinner, and then left the house before Momma came home from work. Sometimes he would come back in the middle of the night and climb into Momma's bed. That's when we heard the fighting the most.

It was late and dark when we got back from Grandmother Jessie's. We all had to go to school the next day, except of course, for my baby brother. Momma put Alfred to bed right away. He grew out of the drawer in a few short weeks and Momma was never able to buy him a bed of his own, but he did get to sleep in the boys' room in one of the bunk beds with Wayman or Donald.

Jessica and I went right upstairs to get our chairs ready for bed. It only took a few minutes to fold the top back and extend the bottom part of the chair. An old sheet and blanket were sandwiched between the cushion and the box spring. It didn't take long but by now we realized that these were not real beds and our bodies ached every day from sleeping on the hard metal frames all night. Marie flopped down on Darlene's bed and went right to sleep.

Donald, Wayman and Darlene wanted to stay up late because they weren't certain what Daddy was going to do. None of us really knew whether Daddy still lived with us or not. Sometimes he came home, but most times he didn't. He spent most of his time at Pop Pop and Granny's basement. Sometimes he would come home late at night and cause such a ruckus with Momma that we had to call Whitehead - the hard-as-nails, kick your ass real fast Colored cop that patrolled the neighborhood - to take Daddy away from our house and down to the Roundhouse. It was embarrassing when the red car pulled up, but we were happy to see Daddy leave. Jail was a good place for him to be.

It was past midnight when Momma finally went upstairs and told everybody to go to bed, except Daddy. Daddy stayed on the slip-covered couch looking at the Magnavox TV.

"Get out, Curtis," I heard Momma say. "Get out. Leave me alone. Leave all of us alone," I heard Momma say. "We're gonna lose this house any day now and you're not doing a damn thing about it."

"Come on...come on, Lucille," Daddy pleaded. He was in there trying to do it to my Momma. I thought they were finished with that. I knew all about doing it because Momma told me if you do it you'll end up getting pregnant, and you better not get pregnant. But that's all that she said. I knew Momma never wanted to be pregnant again. When baby Alfred was born, they wanted to fix her so she'd never have kids again. At thirty-five, the doctor said that she was too old to be having babies. Another try might kill her. But Momma refused, she said she wasn't having no white doctor mess her up for life.

"No, Curtis...I said no!" That time it was loud and clear. I heard it in the girls' room while I was lying there in my chair trying to fall asleep. Everybody else heard it too, and we were just waiting to see if we needed to get up and go in there to protect our Momma. It would be Daddy against all of us: Donald, Darlene, Wayman, Jessica, Marie and me.

The bed squeaked. I heard footsteps on the hardwood floor. Somebody was walking around making a lot of noise. The wood cracked as the lock rubbed against the doorframe that had been weakened by too many efforts to secure the bedroom door from outsiders. A heavy foot hit five of the steps before it was silent.

"Sing'em goldfish," Daddy hollered as he continued to descend down the stairs, "you gotta fresh bowl of water coming." That was Daddy's answer to everything.

13

Best Friends

I went to school the next day just to pass the time. There was nothing else for me to do except wait until the school year was over. Everybody was winding down and most of the students, and teachers, were already brain dead. Actually, the fun part of school was the math bee that was held every Tuesday and Friday mornings. It pitted the boys against the girls to see which team was the smartest. Everybody was excited about the competition and everybody wanted to play. I was disqualified in the second week of class for being too fast and too smart. According to the teachers, no one else had a chance to score. I felt it was unfair, but it was the first time that I realized that I had good brains.

Dress-up day was Wednesday. It was the last big event on the school calendar. I put on my white dress and the lime green cape with the matching cummerbund, my black patent leather shoes (and fancy white headband that I made from the leftover scraps from my white dress) and went to homeroom to show off my best outfit. After the roll was taken and the oohs and aahs were completed, I cut the rest of my classes and rode up and down the El from 69th Street to Frankfort. I got on and off the trains all day, hoping that somebody would notice. They never did.

There was nothing special about Thursday or Friday, and the

week ended the same way it started. Momma still had not made up her mind about sending me to Grandmother Jessie's.

It was a Friday night and I waited outside on the porch to see if anything was about to go down with the Crew. The Crew belonged to me now, instead of Wayman and me. Wayman was a good hustler, a good salesman and a real good brother, but he wasn't a rough and tumble kinda guy like the other Crew members. They were more athletic, good ball players and junior street thugs in training. None of them were as hostile or violent as they pretended to be. Most of it was just for show. I had been a member of the Crew for several years now and I realized that we weren't really a street gang like those we'd been hearing so much about at school and on television. We called ourselves the Crew, but we weren't like the Coast or Barbary Coast that engaged in gang warfare. We wanted to defend our territory, but didn't have knives or guns or anything crazy like that. We weren't about to shoot or kill somebody.

I got to stay with the Crew because I was fast, athletic and didn't have anyone else to hang with. Every year I would win first prize for the fastest girl on the block. That made me special. I won first prize even if I didn't cross the finish line first, like the time last summer at the annual block party when the girl from Walton Ave. beat me by three seconds. Mr. Quillen gave her the first prize, but took it back when everyone complained that she didn't live on Catherine Street.

Every gang had at least one girl attached to it and that girl was gonna be me. I was skinny and flat-chested and unworthy of a hit. The Crew didn't have to worry about me and I didn't have to worry about the Crew.

I waited outside for a long time, but didn't see anybody. I started to get the feeling that the Crew was doing a lot of things without me. Sometimes it just didn't make sense to take a girl with you. And the Crew started to talk about girls in a different way than they did before.

Girls were fine, foxes, boogas or booga bears. They were built, stacked, and had big butter balls or rat titties. They talked about busting cherries and getting some trim all the time and they laughed if I tried to be part of the conversation. I started to feel a little bit like an outcast, but still wanted to hold on. Only Dougie was willing to hang with me all the time.

Dougie was losing his standing with the Crew. He was too weird. Dougie jumped rope, played hopscotch and fought like a girl. He was fussy about the way he dressed and tried his darnest to always look better than me. Butchy said he was a sissy. Lump called him a flaming faggot. And Champ said that everybody would laugh at us if they knew that Dougie was a member of the Crew.

I looked up and down the block several times and I still didn't see anybody. It felt good being outside. Spring had finally arrived and hanging out on the front steps was so much better than being in the house. I walked up to the drug store to buy a bag of five cent Sugar Babies. I crossed the street, pretending to go into the church as I looked around to see if I could find the Crew. There were too many men hanging out in front of Mr. Kelly's Bar, so I crossed the street before I got to the end. It reminded me, too much, of our days on top of the bar on Woodland Avenue. I always kept my distance from drunken men. After exhausting all possibilities, I finally decided to go into the house and call my new best friend Debbie Jones.

I finally found a best friend to share all my teenage fantasies. I hadn't had a close female friend since Monica Stone and I became best friends in the first grade at the Wilson School. I met Debbie Jones at Sayre Junior High School. She was destined to become my ace boon coon. I was only six months older than Debbie, but I was a full grade ahead. Debbie helped to make my eighth grade year at Sayre one of the best years of my life. But seventh grade, that didn't go too well at all.

Not everyone who graduated from the sixth grade at Harrity Elementary school went to Sayre Junior High. Donald went first. When he started Sayre, it reunited him with all the kids on the block that went to Bryant Elementary School. We were happy about that because the divide that was created when they made all the Reid kids attend Harrity was finally over. Darlene would be next, but just when she started thinking about going to Sayre, the school district started a new policy requiring Harrity to split their graduates between Sayre and Shaw Junior High. Mixing up all the neighborhood kids to avoid natural gang formations was the new rule. Sayre, at 58th and Walnut, was within walking distance. We all wanted to go. Shaw was located at 54th and Warrington, much too far to walk. You'd have to travel on the PTC everyday to get to school. You wouldn't be able to ride free, but you could purchase school tokens at a discount for less than a quarter of the normal price. I think that the folks at Harrity decided that the best way to share the graduates equally among the two schools was to alternate the graduating classes. The even year graduates went to Sayre, the odd years went to Shaw.

Sayre was a brand new junior high school and all the kids at Sayre thought they were better than the kids at Shaw. Shaw was a much older school and had lots of traditions and high standards to maintain. The Shaw kids thought that they were smarter. There were more Colored kids at Sayre and everyone thought that was cool. The school district's new policy of alternating years would break up the Reid Tribe. We wouldn't start to return to school in even succession until all of us started to arrive one year after another at John Bartram High School.

Darlene was lucky. When she graduated in 1960, she was sent to Sayre. It was only six blocks away and Darlene had to walk. She didn't seem to mind because Deborah and Sheila got to go to Sayre, too. Wayman was first among us to graduate from Harrity in 1961 and attend Shaw. With his discount PTC tokens, he boarded the bus every day, at 56th and Catherine Street and it carried him all the way up to Warrington Avenue. He had to walk two blocks to get to 54th.

I had my sights set on Sayre when I graduated from Harrity in 1962. Junior high school meant that I was just about to be a teenager and all kinds of good things were about to happen to me. No longer would I have to sit in the same class all day long. I would change classes every forty-five minutes. I would have a lunch break with hundreds of other students and I could hang out in the halls and meet new friends. It was a big school and no one would know that Marie, Jessica, Darlene and me wore the same clothes. I would get a period and a chest, and pretty soon I could start looking for a boyfriend.

Darlene wasn't happy about me going to Sayre. She still didn't want me hanging out with her friends and, up until now, she was the only member of the family in the school. Donald started out at Sayre, but he didn't last for long. He started getting into trouble as soon as he got there. Donald was smart, real smart. He studied science, math and music and excelled at everything. Donald had conversations with teachers like no other student. But Donald was also what they called unruly and undisciplined. He was a troublemaker and never wanted to follow the rules. If you talked to Donald, he talked back and the teachers weren't used to that.

One of Donald's first run-ins was with Mr. Chaney, the gym teacher at Sayre. Whatever he said or did, Mr. Chaney took it upon himself to beat Donald with a paddle. That was a mistake. Curtis, Jr. was my Daddy's firstborn, and no one was allowed to put a hand on him, except Daddy.

Daddy and Donald walked up to Sayre the next day. Daddy asked Mr. Chaney, a young Colored teacher who wasn't that much older than Donald, to step outside. Daddy threatened to kick his ass if it ever happened again. It never did, but that didn't keep Donald out of trouble. Halfway through the eighth grade, they sent Donald to Kato...a school for bad boys. Darlene was left at Sayre, all by herself.

What a relief it must have been to be the only Reid child at the public school. Not having little brothers and sisters hanging around all over the place had to be deep. Just as Darlene was about to enter the ninth grade, I showed up for the seventh. Still, the school was big and Darlene was two years ahead of me. No one would know that I was her sister.

Unfortunately, for me, things started to go bad the very first week of class. My feet had grown over the summer and I no longer had a pair of shoes to wear. I tried to salvage an old pair of Darlene's shoes that were no longer of use to her. The tops fit, but there were holes in the bottom. I cut out a few pieces of cardboard and stuffed them tightly into the shoes so that my feet would not feel the rough cement as I walked the six blocks to Sayre. The first three days went okay, but it rained that Friday. Not only were my feet soakin wet, the old shoes couldn't withstand the onslaught of hurricane force rains that often cursed us in early September and the penny loafers fell completely apart.

This was a real crisis for Momma because she didn't have any money to buy me a new pair. Momma could always make us something to wear with the scraps from Mr. Caldwell's dress factory, but Momma couldn't make us any shoes. I worried all weekend about what was going to happen.

"Patricia needs shoes," Momma hollered at Daddy when he came back from visiting with Pop Pop and Granny in the basement.

"I didn't wear shoes to school in South Carolina," my Daddy joked.

"We're not in South Carolina," Momma responded angrily. "Curtis, something has to be done. Patricia can't just stay home because she doesn't have any shoes to wear. After a few days, they will send the truant officer and put your ass in jail."

"Let them share," Daddy said.

"There's nothing to share," Momma shouted. "She wears a size five. Her foot is too big for Jessica's shoes and too small for Darlene's. She gotta have her own pair." Momma was steaming. She didn't know what to do. I was frightened. This was disastrous and somehow I knew that no matter how hard she tried, Momma couldn't fix this problem any time soon.

"Look at what's happening here," she said, almost crying but only a little bit. "The mortgage gots to be paid. The electric bill gots to be paid. There's no oil in the furnace. The kids need food and now Patricia needs a pair of shoes. That's your Prima Donna that you're supposed to take care of."

Daddy walked back and forth from the kitchen to the living room, smiling, as if nothing that Momma said had any meaning.

"My bills are all due and the baby needs shoes but I'm busted."

Daddy was at it again, belting out a song loud and clear, with his church choir voice, and pretending to be a lounge singer.

"Cotton's down to a quarter a pound and I'm busted."

This time it was Mr. Ray Charles, Daddy's other favorite Negro superstar. But the louder he sang the angrier Momma got.

"I got a cow that went dry and a hen that won't lay,

A big stack of bills that gets bigger each day,

The county's gonna haul my belongings away, 'cause I'm busted."

"Shut up Curtis," Momma shouted. "Shut up."

"Sing'em goldfish. You gotta fresh bowl of water coming." And with that, Daddy grabbed his purple fleece sweater and left the house, leaving Momma and me there to worry about the shoe crisis.

I was preparing to stay home that Monday. I wasn't gonna to walk to school barefooted. Nobody did that in Philadelphia. Everybody was getting ready to leave except me. Then Daddy walked in the front door, smiling and grinning. It was 7:00 in the morning.

"Prima Donna," he sang as he hit the door. "Where's my Prima Donna?"

I went flying down the stairs with the rest of the bunch. *"What did Daddy want? Did he bring me something special?"* Daddy no longer worked at Casa Conti, so whatever it was it wouldn't be something to eat.

Daddy carried a brown paper bag in his hand, but it wasn't a skinny bag with the top twisted tightly around the neck. As soon as he saw my face, he shoved it in my direction.

"Get ready for school," he stated gleefully. Daddy was beaming with confidence, grinning from ear to ear. He hadn't been this happy in weeks.

My Daddy had done it. Once again he proved that I was special. Just when I thought my whole life would be ruined by my inability to attend classes at Sayre Junior High School because I didn't have any shoes to wear, my Daddy came through with a brand new pair of shoes. He was my hero all over again. I was happy as a lightning bug's ass and couldn't wait to see what they looked like.

Nothing prepared me for what I found in the bag. It was a pair of worn out, raggedy, thick soled, dirty brown, old lady shoes. They were horrible.

"I can't wear these," I cried. "They're too big. They're not my size. I wear a size five. These are size six and a half. I can't go to school in these old shoes."

"Put 'em on and go," he shouted. "Your Granny sent you them shoes so you wouldn't have to miss your school work."

"I can't wear Granny's shoes to school. I can't."

"Yes, you can and you will. Kids in China don't have any shoes to wear. They wrap their feet in cloth and walk miles and miles just to get an education. Be thankful that you have something to put on your feet."

I was bawling my eyes out. Tears streamed down my face and snot ran freely from my nose. Momma rushed out the door and went to work. Darlene stood on the front porch and waited for Debbie and Sheila. Wayman headed for the bus on 56th Street. Donald cracked up. Jessica, Marie and baby Alfred stood in the middle of the floor and cried with me.

I stuffed some old socks in the top of the shoes and tied them as tightly as I possibly could. Aside from being the ugliest shoes on the face of the earth, they were too big. I had difficulty keeping them on my feet. For six blocks I struggled, ever so awkwardly, attempting to walk to school as fast as I could. I didn't want to be late. And I didn't want to get the paddle. On the second day of class in my new school, Mr. Chaney, the gym teacher who sometimes took care of disciplinary problems, paddled me, and it wasn't even my fault. Some knotty-headed boys did something wrong, but nobody would point them out. Chaney gave all of us the paddle, just to prove his point. It's a good thing I didn't tell my Daddy 'cause he would have whupped his ass for sure.

I was hoping that no one would notice as I arrived for home-room. I quickly slid into my seat and waited quietly until Mr. Ott, the wise-cracking, buttless music teacher, called out my last name. I don't think he liked his job because he was always sending some kid down to the disciplinary office.

"Reid," he shouted in a booming baritone voice.

"I'm here," I shouted back. You had to be loud if you wanted to be heard. I wanted to be loud so no one would have to turn around and try to find me and the shoes at the same time. He continued to call the roll as I waited to see if any of the new kids noticed anything different about me. I hoped not.

I left homeroom to go to first period class. Everybody was looking at my feet. I had been discovered. They stared, snickered, then turned away and giggled out loud.

"Them shoes, them shoes," one boy hollered. I didn't even know his name.

The whole class was waiting for me by the time I got to second period. I tried to rush through the crowd to beat everyone to class, but the shoes slowed me down. I ended up getting there dead last.

They roared with laughter as soon as I walked through the door. I was embarrassed and humiliated, but there was nothing that I could do.

Gym class wasn't any better. Half the girls in the seventh grade class were in the gymnasium when Miss Certaine cautioned us about the importance of wearing a clean gym uniform and bringing a pair of sneakers for gym classes. *"Hell, I didn't have one pair of shoes. How was I going to get two?"* They were laughing and looking in my direction. Miss Certaine walked slowly down the line until she finally got to the space where I was standing. She had the most pitiful look on her face when she looked down at my feet and then dead in my face. But she didn't say anything.

I dashed out of the gym as fast as I could and headed toward the lunchroom. I was all by myself now because no one wanted to be seen with the girl in the granny shoes. Students were lined up on both sides of the aisle, pointing and laughing as I attempted to get my free lunch.

"Old lady shoes."

"Ancient brogams!"

"Granny boots!" they shouted out. It was the worst day of my life.

I tried to run home, but the shoes were big and heavy like lead. The sides were rubbing up against my ankles, bruising and breaking the surface of the skin, causing me pain. *"How could this happen to me? How could my Daddy do this to me? I'm never gonna forgive him and I'm never gonna speak to him again."*

I thought about killing myself, but it wasn't a good option. I didn't like blood and I didn't like dying. Dying, which I worried about often, got in the way of too many things that I wanted to do.

I got home first. There was a constable sign glued to the large white post that connected the porch to the roof. It meant that the city sheriff was coming to sell everything you owned in your house because you didn't pay your bills. It was another embarrassing thing that I didn't want anybody to see. *"Who would want all the raggedy ass things in our house anyway?"* I thought quietly to myself. I scrubbed off the sign with hot soapy water, making certain not to leave any evidence of its existence behind.

Darlene came home after me. She looked at me with a sad face. *"I wondered if she knew about the shoes."* I think not. Darlene was in the ninth grade, and all the kids who were teasing me were in the seventh. I was glad that she wasn't humiliated like me, too.

When Momma came home, Darlene was first to greet her.

"Momma," she said almost demandingly, "you gotta get Patricia a new pair of shoes. Everybody in the school was talking about the girl who showed up in what had to be her grandmother's shoes. It was so embarrassing. I felt sorry for her. I didn't tell anybody that she was my sister. She can't go to school like that. Not to junior high."

I had to wait until Friday. But when Momma got paid, she took me to Silverstein's Shoe Store on 60th and Locust Street and bought me a new pair of dark brown penny loafers. That's the best thing that Darlene ever did for me.

Debbie Jones didn't know about the shoe incident, because she wasn't there. I don't know if she ever heard about it, but she never brought it up and I certainly wasn't gonna tell her.

I shared things with Debbie that I never shared with anybody else.

Not even Wayman. We talked about hair and boys and shoplifting at John Wanamaker's Department Store and Strawbridge and Clothier. Those stores had beautiful clothes for teenagers that my mamma could never afford to buy. We met before and after school. No matter what happened during the day, we played catch-up every night on the phone. We didn't get to see each other much on the weekends because we lived so far apart. Debbie lived right around the corner from 51st and Market Street on Ludlow. It was exactly fourteen blocks away from my house. Sometimes I would walk that far to see her, but not tonight. It was too late and I didn't feel that desperate.

"Hey. What's going on?"

"Who's this?"

"Who's this? You know who this is."

"Who would you like to speak to?"

"Deborah Jones! It's Pat."

"Pat, this is Carol. Would you like to speak with Debbie?"

Debbie had a big sister too. In fact, she had three big sisters and a brother. And Debbie's big brother, Philip, was simply gorgeous, more delicious looking than Grandmother Jessie's fried apple turnovers. He had smooth brown skin, dark hazel eyes and soft brown nappy hair. I think it was soft and nappy, but I couldn't be sure because I never got to touch it. He was almost ten years older than me, so I dared not say a word to him. He was in the Army and about to go to a place called Vietnam, but I wasn't supposed to say anything about that. He never even glanced in my direction to acknowledge my existence, but I could see him and he was so fine. I woulda traveled back and forth to her house just to get a glimpse.

Debbie was the baby. Carol's voice sounded just like Debbie's and sometimes I made the mistake of thinking that it was her. I tried to remind myself not to do that because I didn't want Carol to know any of our secrets. Carol wasn't a smart aleck and didn't get nasty when I had mistaken her for Debbie, but I could tell that she was annoyed.

"Pat."

"Debbie."

"I told you to always ask for me when you call."

"I know. I forgot. I thought it was you that picked up the phone."

"No. It was Carol."

"Is she mad at me?"

"I don't know. I didn't ask. What's up?'

"Did you see the love of my life today?"

Debbie knew that I was talking about Zak. Everybody loved Zak. He was the cutest boy at Sayre Junior High.

"Yes, I saw him, all laid out in a black and silver outfit. Isn't he gorgeous?"

"Yes indeedy. A real pretty boy - light-skinned, curly hair with hazel brown eyes - and he's tall, too. I may not be the first one to get him, but I might be the second or third. I'll just wait in line."

"Patricia!"

I swirled my head around and caught a glimpse of Momma's eye. She was mad about something and hollering at me for no reason. She caught me by surprise. I didn't see Momma when she came in. I was too involved in my telephone conversation.

"Patricia. Hang up the phone right now," Momma demanded.

"Gotta go," I told Debbie rather hastily. "My mom wants to use the telephone."

I hung the green phone up on the kitchen wall and stared at Momma. She didn't look happy. Maybe she had a bad day at Mr. Caldwell's. Momma seemed more tense and irritable now than she had ever been before with Daddy not working and the kids always needing something to eat. Momma was beat down. I moved quickly to get out of her way and headed for the front door.

"Sit down," she said in a stern voice.

Had I done something wrong? Whatever it was, I couldn't remember. I grabbed one of the old blue chairs in front of the gray-speckled table and plopped my butt down. I was looking at Momma like she was crazy.

"As long as you live," she started, trying to sound like one of those fired-up evangelists, "I better not ever hear you say that you would stand in line just to get a piece of some light skinned, curly-head boy. What were you thinking? You think that light skin is better than dark skin? Is curly hair better than nappy hair? You think that you're less of a person because you don't have light skin with long curly hair? Never judge a person on the basis of their looks. Good looks won't get you anywhere. Good looking people don't develop themselves because they think their looks will get them over. Good-looking men think that they can have all the women. Good looking women think men will take care of them. Light-skinned good looking folks are the worst. You're gonna be a good looking brown-skinned woman. Don't let that go to your head. Keep your priorities straight. I want you to stay in school and get a good education. Get a high school diploma and you won't have to worry about catching some curly-head man to take care of you. You gonna be able to take care of yourself. And don't worry about not having good hair. You can buy all the hair you need."

It was a lesson I would never forget.

14

Trying to get to Heaven

I stuffed all of my precious belongings into the smooth, almost pastel blue, leather suitcase with the lock and key. Well, it wasn't actually leather, pleather (play leather) is what we called it. Momma brought two new suitcases from Woolworth's five and dime store. She got them on sale for $7.99 apiece. We needed real luggage, not old white pillowcases, to pack our things for the six week stay at Grandmother Jessie's. Momma had finally made up her mind. She was happy again, although I kept thinking about what she said about Zak and me: *Never chase after a man who is not chasing after you; one day you'll be a good-looking, brown-skinned woman; Get a good education, a high school diploma, so you'll be able to take care of yourself!*

There were very few things that I could call my own. We shared almost everything. I wanted to pack the comb, brush, Tussy deodorant and jar of Dixie Peach, but they didn't belong to me exclusively. I did have my own toothbrush. A free dental program at school took care of that. I washed and pressed all of my short sets, placed them in the suitcase and locked it every night. The suitcase became my own private space and I tried to fill it with things that had special meaning to me. I was in and out of that suitcase like a traveling salesman. Most of what was packed inside I continued to need on a daily basis and that made it more difficult to keep everything in perfect order.

Momma said that we needed new underwear because she wasn't sending us to Grandmother Jessie's in raggedy draws. But I also needed something else: a bra. My rat titties were gone. There was real swelling around the nipples and my fleshy brown bosoms were starting to fill in. I was so proud of myself. Momma went to John's Bargains and bought me two new bras, size 30AA, for $1.99. Wear one and wash one.

I don't think Momma wanted us to leave her for the summer, but Grandmother Jessie was promising too much: food, shelter, clothing and money for two of your kids for six whole weeks. Who in their right mind would turn down a deal like that? The money part was really gonna be helpful. I needed a job and it was hard getting one at thirteen.

The first time I got paid for anything was last summer when I went to work for Miss Doris down the street. I was twelve. She lived in Mr. Talbert's house, but Momma told me not to call her Mrs. Talbert because she wasn't his wife. I was something like a Mother's Helper, but she didn't have any kids for me to help her with. I worked around the house, washing, cleaning and straightening little things out, and for that, she was willing to pay me $2.00. Miss Doris was the first one who told me about a period. While changing the white linen sheets on her bed, I noticed a dark brown, turtle-shaped stain on the center of the mattress. I scrubbed the spot real hard, but couldn't remove it. She explained that it was caused by her period and that bloodstains never left their spot willingly.

"Once you get your period," she said, "you'll have to be careful."

After a while, we all knew about bleeding women from the square brown bags that everybody's mama purchased at the corner store. Most of the time, they would send one of their kids to fetch the package. No one wanted to get caught walking back from the drugstore trying to hide the brown bag under their arm. The size and shape of the box could only mean one thing: you were transporting Kotex 'cause your mama was on her period.

Mrs. Sorrell hired me next. Debbie Jones got me that job in early spring. She was already working for Mrs. Whitney, the doctor's wife, who was one of Mrs. Sorrell's girlfriends. Mrs. Sorrell was a school-teacher that lived a few blocks away in the Cobbs Creek section across from the park on 63rd Street. The Sorrells had better jobs than the people on Catherine Street and could afford a Mother's Helper every Saturday. They had a couple of uncontrollable, curly-headed kids running around the house, always tearing up the place. I was paid $3.50 to help clean the house and watch the kids. I was so tired after the very first Saturday that I fell asleep on the couch before I finished scrubbing the bathroom floor. I wasn't used to housework 'cause I did everything in my power to avoid learning how to be domestic at home. I didn't want to go back, but I needed the money to pay for my classes at Mrs. Sydney's School of Dance on 61st and Market Streets.

I had been dancing at the Sherwood Recreation Center ever since I moved onto Catherine Street, but that wasn't enough. My distant cousin on Daddy's side, Cousin Marge, was the recreation leader at Sherwood. She had a little dance training in her background and tried to teach us a few dance steps, but it was nothing like a real dance school. Cousin Marge was pretty famous back then, but not because she could dance. She was dating Wilt Chamberlain and everybody thought that was hot. He showed up one time at the Center to see her and people's tongues wagged for weeks. He was rich and famous and everybody prayed that she'd catch him. She didn't. Miss Marge (I had to call her that in front of all the other kids) told me I could be a good dancer, but I needed professional training. She told me about Mrs. Sydney's.

Dance instruction at Mrs. Sydney's cost $2.50 per class. I begged Momma to let me go, and she agreed, as long as I earned enough money to pay for it myself. Momma did agree to pay for my carfare back on the PTC because she didn't want me to walk home by myself that late at night. Walking to the dance school during the daylight hours wasn't a problem. It was only nine blocks to the north. Momma never believed in giving her kids everything. You had to find a way to make money on your own, and once you earned more than $5.00, you had to give Momma half to help support the family. She said that it taught us about responsibility.

I had no idea what Grandmother Jessie was going to pay me, but it had to be more than the $3.50 that I got from the Sorrells, or the $2.00 that I earned at Mrs. Talbert's. Finally, my life had taken a turn for the better.

We were still a week away from leaving for Grandmother Jessie's. Momma said that we couldn't leave until after the 4th. Memorial Day, Labor Day and Independence Day were celebrated big time on Catherine Street and Momma wanted us to be at home with the rest of the family. I don't know why. We didn't do a whole lot. Momma would buy hot dogs and hamburgers and let us grill them out on the back porch. We didn't have rolls, too expensive, but Momma would buy at least two loaves of Bond bread. Darlene would make potato salad and Wayman and I would see if we could hustle up enough money to buy fresh corn on the cob. Everybody pitched in. Donald would come home with a big surprise: cakes, cookies, candy, ice cream… something that Momma could never afford to buy for all of us kids.

Donald would tell us the wildest stories about where he got the money to buy us all of these goodies. One time he said that he was doing days work with Pop Pop. I think that was true because Pop Pop talked about how Donald was such a hard worker that he should go back to Clemson, South Carolina, and take over the family homestead. Sometimes Donald would get up early in the morning and catch a bus (not the PTC) that stopped on the corner to take men to the Jersey farms. It was an old rusted-looking brown bus that may have been white or yellow in another life. He would pick tomatoes, cucumbers and stuff like that with other Colored men from the city. But most of the time, Donald got his money from stealing.

It took us a long time to figure out that Donald was a thief. He would come home with his pockets filled with change and say that he found the money somewhere on the streets. The truth was, Donald had learned about the secret passageways behind the basement at Granny's and visited a couple of the apartments when nobody was home.

Once when Momma needed money real bad, Donald came home with $120.00 and told Momma that he won it on the spinning wheel game at the Transfiguration Church carnival. Momma took everything she had and went down to the carnival to see if she could win some money, too. She lost everything. The truth was, Donald had broken into Mr. Kelly's bar and stole the money from the cash register. Donald would lie like that, but he always brought home his loot and shared it with the rest of the family. He would bring us something special on the 4th.

Our house was not the place to be on the 4th of July or any other holiday. We had the barbeque basics, but very little of anything else. We also had a large patio table with a huge umbrella that took up the entire backyard. Momma was so proud of that one piece of furniture. After finishing off the limited supply of food at the Reid house, I would work my way up and down the block to see who had free good food to eat. And people were always willing to share. Mr. Sarge and Mrs. Bertha had plenty of food and no children; the Quillens had crabs; the Lyons had fried chicken; and the Putmans had everything. All I needed to do was knock on the door and work myself in.

The sun was shining on the 4th of July, and that made it a good day for family barbeques, picnics and other stuff. This 4th of July was the same as others, but different. Everybody was talking about civil rights and civil rights had everything to do with Colored people. It was the most important thing that had happened in our neighborhood since they shot and killed Jack Kennedy. Mr. Adams said it was because he was a friend to the Negroes. Mr. Frazier said not. He said it had something to do with corruption in the unions. Mr. Quillen didn't agree either. He said we were not Negroes anymore, we were Black. Those used to be fighting words, but most folks were nodding in agreement. I still wanted to be Colored because all the women who said they were Black started to show up with nappy heads. I wasn't ready for that.

Mr. Adams kept talking about the March on Washington. He said millions of Negroes were there protesting and demanding their rights. This was especially true for the people from the south, and all the old people on the block once lived in places like Virginia, Mississippi, Georgia, Florida, Arkansas, and North and South Carolina. He said everybody should've been there, but Mr. Frazier said he didn't need to be around that many Negroes. Mr. Quillen said, "the bill had passed, it's time to kick some ass!" It seemed like all the grown people were walking up and down the street talking about civil rights and some new civil rights law, but we still had fun. We danced and played games in the street. I feasted on everybody's food except what we had at our house. Momma stayed home with us all day, but nobody saw Daddy. He probably celebrated the holiday with Granny and Pop Pop in the basement.

I thought a lot about that here lately, about how much our family had changed in the six years that we had been on Catherine Street. How Daddy, without a job, hardly ever came home at night, and how we had become the strange family on the block: all those children without their daddy. Nobody else's daddy had left them. I wondered why?

I didn't see much of Granny anymore. Momma didn't need her to come over and take care of the kids because we were much older now and could care for ourselves. Alfred was only three. Because Daddy didn't have a job, sometimes Momma used to make him stay at home and babysit. When Daddy didn't get home in time from Granny's house, one of the girls would have to stay at home and take care of Alfred. We switched turns so none of us would get into too much trouble and cause the nosy truant officer to come to our house. But we didn't have to worry about Daddy coming home in the summer, and now I think he's gone for good.

I didn't miss much about Granny. Granny was an old lady's old lady. Almost sixty. When she took care of us every day Darlene, Jessie or me would have to take turns scratching Granny's head. White flaky skin would rise up from her scalp, resting all over her clothes and everybody else's. Granny called it "da'ruff" and we had to keep scratching until all of it was gone. When her scalp was clean, we had to spread on the Sulfur 8, which would stink up the place, or Dixie Peach to stop the da'ruff from coming back. I guess it didn't work that well because we were always trying to find a way to get out of scratching Granny's head.

We had to obey Daddy's rules, Momma's rules and Granny's rules. Granny's rules were the worst. Granny would sit in church all day Sunday collecting the rules. Then she would come to Catherine Street on Monday to babysit all us kids and force her holy rules on us. When the rain and lightning came, we had to pull all the plugs out of the sockets so God could do his work. If the sun came out before the rain stopped, the Devil was beating his wife with a frying pan *(Why would the Devil do that?)*. If you got those ringworm looking white spots on your face, she'd get a clean cloth and wash your face in pee. On Good Friday, Donald, Darlene, Wayman, Jessica, Marie and I had to sit quietly in the living room, totally speechless, between the hours of 12:00 and 3:00 because that's when Jesus (not my brother Curtis) was dying on the cross. And we didn't get anything to eat all day until after 3:00. Fasting would make us understand Jesus' pain and suffering, but it certainly didn't make me real fond of Jesus. Granny did everything just like an old country woman would do. I never wanted to be old and country like her and I was happy that she was finally out of our day to day life. But my Grandmother Jessie…that was another story. She was a church woman, a businesswoman, and an Eastern Star. She knew all the important Colored people in Philadelphia. Grandmother Jessie was everything I thought I could be and more. Six weeks at her house would be like Heaven, and in just a few days I would be on my way. If I had only known then what I know now, things may have turned out to be a lot different.

15

Colored Girl

Just one more day, that's all that was left before I arrived at that Heavenly place.

I was on my way to Debbie Jones' house. It was hot and humid and I was sweating like a pig. Fourteen blocks was a long way, and my feet and legs ached the same way they did the morning after dance class when I didn't warm-up and stretch properly. I walked all the way down to 51st street before I cut over toward Ludlow. I walked right pass Chancellor Street. Granny's basement was only one block away, but I wouldn't stop. My Daddy was probably there and I didn't want to see him. I didn't tell Debbie that my grandparents lived two blocks away from her house. I was too embarrassed and didn't want her to know. And I was in too much of a rush to get to her house. Debbie was going to show me what to do with my hair. I remember how disappointed Grandmother Jessie was the last time we stayed overnight. In addition to all that other stuff, my hair was a little too nappy for her. Debbie heard about a new hair straightener called *Curl Free* that promised to take all the naps away.

Giving ourselves a perm was our first great teenage adventure. We went around the strip on 52nd street to find Woolworths, the five and dime department store. We found the *Curl Free* in the beauty supply section. At $2.99, it was a bargain. It would make our hair as straight as the white girl with the blonde hair whose picture was plastered on the outside of the box. We were excited. We hadn't told anybody what we were about to do. We would surprise them with our new hairdos. Debbie's big sisters - Phyllis, Carol and Betty - and her big brother, Philip, would marvel at our good looks.

We gathered everything that we needed and went upstairs in the bathroom to prepare for the transformation. After reading the directions very carefully we both stuck our heads under the spigot to get it wet.

"Look at those nigger naps," Debbie shouted, "nappy, nappy hair," she emphasized.

"Yours nappy, too" I insisted. Her hot-pressed hair had shriveled up from six inches to two, but in truth, it was nowhere near as nappy as mine. But my days of being a nappy-headed niggra were just about to be over. *Curl Free* would set me free.

We sat in the bathroom for twenty minutes waiting for the miracle solution to straighten our hair out. Debbie washed the crème solution out of her hair first. It looked a little straight, but not too much.

"You'll really see it work after we use the dryer," she said.

I was next and the more I washed and shampooed the more certain I was that *Curl Free* should have been called *White People Free*. It didn't straighten out a thing. The perm was for white people's hair, not Colored. I followed all the directions to the tee and my hair was just as nappy as ever. We had failed miserably in our first attempt to transform ourselves into fine young women with a fancy new do.

I couldn't go back home looking like a Banshee woman. We decided to pull out the hot comb and fry my hair the old fashioned way.

The moment the hot comb and sizzling grease hit my hair, I knew something was wrong. It smelt like burning tar that they used for filling the cracks in the asphalt along the trolley tracks. Every time we put the hot comb in my hair, chucks of naps melted away, sticking to the edge of the hot iron. I was terrified. Convinced that I no longer knew what I was doing, I borrowed a colorful scarf from Debbie, wrapped my head tightly like that new African singer Miriam Makeba, and walked four blocks to 55th and Market Street where my Aunt Savannah worked as a hairdresser in Ms. Inez's Beauty Shop.

I peeped inside before sheepishly entering the front door and quickly surveyed the room to locate my Aunt Savannah. Beauty shops were always filled with wild looking Colored women. Their hair, in its most natural state, stuck out in all directions on the top, sides and back of their heads. They were in various stages of the beautification process. There was a young shampoo girl working at the special sink with the hole for your neck. Her job was to get you clean and natural so you would be ready to get your hair fried. There were women sitting under the dryers, shriveled up in various stages from hardcore nappy to wavy almost white girl straight hair. You needed guts, and money, to go to the beauty shop. And while you were waiting, everybody talked about everybody's business.

I spied my Aunt Savannah working on some big red-bone woman's head. She was in the pressing stage—half straight, half nappy—so the woman didn't look too crazy. Aunt Savannah looked like she was almost finished, but I couldn't tell for sure. I locked my eyes on Aunt Savannah and rushed over to her chair.

"Hi, baby."

She always said that. I think my Aunt Savannah knows my name, but she was always calling me baby. I knew she knew that I was one of Lucille's kids.

I paused for a moment to put on my sad face. "Hi Aunt Savannah," I said in a quiet, mousy voice. This wasn't my refined, dignified voice that I used on Grandmother Jessie. This was my, "I'm the pitiful daughter of your little sister who's wrecked her hair with some solution for white girls and I need you to save me as soon as you can, even though you'll lose time and money doing my hair 'cause I can't pay you and neither can my mama," voice. I had faith in my Aunt Savannah. She was one of my good aunts and had the same horror story about her childhood as Momma. However, she remembered the horrors more vividly because she was older. And she tried real hard to forget.

Aunt Savannah continued to lead a hard and difficult life even after they all came back home to Mother. Her marriage to my Uncle Leedy didn't last long. He left for Chicago shortly after my cousin Romaine was born and never came back. I'd never even seen him, even though he's my Daddy's oldest brother and they still talk about him like he's on his way back home.

My granddaddy's dying didn't help, either. Aunt Savannah loved her daddy too much. She was lots of fun before he died but, according to Momma, fell deep into a religious trance after he died so horribly. She's a Jehovah Witness now and every time you see her she's handing out copies of the *Watch Tower*. Momma said don't mention God to her, because all she talks about is Judgment Day when our days on Earth will end and some of us will go into the Kingdom and the rest will be banished into Hell. I only have five years to get ready, because Aunt Savannah says the world will end in 1969. Aunt Savannah no longer celebrated holidays with us and she stopped attending dinners at Grandmother Jessie's house too. Momma said she and Mother didn't talk much to each other any longer. Aunt Savannah spent all of her time at Kingdom Hall and Mother at First African Baptist Church.

You really didn't have to mention God to get Aunt Savannah working on saving your soul. And that's the price I would have to pay: I'd have to confess my love for God and repent my worldly sins if I wanted to get my hair done. I was a sinner, and that's all there was to it.

I shared my horror story with Aunt Savannah and told her that I couldn't show up at Grandmother Jessie's house with my hair looking like this. She agreed. But the failed experiment came at a high cost. In an effort to make it right, Aunt Savannah had to cut my hair to even it out. I worried about the results, because Grandmother Jessie was not fond of short hair, either.

I walked, slowly, back to Catherine Street. I was disappointed that I didn't have the straight hair promised on the *Curl Free* box, but my Aunt Savannah fixed me up real good. My pixie cut was a lot shorter, but cute and fashionable. It made me look a bit older, like a teenager in high school.

My nearly pastel blue suitcase was packed and ready to go. It was pretty hot in the house and the fan in Momma's room, stuck in the window pretending to be an air conditioner, wasn't helping out that much. I decided to sit on the porch and wait until the cool breeze arrived with the late hour. I wasn't going searching for the Crew or anybody else. I wanted my new hairdo to stay put and I didn't want to work up a sweat.

I heard the door slam at Putt Putt's house and figured it was probably him. I hollered down to let him know that I was sitting outside on the top step of the porch. He asked me why I was sitting there, all by myself, and I told him that I was waiting out the time to leave in the morning for my Grandmother Jessie's house.

"Hope you have a good time," he said.

"I will," I promised.

"Aren't you gonna miss your mom?"

"A little bit, but she's happy that I'm going to make some money."

"What about us, Piggy? Are you going to miss the Crew?"

"I'll survive," I said rather smugly. "There's more to me than just the Crew," I convincingly reassured myself.

There wasn't much conversation after that. We sat on the steps for a few minutes more and looked at the lightning bugs swarming around the bushes and trees. Putt Putt caught one, squeezed the bottom just at the right time and removed the brightly colored dot from the bug's behind. It was still shining when he put it on my finger and pretended that it was a ring. I think he likes me.

16

The House of Elegance

Momma had no way of transporting Jessica and me all the way down to South Philly with two big suitcases, so she asked Mr. Earl, Mrs. Gertrude's husband (the Merchant Marine) if he would take us all the way down to South Philly in his brand new, blue and white deuce and a quarter. They lived across the street, down the other end of the block, near Kelly's Bar with a new baby. They always seemed to have everything they needed, and they were willing to share. I don't think Momma had to pay him because she didn't have any extra money.

I could tell by the bright sparkle in her eyes that Grandmother Jessie was happy to see us. She was as sweet and pleasant as ever when we arrived on Saturday afternoon. We didn't get there until after twelve and she was not dressed like usual. Grandmother Jessie was still in her nightgown, and even that was beautiful. It had several layers of deep pink chiffon (that Grandmother later called magenta. What kind of color is magenta?). She was free of makeup and, for the first time, I could see the soft, thin wrinkles on her beanless vanilla face.

Grandmother Jessie showed us to the room in the back on the second floor that would be our home for the next six weeks. I wanted a room of my own, but Grandmother Jessie felt that it was okay for the two of us to sleep in the same bed. It was nice…the big bed, with clean, crisp white linen sheets and two giant soft pillows. Much better than what we had at home, even after Momma finally got rid of the chairs last week and bought two new sets of bunk beds. Now everybody had a real bed to sleep in. I slept on the top and Jessica on the bottom.

There were several bags in the bedroom that Grandmother Jessie said belonged to Jessica and me.

"You'll need these things for the summer," she said.

"Thank you, Grandmother Jessie," we whispered in unison. We wanted to appear refined and gracious in Grandmother Jessie's presence. We knew if we lowered the sound of our voices by a few octaves that it would please her. Young ladies were not loud and rowdy.

"Put your things away in the chest of drawers and join me in the kitchen when you're through," she said as she walked away smiling at the two of us. Grandmother Jessie was happy that we were here. And she had already decided to feed us some good food a few minutes after we walked into the house.

I was pretty darn excited. Grandmother Jessie didn't bring us gifts too often because there were too many of us. Momma wanted all of her kids to be treated equal, and that meant if you couldn't bring a present for all, don't bring any.

I tore open the bag first. I don't know what I hoped to find, but it certainly wasn't mirrored in the goods that I found in the bag. There were two boxy white dresses, very heavy on the starch. At first I thought they were our new outfits for church service on Sunday. They weren't. They were white uniforms, just like the ones you would see in the hospital or at the Dewey restaurants downtown where you could get a cup of coffee, juice and a donut for fifteen cents. There were aprons, too. Plain black aprons that contrasted sharply with the pure white uniforms made especially for Jessica and me. It made me think that I was about to work, real hard. I was happy to find the nylon stockings. It was my first pair and it meant that Grandmother thought that I was mature enough to leave the white ankle socks behind. And the sweet smelling perfume (the bottle said toilet water, but I couldn't think about sprinkling myself with toilet water) was a real treat. It smelt a little bit like the lavender that Grandmother Jessie sprayed all over her room. Lots of good things would come out of our stay at Grandmother Jessie's house.

It was past lunch and too early for dinner. When Grandmother Jessie told us to meet her in the kitchen I guessed, correctly, that we would not be eating. My swift survey of the poor working girl's uniform swept away all of my fantasies and quickly transported me back to reality. There was plenty of food in the kitchen, most of it still in the original package from the grocer. There were lots of chickens, greens and potatoes, and while the kitchen didn't stink like it sometimes did when Momma was trying to clean fish in a bucket of water on the kitchen table, piles of fresh fish laid waiting in the sink ready to be slaughtered.

"There's much you have to learn about being in the restaurant business," she said.

"Yes, Grandmother Jessie," we responded.

"Work gets started long before the doors open," she continued. "First thing we got to do is to get the food ready before we get there. Peoples want some things all the time. Fried fish and fried chicken are good sellers. Big fish sandwiches and quarters of chicken do real well. Dinner guests need more food on their plates. Potato salad, greens, kidney beans and rice will help round out things real nicely. Biscuits and yeast rolls are popular, too. I make all of these things from scratch and it starts right here in this kitchen."

I wasn't the slightest bit confused about what was about to happen. Cooking and food preparation was lesson number one.

For the next several hours, me and Jessica got to wash and cut greens, snap peas, peel potatoes and pull guts out of Porgies and Whiting. We watched as Grandmother Jessie mixed flour, cornmeal and bread crumbs to coat the large cuts of prepared fish and chicken. And she was so careful about cutting the whole chickens into quarters, making certain that nothing was wasted. We had to save all the guts of the chicken for one of her specialties: fried gizzards and livers.

The fish guts, thank goodness, were tossed in the garbage.

We prepared several dozen eggs. Grandmother Jessie said that eggs could stretch any budget. Some were used for the potato salad, others for egg salad sandwiches. We had to boil the eggs in salted water for fifteen minutes. Once cooled, we had to make certain that they would spin on a hard surface. A slow moving, lazy egg meant that it had not cooked long enough. I understood that because when I used to try to sneak out the house to avoid doing housework, Granny used to call me a lazy egg. Soft-boiled eggs were a disaster.

When the yeast rolls or cakes were baking in the oven, we had to walk around the kitchen very quietly. Too much noise would cause the cake to fall, and that would be another disaster.

Chapel's Luncheonette catered to the Colored working folks in South Philly: auto mechanics, janitors, laborers, factory workers and office staff. They worked everyday and could afford to eat out on special occasions—like lunch. It was open from seven to seven on the weekdays, and ten to eight on Saturdays. It was always closed on Sundays. Grandmother Jessie needed to spend Sundays in church praising the Lord, and she believed everybody else in the free world should do the same.

Grandmother Jessie was there at the luncheonette running the show most of the time, but she did allow her short order cook, Roland, to open up the place early in the morning. He didn't have any difficulty fixing up the eggs, ham, grits, bacon and cornbread that folks ordered early in the morning. Hot sausages, liverwurst and corn beef hash sandwiches weren't too difficult either, but Grandmother Jessie needed to be there when they started to serve the real serious food.

We'd been in the kitchen working for nearly three hours when Grandmother Jessie re-appeared. Her face was all dolled-up, but she didn't wear a fancy dress to match. She had on one of those boxy looking white dresses that she had made special for Jessica and me. It hung just beneath her knees and looked just like the outfit she wore to church on missionary Sundays when she gave service as a nurse's aide.

"This is my cooking uniform," she announced ever so proudly

even before I had a chance to ask. "You have to wear the right clothes for the right job."

"Yes, Grandmother Jessie."

"I need to go down to the restaurant, now. Will the two of you be okay if I leave you here alone?"

"Yes, Grandmother Jessie."

I was happy that she was leaving me home. We still had a lot of cleaning up to do in the kitchen. Grandmother Jessie had packed most of the prepared food to take with her to Chapel's Luncheonette, but she didn't take it all. She probably was saving some of it to give to us later. We cleaned up the kitchen, the best we knew how, and fixed a grilled cheese sandwich before we went outside to scrub down the marble steps with Comet cleanser. It was another job that Grandmother Jessie had given us. We finally finished our chores and were free to play outside, as long as we didn't hang around the rough-necks. I wanted to stay up long enough to wait for my Aunt Nita to come home from working for the PTC. It was only six o'clock, but I was dead tired. I went upstairs to take a nap. I wasn't worried about what Jessica was going to do.

They were making enough noise downstairs to wake the dead. At first I thought that the TV in Grandmother Jessie's room was turned up too loud. I heard voices, men and women. They were loud and rowdy, not like the church folks who would visit Grandmother Jessie's house. It sounded as if a party was going on. And then I thought about my Aunt Nita. She was a fine young woman and the loud and rowdy bunch must belong to her.

There was a lot going on, but I was too afraid to go downstairs to see.

"Jessica, Jessica," I whispered. "There's people downstairs."

"Leave me alone," she grumbled. "Stop messing with me."

"Jessica," I insisted, "somebody's in Grandmother Jessie's house."

She sat up on the bed, rubbing her eyes hard to get the sleep out. She was fully awake by then.

"Who's down there?" she questioned.

"I don't know."

"Are we going downstairs?"

"I don't know. Are we supposed to?"

We sat on the bed for the next fifteen minutes wondering what to do. "Should we crash the party?" That woulda been okay for Aunt Nita, but not Grandmother Jessie. We walked out into the hall to listen more intently to what was happening. They were loud and boisterous, just like the people from the bar when we lived in the apartment on Woodland Avenue. Music was playing in the background and we could smell the smoke from the cigars and cigarettes all the way up the stairs and into the bedroom. We walked back and forth in the hallway and slammed the door a few times when we went in and out of the bathroom. Grandmother Jessie finally heard us.

"Are you two sleeping beauties awake yet?" she yelled up the stairs.

"Yes, Grandmother Jessie," we replied in unison.

"Come down and fix yourself some dinner," she hollered back in a joyful voice. She seemed loose and cheerful, happy about something. Maybe she sold a lot of chicken and fish dinners at Chapel's Luncheonette.

We were still dressed in our new short sets and our hair still looked pretty good, presentable enough to meet company. We went down the back stairs to the kitchen. Food was everywhere: fried chicken, fish, pig's feet, potato salad and okra stew. Everything. I didn't know what to take first. The loud people were sitting in the dining room around Grandmother Jessie's fancy mahogany table. They waved and hollered out a few greetings.

"These are two of my grandbabies," Grandmother Jessie announced proudly. We smiled back, politely.

Grandmother Jessie entered the kitchen just as I grabbed a plate from the cabinet above the sink and headed toward the table.

"No, not that," she said rather quickly. "That food is for the guests. Would you like some beans and franks?"

Beans and Franks! I couldn't believe my ears. It sounded as if Grandmother Jessie was taking fried fish, chicken, potato salad and greens out of my mouth and offering me a hot dog instead. Calling them franks and beans didn't change the fact that we were about to have hot dogs for dinner. That might have been a good meal at home on a Saturday night, but we were at Grandmother Jessie's.

"Yes, Grandmother Jessie," we quickly responded nodding our heads. What else could we say?

Grandmother Jessie gave us the package of franks, a can of pork n' beans, and two saucepans to heat our food on top of the stove. We were old enough to cook for ourselves.

We moved quietly around the kitchen. Didn't say a word. I don't know what Jessica was thinking, but I sure was disappointed in Grandmother Jessie. She came back and forth in the kitchen to bring more food out to her guests. She wasn't checking on Jessica and me. While we were sitting there chowing down on the hot dogs (Jessica had two; I had three), a few more of her friends arrived. I spread a few beans around on my plate to make pretend that I was eating them. I never did like beans. Had too much of that at home and Donald said he needed to eat lots of beans in order to fart. I needed to throw a half of cup full in the garbage so nothing would be left over. I didn't want to appear ungrateful for the beans and franks dinner.

We took the back stairs to our room and sat on the bed talking out loud about Grandmother Jessie's party.

"Did you see the fat man?" I said.

"Do you mean Mr. Carter?" Jessica responded.

"No, not Mr. Carter," I snapped. What was wrong with Jessica? Didn't she see what was going on?

"The fat man, with the fat lady, that was eating all the chicken and drinking from the short glasses."

"Yes, I saw him but I couldn't see his face real good."

"You didn't see him stuffing his face?"

"I wasn't paying attention. I was watching Grandmother Jessie having such a good time, acting like she didn't have good manners."

"You think she was having a good time?"

"Why else would she have all those people in her house when it's not a Sunday? And she wouldn't even let us have the real food."

"She's having some kind of party. That's why she treated us that way. But," and I paused for a moment to make certain that I didn't say the wrong thing, "I don't think that they're the people from the church..."

What did we know? To tell the truth, we only saw Grandmother Jessie once in a while. Not as much as we used to see Granny. Granny came over every day. We saw Grandmother Jessie on special holidays. We visited her when she invited us to her house to show us all about fine living. With the exception of Mr. Carter, and a few of the sisters from the First African Baptist Church, Grandmother Jessie's friends remained a mystery to me.

I wanted to get in the shower and go to bed, but I was afraid to walk from the back room to the bathroom. Someone might see me with just the towel wrapped around my body, or me standing there in my PJs. The men and women were coming up and down the stairs, using the bathroom on both the second and third floors. The doorbell kept ringing and as the crowd grew, so did the noise. They were listening to slow, sad songs and people were singing along with the record. They were all eating, drinking, singing and cussin. What the hell had gotten into her? I thought that they were getting a little too wild, but that couldn't have been the case. We were at my Grandmother Jessie's. And this was so unlike my Grandmother.

17

The Church Lady

We had to get up early Sunday morning to get ready for church. Jessica and I brought our Easter Sunday dresses to wear. We had never been to Grandmother Jessie's church, so no one there would recognize our outfits and know that we had already worn them three times since Easter Sunday. At the rate we were going, we would wear them out before Palm Sunday arrived next year. Then we wouldn't have anything to show off the week before our new Easter outfits were made. When we dressed up on Palm Sunday, we'd remind folks on the block of how sharp we were the year before when Momma made all of our outfits from the scraps at Mr. Caldwell's.

Everybody had a different way of doing religion in our family. Grandmother Jessie was a Baptist. She went to church every Sunday and donated lots of her money to the various church funds. Momma, Aunt Nita and Brother Vernard were raised Catholic. Aunt Nita sometimes went to mass on Sundays when she didn't have to work for the PTC. Brother Vernard said he'd had enough religion in Catholic school.

"I don't need mass," he reminded us as we were about to step out of the door. "I've got all the bases covered. Jesus, Mary and them know who I am."

Momma didn't go to mass, and she didn't go to church with us either. She would send all of us across the street to Sharon Baptist for Sunday School classes and Vacation Bible School, but she never insisted that we attend the 10:45 service.

Daddy was raised a Baptist, or so he said, but he never went to church. On one rare occasion, Momma and Daddy came to church together because me, Jessica and Marie were getting baptized. Daddy sat through the whole service and cracked jokes about the Reverend P. M. King, the pastor at Sharon Baptist Church. Right after they called my name to come forth to the sacred pool to get dipped in the holy water Daddy shouted out, "You better get the water real hot for this one." Everybody laughed, except Momma.

Momma didn't approve of the First African Baptist Church and she didn't understand why Grandmother Jessie insisted on attending. According to my Momma, many years ago the church separated the dark Colored from the light. Once when my Grandmother Jessie showed up to church with my brother Hershey, they asked her to go upstairs to be seated. As a near white-looking person who had always been invited to sit in the front pew of the church, she knew instantly what was happening. Grandmother Jessie demanded to see the famous Pastor Harrod, the leader of all the Colored ministers in Philadelphia. She performed. "How dare you!" she shouted at the minister. She talked about her role in the church while, at the same time, professing her love for her dark grandson and for all Colored people. The allegations of color discrimination were denied, and Grandmother Jessie and Hershey were seated in the front. But Momma said that she knew better, and so did Mother.

We got to ride to church in Mr. Carter's car. He dropped us off at the front, but didn't go in. I don't know what kind of religion he practiced.

Everybody was dressed in their Sunday best at First African. All of the men and boys had on suits with long pants. The women wore pretty pastel dresses, some with flowery prints, some without. Most wore hats and the real proper women had white gloves. The minister was a tall, fair-skinned, good-looking Colored man with a heavy black robe draped over his shoulder. *"Much too hot for the summer,"*

I thought to myself. He had to be sweating like a pig under it. There was a choir singing and plenty of church fans waving back and forth advertising some funeral home. I wanted to listen to what the preacher was saying, but I was too busy trying to check things out.

First African Baptist on 16th and Christian Streets was a brightly colored church building with lots of images of white Jesuses everywhere. It was the first time I remembered thinking that God must be a white man. He certainly wasn't Colored. Nobody chose to be Colored. The windows were beautiful, too, but even the angels and the fat babies with wings who came from Heaven were white. That's when I saw the fat man who was stuffing his face with fried chicken sitting at the front of the church. He had on a dark suit with a white handkerchief hanging out of his pocket. He used it to wipe the sweat that kept popping up on his forehead. He sat in the front along with all the other Deacons of the church and didn't look much like he did the night before. The more I looked around, the more certain I felt that maybe a lot of Grandmother Jessie's friends were at the house the night before, but I couldn't be sure. Everybody looked innocent and refined on Sunday morning.

The preacher preached the same sermon as Reverend P. M. King.

"Everybody who's talking about Heaven ain't goin' there." He shouted to a rousing chorus of Amens and Hallelujah Jesuses.

"Stop talking about your neighbor and do some good for somebody."

More Amens, Hallelujahs and thank you Jesuses.

"Don't covet thy neighbor's wife or his possessions. Stop trying to keep up with the Joneses."

Everybody was filled with the Holy Ghost, or was it the Holy Spirit? I think the more you shouted, the holier you got to be. A couple of women jumped into the aisles to do the holy dance. The spirit hit them hard, and they wanted everybody to know that they had been touched by the Lord. I thought they were faking it 'cause I saw one lady looking at the other lady's feet to see if she was dancing better than her. The sisters in white, who were part of the Nurse's Aide Mission, had to rush forth and calm a few people down.

I wondered if the Holy Ghost was gonna hit me, too? I hope not. I'd be so embarrassed.

Grandmother Jessie had church business to take care of after the service. She told us to walk back home. I didn't think that I could make it because my feet had been hurtin' since the moment I walked out of the door. No matter what the size, cheap patent leather shoes always hurt your feet. Walking three long blocks was too much, but there was nothing that I could do about it.

We exited through the back door and made a left on the corner of 16th and Christian. It was a warm day out, much too hot for our lime colored capes, but they looked so fashionably good with our white dresses and matching cummerbund. We sweated our way down Christian as we headed over to the 1900 block. I didn't like walking back to Grandmother Jessie's house all dressed up. The people in South Philly were not like the folks on Catherine Street. There were people hanging on the corners and out of windows shouting to folks running down the street. There were lots of three story houses, but most did not look like Grandmother Jessie's. I saw a lot of nappy-headed kids everywhere, although Momma reminded me to stop thinking about good and bad hair. And the people in South Philly didn't wait until Saturday to turn on the fire hydrant. Water was squirting out all over the place, and the neighborhood folks made a game out of throwing dressed-up people in the water. When Jessica and I walked by the surging hydrant, I was certain that somebody was about to grab me, throw me in the water and, possibly, drown me. We walked fast, keeping pace with the rapid beat of my pounding heart. I thought about how to explain to Grandmother Jessie that some roughnecks threw us under the hydrant for fun.

We got home safe. But we were still wet. The lime green capes, the fast paced walk and the fear of being drowned in a public hydrant was enough to work up a soaking sweat.

We went to our room, rearranged our clothes in the chest of drawers and thought about what we would have for dinner. Dinner was always early on Sunday, and sometimes that meant that you didn't get lunch. I wondered if Grandmother Jessie would give us some good food for dinner, like what she gave to the party-goers the night before.

She didn't disappoint us this time. Grandmother Jessie fixed up all the leftovers from the night before and made us a scrumptious meal. Aunt Nita was home, and so was Hershey, so we all got to sit down at the kitchen table and act like we were a family.

Aunt Nita told us funny stories about all the crazy people that she saw everyday on the PTC. One man jammed a dollar bill down the mouth of the token machine and then asked for change; a lady showed up with five kids on a Friday without any money. It wasn't a Sunday, so children couldn't ride free. She told my Aunt Nita that she would leave them all right there at the underground station if she didn't let them all get on the subway. And some of the people, mostly white teenagers, would just wait until the train came and then jump over the turnstile without paying.

Hershey didn't say much. He never did much talking. Brother Vernard was twenty-one now and had a whole new life that nobody knew much about. He stopped gang-warring a long time ago. He didn't visit us on Catherine Street anymore and had dropped out of school before he got his diploma. Momma was real disappointed by that 'cause she always talked about how important it was for us to get a high school diploma. She and Daddy didn't have one. Brother Vernard did have a job. He was learning to be a bartender and short-order cook at the corner bar.

Grandmother Jessie changed the focus of conversation when she started telling us about what to expect the next day when we arrived for work at Chapel's Luncheonette.

"Just do what you're told and everything should be okay."

"Yes, Grandmother Jessie."

"I want you to learn some things about being a businesswoman that you can use someday."

"Yes, Grandmother Jessie."

"I need to leave quite early in the morning. The two of you don't need to come with me. I'll give you directions and you can walk to the store and meet me there at twelve."

"Yes, Grandmother Jessie."

I started to worry again. I didn't know where 16th and Bainbridge was. I didn't want to walk to work every day in a boxy white uniform. What if I encountered the fire hydrant game patrol?

"I don't want you working all day," Grandmother Jessie said, interrupting my thoughts about how dire the situation had become. "Children are not supposed to work all day. Six hours will be enough. If you get there by twelve, you can leave at six and walk back home. I'll need to stay later than that."

This was not working out the way I'd planned and was certainly not what I'd expected. I'd be walking long distances, working hard and not having much fun. Listening to Grandmother Jessie talk, I realized that we'd be working every day of the week except Sunday. She had every hour of the day planned for us and she never did say how much she was going to pay us.

We cleaned our plates off the table, scooped all the garbage into the brown paper bag, washed and put away all of the dishes. Grandmother Jessie didn't have to tell us to do it. We were quick learners and knew what we were supposed to do.

I didn't mind turning in early. I was tired and still a little bit excited. It was my first real job and I couldn't wait to get started. And the best part of all, I would be loaded with money when the summer was over. I still had a lot to look forward to.

I heard the doorbell ring, but didn't think much of it. It was a man with a deep voice, probably Mr. Carter, but I didn't feel like peeping through the banister at the downstairs hallway to get a good look and to make sure. It was late, after nine. I put on my PJs and went to bed.

At first, I thought I was dreaming. I heard loud noises like I did the night before. Music was playing. Women were laughing. Men were singing. There were more people in Grandmother Jessie's house. Jessica was fast asleep and I wasn't about to wake her this time. I laid there quietly listening to the people downstairs laughing, singing and shouting at each other. They were moving up and down the stairs, again, like they had not finished the party from the night before.

I heard several voices right outside our bedroom in the hallway. I jumped out of the bed to see what was going on. The room was dark but I could see the light coming through the keyhole. I pushed my face flat to the door, scratching my cheek on the rough edges, and tried to peep through the keyhole to see what was happening.

I saw another fat man and a woman with a big ass on the landing of the third floor stairs. He was pushing and teasing her as she struggled to climb the second set of stairs.

'Shhh…Shhh…, childrens up here," he tried to whisper to the woman with the big fat ass.

"Shh…Shh…," she said, spitting back at him. She giggled quietly as her heavy head hit the top of her chest. They both giggled some more as they worked their way up the steps, out of my sight. I jumped back in bed and tried to be quiet. What was going on at Grandmother Jessie's house?

I heard them flop on the bed. The box spring was old and squeaky. It was quiet for a few seconds and then all I could hear was the squeak and the bounce, repeatedly, rhythmically. Squeak, bounce, squeak, bounce, squeak, BOUNCE. They were doing it. I was certain of that. And he was screwing her hard. I heard them moaning and groaning.

"Yea, yea, yea," I heard her shouting through the walls. I had never been this close to people boning before. I tried to go to sleep, but my mind was focused on what they were doing. What was it like? I wondered. *"Who's on top? Who's on bottom?"* I asked myself. *Who were these people banging each other's brains out and doing it real hard in Grandmother Jessie's guest bedroom? What were they doing in Grandmother Jessie's house?* I shut my eyes tight, pulled the cover up over my head and tried to calm myself down. I had gotten pretty excited thinking about the naked people upstairs. Well, I didn't know if they were naked or not, but people had to take their clothes off to do it.

My thoughts of them were grotesque: a fat man with a woman with a big old ass, and tits, rolling over each other in the bed. But then my thoughts turned sensual as I imagined what pleasure must have been involved in the heavy love-making that was going on upstairs.

I finally drifted off to sleep after my imagination had run wild about the pushing and thrusting, moaning and groaning, heavy breathing and wheezing, but not before the thought of all of that sex, sex and more sex, made me have, I think, my first wet dream.

18

The Hussy
_____

I didn't know what to think. Oh yes I did. As I laid there, between deep sleep and bright consciousness, it hit me. Like…like…an epiphany. That's what it was, an epiphany. I learned that word in my seventh grade English class when Jill Fasnault spelled it in one of those spelling bees. I never could spell worth a damn, but I knew the meaning of the word.

The big house, all those bedrooms, picture perfect 24 hours a day. And the sign, the sign in the second floor bathroom about not stinking up the place. I was naïve, but not stupid. Grandmother Jessie was running a house. She was an entrepreneur alright: She ran Chapel's Luncheonette by day and Chapel's House of Ill-Repute by night…or at least that's what I started to think as I thought about rolling out of bed and getting myself ready for the first day of work.

For the next several minutes I laid there perfectly still. Jessica was asleep and I didn't want to wake her. I wanted to tell her about what happened last night, but I couldn't reveal the full story. I was embarrassed about the moist heat I felt in my own white cotton draws when nobody was in there.

I looked at the round porcelain-looking clock on top of the chest of drawers to check the time. It was only 6:45, too early for most, save the milk and bread man, to be stirring around. It was quiet now.

No more squeaking and bouncing. No laughter. No music. No loud noises. No sex. The house had returned to its normal, pristine state.

I heard the doors open and shut. The open, as she moved from her bedroom to a few short steps down the hall to the second floor bathroom, the shut as she entered, leaving the stale air that still stank of smoke and liquor behind. It was my Grandmother Jessie. She was an early riser.

Who would have thought it? Grandmother Jessie. Mother. Mrs. Lester Chapel. Sister First African Baptist Goody Two Shoes!

I heard her butt singing, high notes and low notes. She was full of gas, so her butt was forced to sing a distressful blues song. She wasn't a quick farter. There were short sudden bursts, then long labored ones, like she was struggling to string together the perfect lyrics to make the perfect song. I turned over a few more times trying to adjust my body to a comfortable spot. I liked sleep and dreamland was my favorite travel destination. I wanted to go back there, but I was too restless.

I heard the water gushing out of the spigot and spilling into the tub as she prepared for her bath. There was a shower, but she preferred not to use it. I loved it. A shower was such a novelty item and I was eager to let the warm water sprinkle all over my naked body every chance I got. I imagined her in there testing the water to make certain that it was not too hot or too cold. Cleanliness was next to godliness in Grandmother Jessie's house and that included her body, which served as her own personal temple.

I couldn't sort it all out, but I tried. "Is this what she did on the weekends? How long had she been doing it? Who else knew? What this like...a hoe house?"

The doors opened and shut as she moved a few short steps from the bathroom and back to the bedroom. Guiltless. None of this mattered to her. I was certain that she was in there powdering herself up and getting ready to take on the world at her day job. She would put on a clean white uniform and a thin black hair net that would keep the strands of her straight brown hair from falling into the fried fish and chicken sandwiches. Before she was through, she would paint her face with red rouge and red lipstick and make certain that she would put on a matching necklace and earrings. "Pretty gaudy," I thought to myself.

I rolled over to my right side, curled up like a newborn and looked out of the window. The air was still. It was humid. I could smell the heat. It was gonna be hot today, a real scorcher.

It wasn't a very scenic view: brick houses with elongated windows, most with shades pulled all the way down to the bottom, a few with white lace curtains but most without. No trees or squirrels. I laid still in bed, listening to the drip from the bathroom faucet that continued to leak because it needed a washer. Maybe she thought they were tired and needed some rest? That's why people were upstairs, banging their brains out the night before. I was still listening as she descended the back stairs and worked her way to the kitchen. Was it still messy from the night before?

"What time is it?" Jessica asked rather abruptly. She had moved suddenly after being shaken from her sleep by the clanking sound of milk bottles being dropped off next door by the Sealtest man. I glanced quickly at the porcelain clock.

"6:55," I said just as Jessica was turning over in the bed.

"Are you getting up?"

"In a minute."

"Is Grandmother Jessie up?"

"Uh huh. I heard her washing up in the bathroom. She's downstairs getting food ready to take to work."

Jessica turned over to her left side, grabbed the end of the white sheet, threw it up over her shoulders and snuggled into herself.

"You're not getting up?" I questioned.

"Do we have to right now?"

"I think so."

I knew we didn't have to get up and leave early with Grandmother Jessie. She told us that at dinner last night, but I couldn't lie still in bed any longer. But I wasn't exactly eager to rush downstairs and greet my Grandmother Jessie. I didn't want her to look in my face. What would she see? Anger? Embarrassment? Disgust?

I heard the open and the shut. It was Aunt Nita this time. It was Monday, or Blue Monday as she would like to say, like the singer Fats Domino, and she had to get ready for work. I don't know why she called it Blue Monday because she always had to work on the weekends. But it would be another day of working with all the crazy folks that rode the PTC. "Did she know? Was she down there partying, too? Did Grandmother Jessie ever have to use her room for a drunk man and a fat woman who needed to get it on?"

I wanted to ask my Aunt Nita about what went on at Grandmother Jessie's house, but I couldn't. Innocence lost, I wouldn't admit to her that I suspected the worst of my perfectly devout Christian grandmother.

The doors opened and shut again. It was a good time for me to make my way down the hall to wash my face, brush my teeth and roll on the Tussy deodorant. I bought my own with the last $3.50 I got from Mrs. Sorrell when I quit being her Mother's Helper. I was ready to meet my grandmother in the kitchen.

She was humming… "We're marching to Zion, beautiful, beautiful Zion…"

"You're not going to Heaven," I thought. "The Lord is watching – everywhere – and he knows about the fat lady with the big ass."

"Good morning, sweetheart."

"Good morning Grandmother Jessie."

"Are you ready for today?"

"Yes, Grandmother Jessie." But I was thinking about something else. "What about last night?"

"Bainbridge is not too hard to find," she started to explain. "Take a walk straight down Christian until you reach 16th. Make a left and walk up two blocks 'til you reach Bainbridge. The restaurant is right there on the corner. You can't miss it."

I nodded. I understood. The directions weren't complicated and I could find my way to the luncheonette. It was only five blocks. She went back to humming her religious songs.

"Soon and very soon, we're going to see the King." That's what got on my nerves about church folks. They were always talking about the Kingdom of Heaven when everybody was struggling right here on Earth.

It never occurred to me that I should ask Momma about what was going on. I wondered if she knew and I wondered how she felt.

Grandmother Jessie didn't bother to fix me breakfast. She was too busy. She pointed to the oatmeal on the second shelf in the cabinet and said, "Fix yourself a good, hardy breakfast. You'll need your strength to get through the day." I didn't like oatmeal, but with lots of sugar, milk and butter, I could pretend that it was Cream of Wheat, which I preferred.

It was a little past eight. Grandmother Jessie was packed and ready to go. The way I figured it, she would have to work about nine to ten hours a day at the place she owned. That was putting in a lot of time for the boss.

By the time Jessica got downstairs, Grandmother Jessie and Aunt Nita had gone. Brother Vernard was still in bed. He could sleep late because the bar didn't open until ten and he didn't have to go in until after five. It was quiet. An eerie silence penetrated the whole place. Even Jessica looked a little ghostly when she came down the steps. For a quick moment I thought I was seeing Grandmother Pattie. Of course, she had never lived in the house on Christian Street, but all the surroundings felt the same.

There was plenty of oatmeal left and I made some toast to fill out the breakfast. Grandmother Jessie had a toaster and toast from the toaster tasted real good. We didn't have a toaster at home. It was too hard to try and fix toast on the hot plate. I knew we weren't about to get a toaster because we were still waiting on the stove and sink. Just a few months after we moved onto Catherine Street, Daddy took everything out of the old kitchen so that we could get new stuff. It had been more than five years and we were still waiting for the new stuff to come. The old refrigerator was still there. Thank goodness he didn't throw that out. The hot plate would probably last another month or two. Those were replaced quite often. The slinky wires kept popping and we had to stretch and twist together what was left until it finally broke down for good. There was only so much twisting and connecting that a cheap hot plate could take.

Me and Jessica talked about what we would do for the next three hours. We thought about hanging out, but we didn't know any of these people in the neighborhood, and Grandmother Jessie had already suggested that they weren't like us. TV gave us a choice between Sally Starr, Howdy Doody and soap operas. But there was one other possibility that we never could consider when Grandmother Jessie was home: roaming around the house.

I left Jessica downstairs and went upstairs to peep in Grandmother Jessie room. It was near perfect, as always. I could smell her scent even though she was no longer there. I peeped into Aunt Nita's room, but I was too afraid to go in. I knew it was private and I wouldn't consider doing anything to upset my Aunt Nita. I went upstairs to the third floor. Brother Vernard's door was shut and I was quiet. I didn't want to wake him and didn't want him to know that I was upstairs snooping around. I looked in the bedroom near the front of the house. That was the one right above me and Jessica's room and that's where they were banging their brains out sexing it up the night before. Grandmother Jessie had already cleaned up the place. You could smell the fresh linen. Nothing was out of place and the room looked just like it was ready to receive a good Christian.

I tiptoed back downstairs and left the house through the front door. It was hot and sticky, not even ten yet. I felt sweaty and, I think, nervous. I didn't have good thoughts about my grandmother. I sat there for a few minutes and thought about the house activities: All the food, all the booze, all the partying and all that sex. I became queasy and worried that my stomach and bowels couldn't hold on to my breakfast. That's when I decided to forget about it. What Grandmother Jessie did was her own business.

After a few boring hours we decided to change into our boxy white uniforms with the heavy starch and get ready for work. They fitted us perfectly. Grandmother Jessie had made us these outfits without even trying them on us. I guess she didn't need any of our measurements. We tied on the little black aprons and put on our white sneakers that Momma had bought us at the beginning of the summer.

We walked fast. Everybody stared. We were both short and thin and people probably wondered why these two midget maids were rushing down the street.

Chapel's Luncheonette was a lot smaller than I envisioned. I mean, really, the first thing that I thought was "hole in the wall." There was a counter with six metal stools pressed closely to the edge. There were four small tables with 2 red chairs apiece. I counted. You couldn't feed more than twelve people at a time. There was cooking stuff behind the counter: an old refrigerator, a grill, a sink, a gas stove, but no oven. There was a small bathroom on the right side with a sign tacked on the top half of the door that read PRIVATE. I found out later that Grandmother Jessie wanted to discourage the *patrons* (That's what we had to call the people who were coming into the restaurant) from using it. The place was crowded. Grandmother Jessie and Roland worked the grill and stove, and me and Jessica learned how to take orders and deliver the food to the table with a smile.

It was a busy first day. Lots of people, mostly men, came in to order food. Fish, chicken and pig's feet, those were the most popular orders. They didn't seem to cost much, two or three dollars, and most men gave us a quarter before they left. One man left me a dime and I thought that he was real cheap.

The first three hours were nonstop. People kept coming in ordering sandwiches, mostly take-out. Nobody tipped us when we gave them the brown paper bag filled with piping hot food.

"Who tho' lovely gals?" one cruddy old man asked.

"Those my grands," Grandmother Jessie responded, ever so proudly. "My grands," I thought to myself. I never heard Grandmother Jessie describe us that way. Sounded like ghetto street slang to me.

"The light one real cute; the dark one, too," he felt compelled to add. Grandmother Jessie snapped her head about in a flash,

"Cuse, me, sir," she said in a dignified voice. "You won't be describing my grandchildren that way. They're both good-looking Colored girls. Light and dark ain't got nothing to do with it."

"Whoa...sorry...forgive me ma'am. Didn't mean nothing 'bout it. Just saying they're good-looking gals."

Grandmother Jessie turned her back and continued to cook the hot sausage on the grill. She was like Momma. It reminded me of what I said about Zak. There would be no discussing the benefits of being light in Momma's house or Grandmother Jessie's kitchen. Colored people would make it on their own merit.

Jessica and I sat at the corner table and watched the cruddy looking man leave with his sandwich wrapped up tightly in a small brown paper bag. Grandmother Jessie went back to her humming, although I couldn't recognize which church song she was trying to sing. Things had finally quieted down and the brief moment of rest was a great relief to my aching feet.

Grandmother Jessie put a few more hot sausages on the grill. Who had ordered them? When they were black in the center and crusty around the edges, she pulled them off the grill and placed each one in between two slices of white bread. She placed each sandwich on a small white saucer and brought them over to the end table and handed them to me and Jessica.

"Lunch," she said without a smile.

It wasn't what I hoped for. With all that chicken and fish being fried up in the place, I thought we'd at least get to choose what we wanted to eat.

I was hungry enough, so I didn't complain. After the first day, I realized that a hardy breakfast would not be enough to get me from early morning to three o'clock. But the worst thing about the hot sausage was that it reminded me of the cruddy man who thought it was so important to distinguish light from dark. I was chocolate all right, maybe the same color as Brother Vernard. I wonder if people called me Hershey behind my back.

Six o'clock couldn't come fast enough. My hair and clothes stank of fired grease. I was tired of smiling and waiting on people. I had $2.60 in tips and it was burning my pocket. I think Jessica had about the same. Every time I moved I felt the money jangle in my apron pocket and it made me feel good. I had earned some extra spending change and still would be getting paid for a full day's work. Grandmother Jessie said the tips belonged to us. She never did say how much she was going to pay us.

We rushed back home to Christian Street at the same break-neck speed that we used to get to work in the morning. I rushed upstairs to take off my uniform, hung it out the back window to get rid of the smell and, again, carefully counted my tips to make sure my $2.60 was still there. I changed into a short set and thought about going outside to play. But I was too tired, and for the first time realized that I was no longer interested in playing anything. I had been away from Catherine Street for only 72 hours. I felt like my whole world had changed. Grandmother Jessie wasn't the woman I thought she was. She was no longer my idol. Maybe this wasn't such a good vacation after all. And I still had five more weeks and four more days to go.

19

Party Over Here
___

Tuesday, Wednesday and Thursday brought more of the same: get dressed, fix breakfast, walk fast to Bainbridge Street, work for six hours, walk fast back home and get some rest. Dinners were okay, but not spectacular. I soon realized that our meals consisted of whatever was left over or not a good seller at Chapel's Luncheonette. We had lots of Shad. It was a fish I had never heard of before going to Grandmother Jessie's and it had more bones in it than the skeletal remains of an ancient dinosaur. That's why the patrons never ordered it and I wondered why Grandmother Jessie kept buying it so that it would be left over for Jessica and me to eat for lunch and dinner.

Friday was no different, the same routine all over again. When six o'clock rolled around, I was good and ready to leave, but Grandmother Jessie said that she needed help with a few things. She asked me and Jessica to stay a little longer.

By the time 7:30 hit, I wondered if we were ever getting out of the place. It was almost closing time and people kept coming in, ordering fried fish and chicken sandwiches. I tried not to be too irritable because it was Friday. Friday was payday, or at least I hoped so. Momma and Daddy (when he had a job) got paid on Fridays. All the men on the block got paid on Fridays and everybody always said that the eagle flies on Friday – payday. Grandmother Jessie never said that we were getting paid today, I just figured it.

She finally started locking up the place at 8:15. I was willing, ready and able to walk back to 1911 Christian Street. It was still light out-side and we could make it before dark. No need to worry about the South Philly roughnecks who hit the streets a few seconds past dusk. I must admit that I was real happy to see old man Carter. His black Buick was waiting at the front curb when we walked out the front door.

I stood silently, looking in his direction. He didn't say a word. I rolled my eyes to the right and started walking. We were halfway down the street when Grandmother Jessie shouted, "come!" Thank goodness, we were getting a ride back home.

In less than 10 minutes we were pulling up right in front of the house. Jessica and I jumped out of the car and offered to carry in all the bags of leftovers that Grandmother Jessie brought from Chapel's Luncheonette. We were even smart enough to go into the kitchen and try to put some things away.

Mr. Carter came in behind us and started making himself com-fortable. He was familiar with the place alright. I guess he'd be staying for the evening, maybe even overnight.

"Stay," Grandmother Jessie said as I headed for the back steps. I jerked my body around quickly and stared back at her like she was crazy.

"For what?" I blurted out like the fast, sassy teenager I always hoped to be. What was I thinking? It was, I think, the first time I had the nerve to question my Grandmother Jessie. Now she was looking at me like I was the crazy one.

"A few of my friends are coming over," she said pleasantly but in a sharp, clear and direct voice, "and I'm gonna show you girls how to be a good party hostess."

Now I was steaming. Did Grandmother Jessie expect me to work on the weekends, too? Did I really need to learn how to be a host-ess? And who did she think she was - that white woman named Emily Post?

I rolled my eyes, but only a little bit, and walked back over to the kitchen table. Grandmother Jessie had pulled out all the large, shining silver serving platters (most recently polished by me and Jessica), and started to load them up with food. This time, I really didn't care what she was serving. I was still steaming about my new role as a domestic servant.

"Go change your clothes," she said.

"Into what?" I snapped. What the hell was wrong with me? I was standing up and challenging Grandmother Jessie like she was some raggedy-ass sister on the block.

"Something a little prettier than your work clothes," she responded in a terse voice.

We were working so hard that we hadn't even noticed that Grandmother Jessie had slipped away and changed into her party outfit. I heard the door bell ring, but I was too pissed off to go and see who was at the door.

"You lookin good," the two crusty old men said when she answered the door. They were right. Although Grandmother Jesse was every bit of a 220 pound, fifty something year old woman, she sure knew how to dress. You woulda thought she was on her way to a cabaret or something, instead of a house party. She wore a lavender and pink party dress with matching pearl necklace, earrings and bracelet. And she had on a colorful pair of pink leather heels.

"What we gonna wear?" Jessica asked.

"I don't know," I snapped. "It's not fair for Grandmother Jessie to make us wait on people at her party." I was way past steaming by now. I wanted to curse Grandmother Jessie out, but I didn't dare. Being slapped into tomorrow woulda been a reality if I sassed my grandmother.

"We only have one dress!" Jessica responded, completely ignoring my complaints about Jessie Chapel. I guess she wasn't old enough to challenge the old lady. I pretended I didn't hear what she was saying.

"I don't want to wear that dress without the cape," I protested.

"Don't matter," she said. "You don't have anything else."

And I knew she was right.

I didn't bother to shower. I took off one boxy white dress and traded it for a sleeveless, form-fitting one with an A frame skirt. I put on my lime green cummerbund. It added a bit of colorful flair to the drab-looking white dress. And the coffee-colored Kashmir stockings provided the final touch that made me feel like a grown woman.

It was like being at the luncheonette all over again: fried chicken breast, potato salad and greens on one plate; fried fish, salad and greens on the other. But what truly shocked me is when people started to pay for their meals.

"Here you go!" one woman shouted waving two dollars in her hand. The man with her could barely wipe the grease off his fat smelly hands before he reached into his pocket and pulled out two more. I took the money and carried it back to the kitchen. Grandmother Jessie just pointed to the beige, black and brown cigar box. I lifted the lid and dropped in the bills, right on top of two fives, a ten, and a bunch of ones.

I had gone back and forth to the dining room a couple of times serving up chicken, fish and pig's feet, collecting two dollar bills and a few pieces of loose change. When Grandmother Jessie handed me two small shot glasses, pointed me in the direction of the two crusty men who had arrived to the house first and said, "get fifty cents apiece," I was through - done enough to stick a fork in it.

"The meals were two dollars, the drinks fifty cents. How much were the rooms? I wondered. What did they call this place? A Brothel? A speakeasy? A whorehouse or what?" The thought of every word brought more distress and discomfort. But before we had time to think about it, we were serving alcoholic beverages to everyone in the place. The more they drank, the friendlier they got. They were smiling and grinning, talking trash and saying how cute we were. By eleven o'clock, they were flying high. They started giving us tips every time we walked into the room. And there was a steady stream of hollering, "Come on over here!"

I stopped being mad and started to think about all the extra money I was getting in tips. As long as the food kept coming and the drinks flowing, nobody seemed to care about anything. The music was loud.

Folks were laughing and singing. I even got out on the floor to do a little dance to *Shimmy, Shimmy Ko Ko Bop*. I was shaking, turning and twisting much better that I did when I was a little girl dancing on top of the bar on Woodland Avenue. I rolled my hips from side to side, shook my shoulders and flat chest in perfect timing with the rhythm. I learned how to do that at Mrs. Sydney's Dance School. People were smiling and grinning, and some people clapped their hands to the beat of the song, so I danced harder. I saw the skinny man and fat woman heading up the front steps to the bedroom on the third floor, but I pretended that they weren't even there.

Jessica went to bed first, but I stayed up serving liquor and providing a little dance when requested. I ate fried fish and chicken and partied with the old folks until Grandmother Jessie told me that I had had enough. She didn't say so, but I sensed that she was so very proud of me. I was becoming a party girl.

20

Saturday Night

I got up late Saturday morning. I was tired, achy and emotionally exhausted. My head was still swirling from all the activities of the previous night. It was fascinating, but scary at the same time.

I thought about all the people who were in and out of Grandmother Jessie's house. Some were old - some young - lots of smart people with good jobs and good pay. I heard Grandmother Jessie say they were the "cream de cream" of Philly's Colored community. The cream part must have had something to do with so many light skinned people being in the room.

My butt dragged around Chapel's Luncheonette all day. I ran back and forth from the tables to the counter and tried to give good service with a smile. But I was bone tired, and I really didn't like these people. They slobbered all over their food, sucked the grizzle out of the neck bones, and then we had to clean up after them.

Before the end of our work day, Grandmother said, "That's enough."

"What's enough?" I thought to myself.

"Jessica, Patricia," she announced, "you can wrap it up here and go home."

I stared at Grandmother Jessie for a few minutes. *"Aren't you going to say anything else?"* I thought quietly to myself. *"Something like, here sweetheart. Here's your pay for a whole week of really hard work."* I looked over to Jessica. She was wiping down the square tables for the last time. *"Couldn't she read my mind? Was she gonna ask Grandmother Jessie about our bread?"*

Jessica didn't say a word and neither did I. I wanted my money badly, but I didn't have the courage to ask for it. Besides, I had earned $3.50 in tips from Friday night's house party and that would probably last me all weekend.

I jumped out of the boxy white uniform, threw it on the floor and plopped down on the double bed. It was only 5:15, but I needed a nap. I didn't have to report back to work until Monday and I wanted to rest up for Sunday's excursion around town and into the neighborhood. Me and Jessica had decided to get dressed up, walk to the bus stop and stand next to people who looked like us. When the bus came, we could jump on and pretend they were our mom and dad. We never forgot about children, twelve and under, being able to ride free on Sundays and we planned on traveling all over Philly as long as we stood next to the right people. We were both over twelve, but we were short, skinny and undernourished. We could fool the bus driver quite easily. A long nap followed by a good night's sleep is just what my body needed to get ready for the next day.

Grandmother Jessie tugged gently on the covers as she called out my name.

"Patricia, Patricia," she whispered "Sweetheart...it's time to get up." I rolled over a few times, forced my eyes open and took a quick glance at the window. It was pitch black outside. Had I slept through the night? Did I miss anything? Why was Grandmother Jessie in here waking me up?

"Patricia...Patricia," she repeated again. "This is for you."

With that I sprung forward like time, stood at full attention and struggled to focus my eyes on what she had for me.

"Good morning Grandmother Jessie," I blurted out, trying to be polite, but still wobbly and disoriented from a long night's sleep.

She smiled. "It isn't morning, honey. It's 9:00 in the evening. Here, I brought you a present." She laughed a little after that. I smiled too as I reached for the brown paper bag. Inside was a beautiful black and yellow sundress. It wasn't a Sunday kind of church dress, but it was much fancier than the play outfits that I used to wear when I was six and eight. It was ribbed across the chest and the waist was high like an Empire dress.

"Thank you, thank you very much," I gushed while pressing the sundress against my chest and tried to sneak a glimpse of myself in the mirror on top of the vanity top table.

"Get dressed," she said. "You can wear it this evening."

Within fifteen minutes of the wakeup call I found myself back in the kitchen. Jessica was already there working. She had on her present, too - an Empire-looking sundress just like mine, but hers was red and white.

The doorbell started ringing; plates of fish and chicken were flying back and forth from the kitchen to the dining room to the parlor and back to the kitchen again. There was mundane chit chat spilling out of the smoked filled rooms and in the hallway where everyone stopped first to greet my grandmother.

"Is it good today?"

"Always is."

"Got the usual?"

"Sure do."

"We'll have two."

"Be right with you."

"Which room? Front or back?"

The Saturday night party was more crowded than the night before. There were wild looking people everywhere. They were loud and boisterous and couldn't keep their hands off me and Jessica. "I'm gonna make a lot of money tonight," I thought to myself.

Me and Jessica, we were working real hard. These folks were

generous and it almost made me feel happy that I was still working. But I still wondered about my Grandmother Jessie.

I didn't know Aunt Nita had arrived home until I saw her standing in the kitchen doorway. It was a few minutes past eleven o'clock. The chimes had just finished singing and the party was in full force. She was sharp, as usual, in her navy blue and white John Wanamaker suit. It was one of her PTC outfits. She hadn't changed into her party clothes yet.

"What are you doing?" she asked, crinkling her nose up and distorting her face into an unpleasant frown.

"Serving," I said first and then Jessica followed.

"Did Mother tell you to do this?"

"Uh huh," Jessica responded. "She didn't have enough help. We did it last night, too. Patricia got $3.50 and I got $4.75 from tips."

"Where did you get those outfits?'

"Grandmother Jessie," we both said in unison.

Neither one of us had time to play chit chat with Aunt Nita. We were too busy. People wanted their food and drinks in a hurry. And the nicer we were to the party people, the better the tips.

Aunt Nita didn't stay. She looked around the kitchen and watched Grandmother Jessie fix more dinner plates and pour liquor into the short little glasses. She went upstairs to her bedroom, which was never used for company, and stayed there the rest of the night.

Brother Vernard didn't get home in time to join the party. He was too busy working at the bar serving drinks himself.

It was close to midnight before Grandmother Jessie told us to go to bed. I was tired, but it was a good night. I had $5.10 and Jessica had $6.00. As soon as we got our regular pay from Grandmother Jessie, we'd be as rich as we wanted to be. I planned on spending some of that money the next day at the Penny Arcade on 15th and Market Street. I wanted to get a picture taken with the words, "Always thinking of you" at the center of the big heart in the background.

I snuggled under the clean, pressed white sheets and dug my face into the pillow. It smelt so good. I was just about to drift off into dreamland when I suddenly remembered. I jumped out of bed, ran to the door and turned the switch into the locked position. There were too many strangers in the house, eating food, drinking liquor and roaming from room to room seeking sexual pleasure and enjoyment. I had to try to protect Jessica, and me, from harm.

21

Aunt Nita's Stand

This time, it was my aunt Nita who told me to pack my things and get ready to go home. That's all she said when she entered the second floor bedroom at the front of the house early Sunday morning. At first, I thought she'd come to tell us to get up and get ready for mass. We attended First African Baptist last week and a switch to Catholic service woulda been good. All it took was one hour and you were out of there for sure. Catholics had all of their stuff worked out ahead of time and it was the same routine over and over again. Michelle told me that once you remembered the Hail Mary, you'd never forget what you needed to say. You were home free after that.

Aunt Nita didn't say anything else. She looked like she was mad about something, but I know that I hadn't done anything wrong. In our white and blue cotton PJs, still damp from the nighttime sweat, me and Jessica jumped out of the bed and started packing. I don't know what Jessica was thinking, but I was certain that packing our bags this time had something to do with Grandmother Jessie and all of her wild, hard-core drinking, eating and greasing partying friends. What else could it be?

It was, I admit, a bit too much for me. Overwhelming! That's what it was, overwhelming. The food, the drinks, the smoke, the music, and all those people traveling back and forth from the first floor, to the second and then to the third. As it turned out, everything in that house was for sale. I mean everything. When did all of this happen?

We carried our pastel blue pleather suitcases downstairs and waited at the front door. Aunt Nita didn't say anything about eating and I didn't ask. I thought I was hungry 'cause my stomach felt like it was about to growl. I wasn't. I was feeling jittery and uneasy. I was nervous about what was going on. I didn't know who we were waiting for, but somebody was coming to take us back to Catherine Street.

Grandmother Jessie wasn't there. It was Missionary Sunday. She'd left for church services early in the morning in her white dress, white shoes, white silk stockings, white hat and a pair of white gloves in her brown leather purse. *"What would she think when she got home and found out that me and Jessica were gone for good?"*

Momma was the last person I expected to see. The way she hugged and kissed us you woulda thought that she hadn't seen us in a month instead of eight days.

"Are you alright?" Momma asked.

"Yes Momma…I missed you," Jessica said.

"I missed you, too," I quickly chimed in, making certain that she didn't think that Jessica loved her more than me.

"What happened here last night?" Momma questioned.

We fought, verbally, to get the story out. Jessica wanted to go first, but I wanted to tell my side of the story, too. We told Momma about the parties, the drinks and all the people who were in and out of Grandmother Jessie's house. I didn't say anything about the people in the bedrooms, and neither did Jessica.

"Grab your things," Momma said.

"Are we leaving now?" I asked Momma who stared back at me with a blank face, which meant don't even look at me and think about asking another question.

"Are we coming back?" I wanted to know. Grandmother Jessie may have done some bad things, but I still wanted to be there in the house that she shared with all the wild people.

"Go, do it now," Momma said firmly.

Momma turned to Aunt Nita and hugged her a few times. They went into the kitchen to talk and me and Jessica waited outside on the marble steps that no longer had that clean Comet Cleanser look or smell.

Nobody else came in with Momma and I wondered whose car she was going to use to take us home. When Momma came out of the kitchen, she told us to grab our bags and walk to the corner. We were getting on the PTC. And while kids were supposed to ride free on Sundays, the bus driver took one look at me and Jessica and said we were too big to pretend that we were under the age of twelve.

22

Liar, Liar, Pants on Fire

Everybody thought that I was such a liar. Every time I told people that I'd be gone for a long time to visit with my Grandmother Jessie in her big, grand and elegant house down in South Philly, I always came back early.

Jessica, Momma and I walked through the front door looking tired and weak. We had carried those heavy bags all the way from South Philly on the El and two buses. Darlene and Wayman didn't say much. I don't think they wanted us to go in the first place. Marie was happy to see us. She'd missed Jessica a lot. They were so very close and had the kind of sister relationship that Darlene and I could only dream about. Alfred couldn't remember how long we had been missing. And Donald...he was in jail.

While me and Jessica were down in South Philly learning the ways of the world, Donald had graduated from robbing homes to robbing stores. When he broke into Mr. Perry's bakery around the corner on South 57th Street, he left a whole lot of evidence that led the detectives right to our front door. Donald didn't just steal the money and ice cream, he took all the cream and jelly donuts that he could find. He left a trail of powdery sugar that any dumb squirrel coulda followed. And Donald was too generous with the stolen goods. After he shared his loot with Darlene, Wayman, Alfred and Marie, he went up and down the block and shared the wealth of goodies with the Crew and anybody else with a sweet tooth. Musk, Lump, Putt-Putt, Denny, Champ, Dougie, Bucky, Butchy and Donnie (the youngest brother) stuffed their faces with jelly donuts until their bellies ached. When the detectives came around the next day to investigate, the trail of evidence led them straight to our front door. He was caught red-handed, but not before he tried to tell a few lies to get himself out of trouble.

"A truck crashed on the corner of 57th and Cedar and boxes of donuts were just lying there on the ground."

"What truck?" the white detective wanted to know.

"I think it was the one on its way to Panty Pride," Donald offered with a straight face.

"I just picked up the boxes to make certain that no one got hurt and that having all those boxes in the middle of the street wouldn't cause another accident."

It didn't take long before the detectives grabbed Donald by his shoulders and put him in the red car.

After we settled in, Momma told us the reason why Donald was gone. He had been sent to the Youth Study Center, a jail for bad boys. He'd be locked up for months and we were only allowed to visit him on Sunday afternoons. Donald would miss his first Sunday visit from Momma because she'd spent all of her time coming down to South Philly to get me and Jessica. It would be a good two weeks before anybody would go down to the Youth Study Center to see him.

Momma was sad about Donald, or maybe she was sad about us. She never said why she rushed down to Grandmother Jessie's and plucked us out of there in a hurry, but I knew why. Momma was always worried about letting us go. Now she was angry for making a bad decision. She didn't stay to say hello to Mother, and she didn't stay long enough to let us say goodbye. I was sad, too. My view of Grandmother Jessie, who I loved, admired and cherished more than anyone else, had been shattered. I could no longer hope and pray that I would be like her when I grew up. But the worst part...we'd left there without getting paid. All I had in my pocket was a handful of change that I'd earned in tips at Chapel's Luncheonette and from the Friday and Saturday night parties at Grandmother Jessie's house.

I wasn't looking forward to being back at home. Things seemed so different. Daddy was still coming and going. He didn't have a job and we'd come to understand that things would never change. While Daddy didn't worry about paying any bills or putting food on the table, he wasn't giving up his claim to us or Momma. When Daddy was home it was Daddy's house. We did whatever he said and talked about him behind his back. We started to tell Momma how unhappy we were with Daddy being there, but she didn't say much about it. Brother Vernard, Donald and Darlene said it was time to "put his ass out," but Momma didn't seem to know how to do that.

I didn't know what to do for the rest of the summer. All my plans had been shot to hell. I was too young to get a real job and I wasn't going back to cleaning nobody's house. It wasn't that Miss Doris and Mrs. Sorrell weren't nice to me; I just wanted to be something better than that. And Grandmother Jessie said that none of her grands would end up being a domestic.

I thought about spending my time training to be a dancer. That was one of my new passions. I was gonna dance, and it wouldn't be that prissy ballet stuff. I'd seen a short woman with natural hair (folks stopped calling it nappy that summer) doing interpretive dancing to the rhythm of African drums. Every time I peeked into her class I saw wild, sweaty women moving their hips, shoulders and behinds to every single beat of the drum. The vibration of the drums penetrated every part of my body and I wanted to tear my clothes off and jump onto the center of the floor and get down. The classical chords of Bach, Beethoven and all of those other dead white men didn't inspire me anymore. But the rhythm of the drums tore into my soul and made me want to claim myself as a free and independent Black woman. I couldn't wait to get back to Mrs. Sydney's. If I tried really hard, I could end up being a star.

But spending my free time dancing was not a viable option. I didn't go to dance school in the summers. The recital was over in June and most people didn't bother to come back until September. I met new friends at Miss Sydney's School of dance and I was happy to be hanging out with the girls rather than the boys.

Sharon, Maxine and Anita were just like me. Actually, they had more in common with each other than with me. They were all in the same grade. I was a year ahead. They were at Mrs. Sydney's long before me. I think Sharon started when she was three or four (hoping to be another Shirley Temple), Maxine when she was eight, and Anita about nine or ten. Sharon was already on toe when I first started and I quickly realized that she was one of Mrs. Sydney's favorites. Sharon was also real popular at Sayre Junior High School, especially after she danced on toe to "Maria" from West Side Story. And she was also a target. All the girls who thought they were boogas always wanted to pick a fight. In fact, Anita and Sharon both started at Tilden Junior High, but had to transfer after repeated threats of being jumped by a group of jealous teenage girls. These girls were mean and vicious, with bad ass attitudes, and everybody had to take their threats seriously.

The three of them were short and tiny, not quite five feet tall. I stood at 5'3" and weighed 110 pounds. I was the tallest and the biggest of the bunch. Everybody had good looks and that was a real plus. We didn't have to fight with one another about being pretty. We shared a love for dance while struggling, at the same time, with who we were and what we wanted to be.

Our friendship was important to Sharon because she was an only child. Anita had a sister named Jeanette who was one of Darlene's friends, and Max had more than a couple sisters and brothers. Anita, Sharon and I didn't have to travel far to get to Mrs. Sydney's, but Max came all the way from North Philly to attend classes. She was really dedicated and danced like she was going to be a star.

I didn't know if my new girlfriends had planned anything exciting for the summer, but I wasn't gonna call and tel'em that I had nothing to do. I already lied, or so it seemed, about spending the entire summer with my uppity grandmother in a fabulously wealthy house in South Philadelphia. I knew that for the next six weeks, I'd be spending my time with the Crew, and talking on the phone to Debbie Jones.

I'd remembered that my Aunt Marge always encouraged me to come back to the recreation center and enjoy the free city-sponsored activities. On Monday morning, I got dressed, fixed some oatmeal for breakfast and walked over to 56th and Christian. I told my Aunt Marge about what happened at Grandmother Jessie's. She didn't seem too surprised. Now, I needed something to do because my plans for the summer didn't work out. She signed me up for the women's softball team. I couldn't play worth shit. The all white opposing teams didn't know what to do when I stepped up to bat. Most of the time, they allowed me to walk because I was a cute little Colored kid. I quit when I found that out.

The summer days were hot and humid and nothing seemed to be going my way. I didn't find a job and I'd spent all of my tips in two weeks. I did go with Momma to the Youth Study Center to see Donald. It was such a long trip, and even when we got there we had to wait in the Rec room until it was time to let Donald out of his cell. Why would Donald want to be in a place like this? He had to wear the same clothes everyday and there were all kinds of rules he had to follow if he wanted to get out in four months. Momma always brought lots of change to buy Donald candy and cookies from the vending machines. She wouldn't buy anything for me and Donald didn't want to share his stuff.

Donald didn't say much to me, only Momma. He told her how bad it was, how the boys there were the roughest and toughest he'd ever seen and how much he missed being at home. He promised Momma that he would never steal again and Momma promised him that if he did and was ever sent back to the Youth Study Center she would not visit him again.

Momma and Donald were never close. Momma said she loved all her children equal, but Donald said that after Wayman got hit by the greasy headed man in the green Chevrolet that Momma loved him less. She blamed him for the accident and didn't trust any of us kids to his care. I didn't think that it was true, but it didn't matter. Momma and Donald grew further and further apart and Donald started to think about finding a new home.

As the summer dragged on, I hung out in the streets with the Crew. We were all teenagers now and started to approach the world in a much cockier manner. We were at the center of the universe and planned our activities around our own special needs. We walked back and forth to Cobbs Creek Park, hiking through the woods and admiring the large brown, black and white-spotted horses that we never got a chance to ride. Even though we all looked forward to Sharon Baptist Church's annual Sunday school picnic, we'd plan our own picnics, stealing most of the food we needed from the Pantry Pride. Musk was the master thief among us, successfully stealing a whole ham from the A & P Supermarket on 60th and Cedar just to show us that he could.

I tried stealing food for the picnic once. I carefully scoped the candy aisles at the Pantry Pride before grabbing a bag of Hershey Kisses and slipping it into the sleeve of my blouse. I was heading toward the front of the store when I got caught. A young white man with sandy hair and brown eyes in a clean white shirt that smelled like Aqua Velvet dragged me to the back, behind the meat department, and hollered for his boss.

"Mack," he yelled. "Mack!"

As soon as he leaned in a little further and yelled "Mack" the third time, I tore my arm away from his grip and hauled ass back to the front of the store. I tripped over a few shopping carts and smacked the white lady who tried to stop me. I didn't stop running until I reached Carpenter Street. I was breathless. My heart was pounding and I couldn't stop crying. My clothes were sweaty and I was totally exhausted, but I was safe. I never tried to steal anything else again. *What if I got caught? Was there a Youth Study Center for girls, too?*

On the weekends, or when the folks were not home, we had blue light parties in the basement. By the time I got back from my

Grandmother Jessie's house, Putt-Putt finally had the nerve to ask me if he could stand a chance. He was, I think, my first real boyfriend, except for Woolworth Davis who I fell in love with in the first grade. When we tried to party like adults in Butchy's, Denny's or Putt Putt's basements, we got to dance together to the Miracles "*You Really Got a Hold On Me.*" We all waited for the part when Smokey hollered "tighter" just so we would have an excuse to squeeze each other and practice doing the grind up against the wall or any hard surface that we could find. We played the record over and over again until everyone got to grind and feel good.

Aunt Nita visited us a lot. Every time I asked about Grandmother Jessie, Aunt Nita would say, "She's fine." Nothing else. I finally got up enough nerve to ask if I could go back home with her to 1911 Christian Street to spend the rest of my summer down in South Philly.

"No," she said. "I'm not going to allow you to be pressed into service."

Pressed into service? What did that mean? My close relationship with Grandmother Jessie was probably over. It reminded me of how I felt when I lost my daddy.

23

A Change is Gonna Come

I was in Sayre Junior High all by myself. Darlene, Debbie and Sheila graduated and moved on to John Bartram High. Donald was there when Darlene arrived. He'd gotten out of the Youth Study Center and promised Momma that he would stay out of trouble. Momma hoped that it would be true. Wayman was there at Bartram too. He just graduated from Shaw where Jessica was now going to school. Marie was still in Harrity, and we were still taking off days at a time trying to take care of Alfred who was only three years old.

The summer of '64 was busted, but with great anticipation, I thought my final year in junior high school would be spectacular. I was hoping to make new friends and meet some new boys. I needed a boyfriend. My relationship with Putt-Putt fizzled after just a few weeks. A new girl named Connie moved on the block and Putt-Putt had his eyes on her. He was working hard on busting her cherry before anybody else got to it.

When the Crew asked if I was ready to give it up, I assured them that it would never happen in their lifetime. I think they may have been thinking about pulling a train, but I woulda fought tooth and nail to prevent that from happening, and they knew it. I wasn't gonna give it up to anybody. And while my relationship with Putt-Putt never truly flourished, I did have my eyes on that guy named Butchy.

I was fourteen; Butchy was fifteen. We had known each other most of our young lives and never thought about being boyfriend and girlfriend. But overnight, Butchy had matured into a gorgeous young man. He was tall, dark and handsome, just what everyone always sang about. Butchy was six foot two, thin and every bit as chocolate as Hershey. And Butchy had processed hair. I remember the very first time I saw him coming out of his house with straight black hair slicked down on the right side. He looked just like David Ruffin and I woulda done anything to get that close to a Temptation. We became the Crew couple and Butchy made it clear that I was officially off limits to everybody. These were his boys, his closest friends and they would do whatever was necessary to protect him and me, too.

I was about to live a charmed life. By now, Denny was sixteen and his daddy had given him an old, beat-up, blue and white car. It was the Crewmobile. They took me where I wanted to go, carried me back and forth to the dance school, and left me and Butchy to sit in there alone and cuddle up late at night. The Crew protected me from gangs of girls who were always threatening to kick my butt, and they never again talked about busting my cherry. What they got in return was my commitment as a member of the Crew, and a promise not to bring any boys from some other territory on our block. How hard could that be?

I was always hoping for the best, but as it turned out, all of ninth grade was wasted. We weren't learning a thing and I was tired of going to school every day just to be bored to death. It was like my brains cells were on a diet - no nourishment whatsoever! There were lots of gang fights in the neighborhood, and the friction between the groups spilled over into the junior high school. Finding ways to control our unruly behavior seemed to be the school's number one priority. Quite often we were sent to the vice-principal's office for disciplinary action. And everybody at Sayre got to know Mr. D'Antonio.

Mr. D. (that's what we called him) was the new disciplinarian. He was a short, pudgy Italian man with lots of hair. Everybody said he was Mafia, but he still looked pretty good for a white guy. After I talked back to that buttless music teacher Mr. Ott, I was sent to Mr. D. for disciplinary action. Mr. D. was trying to be tough, but I wasn't afraid of him. He seemed soft and hard at the same time.

"What you here for?" he asked.

"Nothing," I shouted back

"Are you trying to be smart, young lady?" he continued.

"I didn't do nothing," I insisted. "Mr. Ott doesn't like me because I said something to him in class about all the dumb songs he made us sing."

"What's wrong with the songs?"

"They don't feel right. There's no soul to them"

"You're not here to get soul," he said with a smirk. "What do you need soul for?

"You can't do anything with that music that Mr. Ott teaches. I'm gonna be a dancer someday, and I bet I'll never have to dance to "*Oh What a Beautiful Morning.*"

Mr. D. laughed when I said that. He was supposed to do something bad to me, but he didn't. He started asking me questions about what I thought the other kids wanted to do. Of course, all I could talk about was dance. Mr. D. promised that he would look into more 'suitable' music activities for the kids at Sayre. I was hoping that he would.

Mr. Ott still got what he wanted. I was removed from academic courses and placed in home economics with kids who were far less smart than me. Mr. Ott said that it would teach me to keep my mouth shut. Now, I had to spend my time sitting in front of a Singer sewing machine and listening to some old biddy telling me about how to make a dart. This old fart couldn't teach me a thing about sewing. Momma had already done that. I could make a whole outfit in less than two hours, complete with interfacing, zipper and buttonholes, and guaranteed to look real good. The sewing instructor was trying to teach us how to use a treader to tread a machine. All you had to do was to break the tread and spit on it. It woulda slipped right through the needle. Now my biggest challenge was sitting in class and pretending to be stupid. This was gonna be tough.

About a month after my first meeting with Mr. D., he came to the lunchroom to announce a new innovation for recess activities. The aides rounded us up, like criminals, and took us to a basement room. Actually, it looked like a cage in that movie about the insane asylum. Mr. D. and the aides stood on the second floor level looking down at us at the bottom of the pit. All of a sudden we heard music. It wasn't that boring white stuff, but popular dance music to do the Cha Cha. Nobody knew exactly what to do when we heard *"Hello Stranger"* blaring from the speakers.

"Dance," Mr. D. shouted. "How come you're not dancing?"

The girls giggled, but the boys laughed out loud.

"We can't," someone shouted back. "You up there watching us."

The music kept playing, but everybody stood against the walls and refused to dance. I wasn't going to let this opportunity pass me by. I grabbed a boy named Terry Horn and jumped out on the dance floor doing my best Cha Cha steps.

"Don't let that girl squirrel you," one of Terry's boys hollered out. That made Terry work even harder. But he had nothing on me. I'd been taking dance lessons at Mrs. Sydney's. I had rhythm, time and choreography. My feet never missed a beat.

We weren't out there on the floor by ourselves for long. Before we knew it, everybody else was trying to crowd us out. But it was Terry and me who got to be the king and queen of the Cha Cha.

Dancing for a brief period of time during the lunch break was one of the best things about being in the ninth grade. And when I wasn't thinking about school work, I spent much of my time trying to look pretty. That's one of the valuable lessons that I learned from hanging around at Grandmother Jessie's house. Men liked pretty women. I was still skinny and raggedy, and didn't have much to work with, but I tried real hard to do my best. And Butchy had convinced me that I looked pretty good. I still needed some good store bought clothing to add to my fabulous handmade creations and my well-worn, but still fashionable, hand-me-downs. For that, I could always rely on my Aunt Nita.

When Aunt Nita called crying on the phone, asking to speak to Momma, I knew somebody had died. We were about due; it had been two years since Aunt Ida on my Daddy's side of the family had passed on to glory and I knew we wouldn't escape the Grim Reaper for too much longer. But the news was worse than I ever imagined. Jessie Chapel was in jail.

Grandmother Jessie was busy running her weekend fried chicken and fish, fifty cents a shot brothel specials when the black and white unit walked through the front door and sat down at the large mahogany table in the dining room. After asking everybody how they were doing, they ordered a few drinks and fried fish sandwiches. Just as my Grandmother Jessie asked for her money, the Colored cop reached into his pocket, pulled out a set of silver handcuffs and slapped them on her wrists. She had been busted for engaging in "illegal activity."

Aunt Nita saw everything. The cops called for back-up and escorted Grandmother Jessie out of the front door and into a squad car. The church people started to scramble, acting like they didn't even know what was going on.

My Aunt Nita called Momma 'cause somebody had to go down to the Roundhouse to bail Grandmother Jessie out of jail. And they needed money to do it. Momma never had any extra money and I didn't know what my Aunt Nita expected her to do.

I just couldn't believe it! Jessie Chapel in jail! Behind bars! She was the most upstanding (or what they called boushee), Colored lady in all of South Philly. How could she get arrested? It had to be, I thought, the most embarrassing thing that ever happened to her in her life. Momma said not.

Momma said they worried about Mother going to jail when the white man who had been visiting her went home and died in his bed. He had just left Mother's house. Nobody understood the nature of the relationship between Mother and the white man, just that he visited her a lot. Momma said he was white; Aunt Doretha said he was a real light-skinned Colored man. Momma said he was a preacher; Aunt Doretha said it didn't seem like he was filled with the Holy Spirit, but she was sure that he was a friend of the Devil.

Nobody was home when it happened, but according to my Grandmother Jessie, the two of them had words on the second floor and he tripped on the stairs and fell all the way down to the bottom. That's not what the white man told his wife. He said that he was beaten by Jessie Chapel and that she pushed him down the stairs. No one knew what really happened for sure. He was dead by the next day and it was Grandmother Jessie's word against his wife's. Who you gonna believe?

Momma called somebody. Mr. Carter, I think. He went down to the Roundhouse and took care of everything.

That following Sunday morning, Grandmother Jessie was back in church, sitting on the front pew, staring down all of her Christian friends, and praising the Lord like nothing had ever happened. This woman had nerve.

24

More Bad News

I was thinking about how great tenth grade was gonna be at John Bartram High when I found out that Momma was pregnant, again.

"What's wrong?" Jessica asked as she came out the front door. I was sitting on the right edge corner of the front steps, crying my eyes out.

"It's Momma," I said.

"What's wrong with Momma?" Jessica wondered. She was already in a panic. Jessica was so protective of everybody. The very thought that something might be wrong with Momma overwhelmed her, instantly.

"She's gonna have another baby," I sniffed, trying to wipe my eyes and nose at the same time.

"So why are you crying?"

Jessica just didn't get it. I remember what happened when Momma was pregnant and had baby Alfred. "No more kids," the white doctor told her. "Having more babies could kill you!" How was Momma gonna pull this one off? She was thirty-nine years old, old enough to be a grandmother. She couldn't possibly make it through this time.

I didn't want to tell Jessica that I thought Momma would die if she had another baby. It might make her completely hysterical. Jessica hugged me and told me that Momma was gonna be alright, but what did she know? It was me who told her about Momma's big belly.

Daddy was always f...king up everything.

It was early in the morning when we heard Momma and Daddy fighting. Daddy had snuck back into the house in the middle the night. He was there for one reason and one reason only, to start some trouble. Momma was screaming at the top of her lungs and crying uncontrollably. Whatever she was saying didn't make any sense. By the time we jumped out of the bed and ran downstairs we didn't know what to do.

We all gathered around in our underwear and tried to hold and squeeze Momma. She waved her arm in the air and pushed all of us away. She didn't seem to recognize any of us, not Donald, Darlene, Wayman, Jessica, Marie or me. She couldn't stop crying and started to roll her eyes toward the back of her head.

"Whatcha do to my Momma?" Donald shouted at Daddy.

Daddy yelled back right back. "Don't make me whup your ass, boy. This is my house."

"I'm ready for your ass," Donald hollered, "I'm gonna jack you up."

Darlene screamed at them to stop. Mr. Smith next door, or somebody in his house, was banging on the walls. They were signaling us that they knew we were in there acting crazy. Alfred, Marie and Jessica were screaming and crying. Me and Wayman stood there, trying to look hard. We were all falling apart and still didn't know what to do.

Daddy was walking in and out of the house, threatening Donald, but reluctant to beat him up in front of the six of us.

Momma was hysterical. Yes, that's what it was. She was hysterical, unable to calm down, speak rationally or control her crying.

"I'm gonna call Whitehead," Donald shouted at Daddy.

"Go right ahead, you pissy-ass boy!" Daddy yelled right back in his face, so close that you could smell the Thunderbird wine from the night before last. "I'm not afraid of that sorry-ass cop."

"Don't be stupid," Darlene hollered at Donald. "What's a dumb cop gonna do?"

I sat next to Momma and held her hand. Alfred, Jessica, Marie and Wayman were crowded in there, too. Darlene went in the kitchen and called Grandmother Jessie.

I don't know what Darlene said, but in less than an hour, Grandmother Jessie came barreling through the front door. She was a sight for sore eyes. She was caught in the middle of her Sunday morning ritual, halfway between ready and not. Her hair had hot pressed, uncombed curls on the left side, but it was still straight and raggedy on the right. She wore a housedress that was good for cleaning and nothing else. She did have on a pair of 'worn-out, raggedy-ass, the dog had just dragged in' house shoes to match. No stockings, no jewelry, and no make-up whatsoever, but she smelt pretty good. She was on a mission - to save Lucille - and nothing was getting in her way.

She pushed my Daddy aside and stood in the center of the floor.

"Lucille, Lucille," she shouted, "Look at me!"

Momma couldn't or wouldn't respond. Grandmother Jessie was furious, but not with Momma.

"I knew this would happen," she shouted. "The Devil's up in here. The Devil's up in here!" she repeated over and over again. And then she summoned all of us to gather in a circle at the center of the room and started to pray. Everybody was crying by then.

"Precious Lord," she said, "save this troubled family. Rid this house of evil. Be merciful, oh Lord, and help these children. Give me the strength to…" and on and on and on. I knew we would be standing there for a very long time.

When Grandmother Jessie finished praying, she wrapped Momma in a soft blue blanket that Momma bought from Woolworth's that was supposed to stay put on Marie's bed. She motioned to Mr. Carter to give her a hand. They carried Momma out the front door, put her into the back seat of the black Buick and drove away.

What were we gonna do now?

25

One More Coming

The fatter Momma got, the less we saw of Daddy and Darlene and Donald said Daddy wasn't coming back, that he didn't live here anymore.

We all did what we could to help Momma. Darlene worked, part-time, at the Navy Yard, Wayman hustled newspapers, I went back to cleaning Miss. Doris' house and Donald kept on stealing, bringing it home and giving it to Momma. We started a campaign collecting S&H green stamps, hoping that we could get enough to buy Momma some of the things she needed. Every time the A & P Supermarket had some kind of contest, we went back and forth, buying one or two items at a time, hoping to get a winning game piece. Me and Darlene celebrated big time when we finally won the grand prize. We rushed upstairs to tell Momma. She looked at the winning ticket and, amused by our enthusiasm, told us that we were mistaken. We had applied weeks of stickers to the same card. We hadn't won a damn thing.

But with all of our efforts, things were getting worse. We still didn't have a kitchen and we were constantly running out of oil. Heat and hot water were in short supply. Half the ceiling had fallen down from the second floor and you could see straight through to the roof. We were too embarrassed to ask anybody to come to our house.

When my Cha Cha king friend Terry (he didn't know that boys weren't supposed to visit me on my block) came to see me, he walked into the house, quickly focused his eyes on the ceiling and saw the big hole. You couldn't miss it.

"Why's that hole there?" he asked "Are you trying to tell time by looking at the moon?" He thought he was funny. I wanted to slap him for making fun of me.

We were really frightened when the Health Department paid us a visit. The neighbors started to complain about a foul odor that permeated the air. We knew it was our house that was stinking and smelling up the place, but we tried to pretend that it wasn't. The sewage pipe burst several weeks earlier and everything from the bathroom tub and toilet ended up on the basement floor. Twice a day we would put on rubber boots and try to shovel the shit back into the big hole where the pipe had broken. Big and little turds were floating around the place and we had to be careful not to step on one and squash it into the floor. All that shit stunk up the place.

When the Health Department tracked the stench to 5828, they said that the house had to be condemned. We were worried, and Momma was too. For the first time she started to think about losing her kids to the State.

I'm not sure how it happened, but in a few days some men showed up in giant black boots and yellow plastic suits. They fixed the pipes in the basement. Didn't charge us a dime. Even if they had tried, we had no money to pay for such expensive repairs. After we cleaned up for the last time, the city came around and fumigated the place. We were out of the shit shoveling business.

By the time the Christmas season rolled around, things were about as bad as they could get. The pregnancy wasn't going well and Momma missed a lot of work. Money was scarce and Momma was talking about foreclosure. Things were far from jolly.

We didn't see much of Daddy. He never visited, but sometimes we would see him in a drunken stupor on 52nd street near Granny's basement apartment. Cody Blue, who was good friends with Jessica and Marie and drove around in brand new Cadillacs pretending to be a mobster, told us that Daddy had been mugged a couple times by street thugs. They threw him face down on the cement ground, punched and kicked him around a few times and then took away all of his money. I didn't want anybody to do that to my Daddy and I wept, silently, when I heard the story. Blue said that he would have tried to protect him if he had known that the bum was our father.

We didn't see Granny, Pop Pop or anybody else. Grandmother Jessie was no longer in the luncheonette, speak-easy, brothel or whatever she wanted to call it business. She was a domestic for some rich white family in Cape May, New Jersey. Boy, she must've hated that. I was just hoping that we would have a good holiday.

Six days before Christmas, Momma went shopping at the John's Bargain Store for presents. She took Darlene with her. Just as she finished paying for four mohair sweaters and four slips as presents for all the girls, water splashed from right up under her dress onto the floor. Darlene thought that Momma had peed on herself. She didn't. It was time for the baby to come.

Momma rushed to the back of the store to find the bathroom.

"Employees only," is what some snot-face white woman told Momma.

Momma looked at her and shouted, "I don't think you can stop this baby from coming!"

When Momma explained that her water broke and that she was in labor, Miss Employee quickly jumped aside. Momma rushed in and filled her pants with paper towels. She gave Darlene the four slips and mohair sweaters and told her to go home. Momma was going to board the PTC and make her way to the hospital.

Momma came home on Christmas Eve with a new baby girl. Her name was Suzette. She was a plump, brown baby with a round face and jet black hair. She looked just like all the rest of us. This time I got to clean out the big dresser drawer with Clorox bleach and pretend that it was a baby crib. I soaked the pillow case in hot, soapy water, but it still came out looking dingy and gray. I didn't have any money for Johnson's Baby Powder.

The next day Aunt Nita showed up with a package from Grandmother Jessie. It was a layette, I think, but the baby had already been sent home in her diaper, undershirt and a hospital gown. Daddy was nowhere to be found, and Granny didn't visit us, either.

We were all a little happy and a little sad. It was Christmas Day, but we didn't have a tree and we knew that we weren't getting any presents. After Darlene went into the closet to retrieve the package that she thought was hidden from us, Momma handed me, Jessica and Marie the John's Bargains bag with the four slips and mohair sweaters still wrapped in the plastic covers.

"I couldn't do any better," she said, almost crying.

"This is great!" we shouted. We wanted Momma to feel good about what she tried to do for us and showered her with hugs and kisses.

Wayman and Donald didn't get a thing. Momma never got around to shopping for the boys. Darlene, who every day was acting more and more like she was Momma, did manage to go shopping for a few toys for Alfred. She brought plenty of cheap cars, trucks and a gun and holster set. He seemed real happy with that. But in my heart, I thought it was the worst Christmas ever. No presents. No big happy meal. And no money.

Having a new baby in the house made us all feel good, but Momma told us not to get too attached. Mrs. Sara, Momma's best friend from Caldwell's Dress Company, visited Momma in the hospital and asked her if she could have the baby for herself. Mrs. Sara and her husband Oliver didn't have any children. Momma said she couldn't because of female troubles.

Mrs. Sara was a dark brown, small, thin woman who was a hair taller than me. She was one of the nicest women that I knew. I used to stop by and visit her home on Ithan Street on my way to Debbie Jones' house. She would always give me something – food or money. She and Mr. Oliver were always good to me, and I knew she would be a wonderful mother and he a great father.

"You already got too many mouths to feed," Mrs. Sara told Momma at her visit to the hospital. "You can't afford one more."

Momma didn't say yes to Mrs. Sara, but she didn't say no. When we found out, Donald, Darlene, Wayman, Jessica, Marie and I were pretty close to being hysterical. Suzette was the latest edition to our family clan and we felt that she belonged to us. How could Momma even think about giving her up? Wasn't that just like the State taking one of her kids and making them foster? Momma said this would be different. The State would not be involved. The courts would have nothing to do with it. Papers would not be signed. She would just give the baby to Sara and Oliver and they would raise her. Black folks did it that way all the time, or so she said.

Over the Christmas break we were all able to stay home and help Momma take care of the new baby. Momma said that this would be her last. They wanted to fix her and, this time, she let them do it. The doctors tied her tubes up so no more baby eggs would be flowing up to her belly. They took care of everything before they turned her loose.

We worried every day about losing our baby sister. And every time Momma talked about giving Suzette away, Jessica and Marie would start crying. Darlene told them to shut up. All those tears were good for nothing.

When Miss Sara and Mr. Oliver came over to see the baby, we thought about locking them out on the front porch. We didn't have a doorbell for them to ring, so they kept banging, with heavy fists, on the door. It was pretty cold outside and we were hoping that they would turn around and go back to their own house on Ithan Street, but they didn't. So we had to let them in.

The two of them rushed through the front door, smiling and grinning.

"It's freezing out there!" Mr. Oliver said.

Momma was lying on the slip-covered couch, holding the new baby. We stood around, guarding her like a militia. She looked down at the baby and smiled. Suzette opened her eyes. They were an unusual color, somewhere between amber and hazel.

"No," is what Momma finally said. "No, I can't do it. I won't give her up. Suzette is my daughter and I'll find a way to raise her."

We all parted our lips and smiled big smiles with big grins. Wayman and Darlene started to do a little party dance.

Miss Sara and Mr. Oliver were real disappointed. They left empty-handed. Nobody would be calling them mommy and daddy, but Momma did make them godparents. That meant that they still would be hanging around doing what good people do. But Suzette, our baby sister and the last Reid descendant of Curtis and Etrulia, would be staying with us, forever.

26

The White Woman
in the Blue Dress

It was cold and I was walking fast. The bus stop was only a block and a half from the house, but in the dead of winter, small trips turned into a major expedition if you didn't have the right clothing or equipment. And what I had didn't seem to be enough.

I got off the bus at 60th Street. I liked taking that route home from the high school.

Riding on the bus every day was a wonderful experience, although you had to be careful that some nasty boy didn't get too close and start to grind on you. There was a whole new crowd that I hung out with every morning and afternoon, and another set of kids when I changed classes every forty-five minutes.

None of my close friends ended up in Bartram with me. Deborah Jones was just starting ninth grade at Sayre Junior High School along with my close dancing friends, Sharon and Anita. They would all end up at West Philadelphia High the following year. Maxine, who lived in the Richard Allen Projects on Diamond Street in North Philly, was hanging tough all by herself.

The Crew was spread out all over the place too. Denny, Dougie and Champ were in Bartram with me. Butchy went to Bok Technical

High School and Putt-Putt, with his brainy self, went to Central High School for Boys. Bucky, Lump and Musk hadn't decided where they wanted to be.

I got to join the dance club as soon as I entered the high school. It was one of the most exciting parts of the day. Bartram was so much bigger than Sayre, and it was easy to get lost in the crowd. The kids at Bartram were different, too. Half the school was white, and, the other half Colored. I didn't think that it would be hard for me to make some new white friends. I didn't know a whole lot about white people, but I remember Momma telling me to "stay with your own kind." I didn't realize it at the time, but what Momma was trying to teach me was that Black folks would always be my people and I always needed to be able to way to find my way back home; white folks could reject you at any time.

They put me in Commercial Clerical, instead of Academics. My fight with Mr. Ott had followed me right into John Bartram High. I spent a lot of time learning how to operate office machines and mastering my skills as a keypunch operator. I was finished learning everything I needed to know in just six weeks, leaving my mind free to roam around and do nothing.

Momma went up to the school to see the principal about the "dummy down" approach to my education. Mr. Smith said that he didn't make those kinds of decisions. He sent her to the guidance counselor. Momma told the guidance counselor that I was too smart to be in Commercial Clerical classes.

"How many children do you have, Mrs. Reid?" the snotty old woman wanted to know.

"Nine," Momma said ever so proudly.

"Is your husband at home with you?" she continued to question.

"What's that got to do with anything?" Momma snapped. "That's none of your business."

"Well, Mrs. Reid, I think it's in Patricia's best interest if she prepares herself for a job. She has straight As in the office courses and she should be able to get a good job as a clerk or something like that when she graduates. You won't be sending her to college, right?"

Momma was steaming now. I sat there and watched as she tried to argue for a change in my educational program. It was no use. Momma couldn't make that guidance counselor do what she didn't want to. I wanted Momma to go talk to Mr. D. He, too, had followed me to Bartram and would be the new Vice Principal. I thought he would kind enough to help me out.

"Not now," Momma said. "We'll have to deal with this later."

We never did.

My feet were cold, even though I had on a new pair of boots that my Aunt Nita bought me on sale just a few days after Christmas. They were size seven, brown leather (pleather for real) with a little heel. It was a good present from a good store, John Wanamaker's, but Momma told her not to buy me anything else. Ever. If she couldn't buy for all, she couldn't buy for any.

I picked up the pace, walking as fast as I could. The hawk was out, tearing my butt up. All I could think about was getting through the front door and hoping that the furnace had enough oil to cook up some heat.

I didn't bother to search for my door key. Momma was still at home with the new baby and she always kept the door unlocked.

I saw her sitting there; a young white woman in a flowery, dark blue dress. I knew something was wrong because white people never visited our house. When she asked if she could hold the baby, that's when I knew she was from the State. She was here to take Suzette away from us. And Momma seemed pretty damn happy about it. She was smiling and grinning like a goddamn Cheshire cat as she turned our baby over to that white lady. I started to snatch Suzette right out of her arms. I didn't want her to end up in one of those foster homes that we heard so many bad things about. That's where they beat and tortured kids and everybody thought it was all right.

Turned out I was wrong. The white lady in the flowery dark blue dress wasn't from the child protection agency. She was from the city welfare office.

"I'm here to help your mother," she said in a mousy voice.

"How you gonna do that?" I wanted to know.

"By sending her welfare checks each month," she boasted. "It will to help take care of you and your new baby sister."

It was, I thought, the best news I had heard all day. I knew a little bit about welfare, but not a whole lot. Poor people got welfare. Nobody wanted to be on welfare, 'cause it was like admitting that you couldn't make it on your own. Poor people in North and South Philly were on welfare, but not the people in Germantown. And poor people in the projects, where my friend Maxine lived, were on welfare, too. And now we were on welfare. We were, officially, poor.

As I sat there listening to the white lady talking to Momma, it was the first I'd heard that Momma couldn't go back to work. Momma was a lot sicker than she'd led us to believe. Continuing to operate a sewing machine was out of the question. She tried to get some help from the INTERNATIONAL LADIES GARMENT WORKERS UNION, but they said that there was nothing that they could do for her. What kind of union was that? What was it good for? Momma had been working all of her life, paying union dues and paying taxes, too. Now that she needed some help, nobody was there for her. But none of that really mattered anymore. Momma said she turned to welfare because, "there was nothing else that I could do." Welfare was our last hope.

"What do you want to be when you grow up?" the white lady asked rather suddenly,

"I don't know," I responded too quickly without even thinking. "Maybe a dancer," I added a few short seconds later.

Momma laughed. "She has starry eyes," she said between her smiles. I hadn't seen or heard Momma laugh in so long I thought she'd forgotten how.

"Ever since she started taking lessons at that dancing school," she added, "she can't stop talking about going to New York City to be a dancer. That's why I call her starry eyes. She thinks she is gonna be a star some day."

"What if you don't make it on Broadway?" the welfare lady asked.

"I don't know," I said, shrugging my shoulders and shaking my head at the same time. I was getting mad at Momma for teasing me in front of this white stranger. I could dream big if I wanted to, and Miss Certaine, the gym teacher at Sayre, had already told me that I was one of the best young dancers she'd ever seen.

"I'm a social worker," she volunteered, proud of her chosen profession. "I went to college and got a degree in sociology."

I didn't care. I didn't know anything about social workers or college. And I didn't know anything about a degree and something called sociology. I did know that she was getting on my nerves asking about my business,

By the time she left, Momma was real happy, almost giddy. Checks would start coming immediately. Our rent would be paid and we wouldn't get kicked out of the house. The lady told Momma that the State would put a lien on the house, but we didn't know what that meant.

When Darlene, Wayman, Jessica and Marie came home I told them that we would be getting welfare. (I couldn't tell Donald. He was back in jail at the Youth Study Center.) We started singing that new Temptations song, *"Ain't too Proud to Beg."*

27

Am I Still One of the Crew?

Things couldn't have been any better. Daddy was gone for good, the welfare checks kept coming, school was out, and I had a summer job with the Neighborhood Youth Corps. I made a dollar and fifteen cents an hour, almost thirty dollars a week. I thought I was loaded when I got my first full paycheck, until Momma made me give her half.

We all stayed close to home and tried to help Momma take care of the house. It was still falling apart, but we were staying. No matter what went wrong, we'd find a way to patch things up. The neighbors seemed awfully helpful, too. We were always eating at somebody else's house, and Mr. Sarge, Mr. Jenkins and Mr. Quillen would give us fifty cents from time to time.

When the City came out and shut off our water because we couldn't pay the bill, we knew we were in serious trouble. How can you live without water? Mr. Smith, our closest neighbor, knocked on the door just a few minutes after the water department left. He had stuck a green garden hose through the backyard fence, connecting our house to his. He told us to get as much water as we needed.

Momma had some kind of sickness, but she was still acting like Secret Squirrel. Butchy was still my boyfriend, but Deborah Jones was my girl. We spent most of our time running back and forth from Catherine to Ludlow just so we could hang out together. It was a long walk to Deborah's house in the heat, but I didn't mind. She, on the other hand, had an extra incentive to walk all the way over to Catherine: she had her eyes on that hazel-eyed Bucky, who looked just as good, if not better, than his big brother. Having a boyfriend was a good thing for both of us, but we still spent most of our time trying to look good and flirting with all the boys we could find.

One Saturday night we got dressed up in homemade matching outfits that took less than two hours to make and only cost us three dollars apiece. They were black bell-bottom pants with a matching vest trimmed in white zig zag ribbon. We used the trim to spell out RPG (Respectable Playgirls) on the right side of the vest just above our breasts. We walked from Market to Catherine, 52nd to 61st looking for boys and showing off our homemade clothes.

"What that mean?" they often shouted.

"Respectable Playgirls!" we'd shout back

"That's an oxymoron," one cute nearly bald-headed guy shouted back.

"What's an oxymoron?" we both thought silently to ourselves.

By the time we finished the hunt, it was too late for Deborah to walk back home. I waited with her at the 60th Street bus stop and then made my way back to the house.

I was sitting outside on the front porch, still in my RPG outfit, when I saw Butchy come out of Dougie and Denny's house. By then, Dougie had announced to the world that he was queer and I didn't know why the Crew still hung out with him. Dougie's new passion was trying to outdo me in every which way that he could. Dougie fought like a girl, and he did it a lot better than me. He was a champion Double-Dutcher, played hopscotch instead of Skullys and still did both better than me. If I got my hair done, Dougie went out and got his processed, with waves. When I stepped outside looking sharp in my homemade white sailor suit with the bell-bottom pants, Dougie went downtown to Gimbells Department Store and found a form-fitting uniform that looked so much better than mine. But when

Dougie challenged all of the Crew to pull a train, I thought he went too far. "Who would want to do it to Dougie?"

When all of the Crew rolled out of Dougie's house that evening laughing, joking and comparing notes, I knew something had gone wrong. For the first time Butchy and I fought. I wanted details on what had happened in the house.

"It doesn't mean anything," Butchy insisted.

"What doesn't mean anything?" I demanded to know.

"It's not what you think."

"What's not what I think?"

The Crew gathered around as Butchy and I continued the fight. They all looked nervous and suspicious to me. I may have been the love of Butchy's life, but they were his boys. They were there to protect him and he was not about to violate their trust. I may have been a member of the Crew, too, but I discovered that night that we weren't as tight as they led me to believe.

"What went on at Dougie and Denny's house?" I continued to wonder. *"Had the Crew accepted the challenge?"*

Dougie came flying out of the house, grinning from ear to ear, in his tight pants and cut-off shirt. He joined the rest of the Crew on my front steps. He looked me dead in the face and didn't say a word.

"I hate your guts!" I wanted to scream out. I even thought about jumping on top of him and, beating him down. But I was careful not to try that. Last summer, Dougie beat both me and Connie up at the same time. He acted like a girl, but he was as strong as an ox. I hated him for that, 'cause Dougie threatened me in more ways than one. I stormed in the house and slammed the door in their faces.

I'm never gonna give it up to anybody.

"Stop the racket!" Momma yelled. "Didn't I tell you kids about slamming that door? If you keep it up, it'll fall off the hinges." I paid her no mind. The damage had already been done.

Sometimes I would pretend that I was special when I was at Sydney's Dancing School, but I knew not to act like Miss Special K in the house. I sat on the couch and started to pout. I was pissed off and didn't know what to do about it. When the telephone rang, I knew it was Butchy trying to make up and explain to me what happened at Dougie's house.

"Tricia?"

When she called out Tricia, I knew it was my Aunt Nita and that the phone call was for me. My Aunt Nita cared a lot about me and I knew she wanted to help me out. She couldn't buy me any more presents, but she did call from time to time and tell me about the crazy people on the PTC.

"Hi, Aunt Nita," I responded with excitement and enthusiasm. Just hearing her voice made me feel a lot better.

"Is Momma there?" she wanted to know.

Of course Momma was here. She stayed home every day taking care of the baby and resting. I still didn't know exactly what was wrong with Momma, but it had something to do with her blood. She was anemic, and that meant Momma had to drink a lot of dark port wine to make her blood cells red again.

I called to Momma to let her know that Aunt Nita was on the phone. I tried to strike up a conversation while Momma made her way down stairs, but Aunt Nita didn't seem interested. Aunt Nita didn't say much, just that she wanted Momma.

I wondered what Jessie Chapel had done this time? Was she running a house? Selling little shot glasses filled with liquor? Or had she been arrested, again? I wanted to hang around the kitchen so I could easedrop on the conversation, but Momma would've known that I was being nosey.

"Is everything okay?" I asked as soon as Momma hung up the phone.

"No," she said. "Mother is dead."

28

Scandalous

Nothing had prepared us for Grandmother Jessie dying. How old was she anyway? Fifty-eight? Fifty-nine? How could she be dead? She wasn't sick or anything, not that we had heard about.

Grandmother Jessie's death brought out the worst in everybody. First, it was the sisters from the First African Baptist Church. They came by the house to mourn and to help with the preparations for the homegoing service; they left with the crystal, the silver and much of the fine linen that was Jessica Chapel's trademark. Said something about what was promised them and what Mother would have wanted them to have.

Next came the deacons, deaconesses, and members of the Missionary Board. Certainly they were there to arrange a glorious service that would celebrate her many, many, contributions to the church. Apparently not. Jessie Chapel had created too much scandal within the congregation to be laid to rest in front of the church altar. Her episode with the law must have shaken them up for good. However, that was only part of the story.

Jessie Chapel had a long-standing, intimate relationship with the famous and ever so righteous Reverend Dr. Harrod. Aunt Dorethea said she had been seeing that man forever and the women in the church didn't like it, but there was nothing that they could do about it. When she was a young girl, he would come to the house to visit and spend time with Mother. *When did she have time for all of that?* At any rate, the Reverend Dr. Harrod had been dead for almost twenty years. Who woulda remembered? Apparently. somebody did, perhaps one of the church elders. And there would be no service for Jessie Chapel at First African Baptist Church.

The sisters from the Eastern Star paid a visit to the house, too. Would Grandmother Jessie be receiving some special tribute or ceremony because of her membership in the organization? Apparently not. If Jessie Chapel was an Eastern Star, they didn't have a record of it.

By the time Momma, Uncle Junior, Uncle Edward, Aunt Savannah, Aunt Dorethea and Aunt Nita all got together they were certain about one thing…It was time to call Mr. Chew.

By early Tuesday afternoon, all the arrangements had been made. The service would be in Mr. Chew's Funeral Parlor at 2125 Christian Street. She would be buried in Eden, on top of Grandmother Pattie, who had died just eight years earlier.

Momma said we all needed to be there with the rest of the family. I was terrified.

The thought of seeing my Grandmother Jessie lying dead in some coffin was too much for me. I had memories of my visit from dead Uncle Andrew and thought about how horrible being dead must be. *What do dead people think about?* I became emotionally and physically ill and began searching for ways to get out of going down to Mr. Chew's.

When Momma said the baby was too young to be at a funeral, I jumped up, grabbed Suzette and shouted, "She can stay here with me!" Nobody else moved fast enough. Suzette was in my arms and I was clinging to her like white on rice. She was my only hope of avoiding the coffin and the graveyard. I had dodged another funeral bullet. After that was settled, the only thing left was getting everybody a set of funeral clothes.

Momma wore black, but she made Darlene, Jessica and Marie wear white. She said it was a sign of respect. I knew white had something to do with dead people. On Mother's Day Sunday, all the people with dead mamas wore white carnations. If your mama was living, you wore red. Donald and Wayman wore the only suits that they had and, at the last minute, Momma decided to leave Alfred with me, too.

On the day of the funeral, a large black, stretch limousine pulled up in front of our house to gather the whole family. All the neighbors came out to watch. I don't think anybody had ever ridden in a car this big before. There was a seat for everybody. Momma, Darlene, Jessica, Marie and Wayman piled in the back. Donald jumped up front and sat with the driver. Daddy was nowhere to be found.

We watched as the limousine drove away. I felt real sad about Grandmother Jessie dying, but I was happy that I was not on my way to the funeral. I was responsible for playing with Suzette and Alfred.

By the time they came home, I could hardly recognize them. Jessica and Marie's white dresses were dirty and their hair was shooting out in all directions all over their heads. Momma was mad, Darlene looked angry, and Donald and Wayman looked like they had been in a fight. They had been!

The trouble started when they first gathered at the house on Christian Street. There was food for everybody, and plenty to drink, too. Both Uncle Edward and Uncle Junior needed something to calm their nerves. They started disagreeing about Mother's legacy even before they got to the funeral. And the fight seemed to get started over who would be the first to eat the Brussel sprouts that were left in the refrigerator.

"Mother always liked you better than me," Uncle Edward shouted at Junior.

"That's a lie," Junior responded, "I didn't get to know Mother until I was seven or eight years old. You were here when we got back."

Brother Vernard was shouting, "She was my Mother, too," which only upset my Momma, 'cause Vernard was really Momma's child.

Trouble was brewing and everybody knew it. Momma, Aunt Dorethea and Aunt Nita did their best to keep Edward and Junior apart. The service hadn't started and already things were getting out of hand. Aunt Savannah was no help at all. She sat there, stone-faced, as if she was incapable of expressing her grief. Maybe she was in a religious trance or something.

When they all got to Mr. Chew's the white coffin was there, sitting up front, surrounded by flowers from the family. However, there would be no viewing. Mother died of some kind of cancer (Although Momma insisted that her death was caused by a kick in the side from a horse sometime when she had gone down to Danville, Virginia to rescue the three of them). The chemotherapy that she received caused her skin to darken, almost to the color of Hershey's. Momma said that Mother woulda died if anyone saw her that way. Imagine that.

By the time they got to Eden, Uncle Junior was looking for somebody to vent his anger.

"Where's she gonna be buried at?" Uncle Junior demanded to know.

"Right here, sir," the undertaker said kindly.

"Where's my Grandmother Pattie?"

"I don't know."

"She's supposed to be in there with her."

Uncle Junior was confused, and why wouldn't he be? They dug a hole in the ground at the place where they said Grandmother Pattie was buried. Who coulda known for sure? It was an unmarked grave. And when Junior left the cemetery, he was angry as hell.

The repast delivered even more excitement. Food and drinks were flowing, just like when Grandmother Jessie had one of her parties. Everybody was talking about the great Jessie Chapel, but when the conversation turned to who was getting what, things got ugly.

Grandmother Jessie lived in a fine house, but she didn't own it. What little possessions were left would be divided among the six adult children, and nobody knew just how to do that.

Aunt Savannah became hysterical first. She started screaming and hollering that she didn't want anything. She was mad at Mother for sleeping with her boyfriend, Joe. Apparently Joe didn't see any conflict in sleeping with mother and daughter. They were both seeing him at the same time. Mother and Joe knew about their special relationship;

they just didn't tell my Aunt Savannah. She had been holding in her hurt for a long time, but now was just as good a time as any to let it all out.

Nobody seemed surprised by her accusations. Evidently, they all knew about the special arrangement. And Grandmother Jessie knew for sure. She and Savannah were being screwed by the same man. What was she thinking?

Aunt Savannah stood in the middle of the floor, venting her frustration and talking about Judgment Day. Jessica and Marie must have been terrified.

Uncle Edward and Uncle Junior started arguing again about who Mother loved and who was treated better.

Momma and Aunt Dorethea went upstairs to Mother's bedroom to search the place. If Grandmother Jessie had money, nobody knew where she hid it.

"It's gotta be here, it's gotta be here," is what Momma kept saying.

"What's gotta be here?" is what Aunt Dorethea wanted to know.

"The papers," Momma responded. "I've got to find the papers."

Aunt Dorethea was searching, too. For what, I'm not sure. But what she found was a lot more than she had bargained for.

In the bottom drawer of the chest of drawers laid a metal tin box with official looking papers. There was the marriage certificate for Mother and Lester, the death certificate from five years ago, and, a family Bible with the names of all the children. There were birth certificates, too: one for Savannah Chapel, Lester Chapel, Etrulia Chapel and Bonita Chapel. Who was Bonita? After comparing the dates, she realized that Bonita was my Aunt Nita. The birth name was different from what she had known. She found another birth certificate for a Vincent Chapel. He had been born in 1937 and died shortly thereafter. No one ever spoke of him. And then she found her own.

Hattie Womack, that's what the birth certificate said. Hattie Womack. Hattie's date of birth was the same as my Aunt Dorethea, but the name did not match. She flipped the certificate over to the backside to find this little note: *please change this girl name to Dorethea. I'm her mother, now.*

Aunt Dorethea kept on searching. She couldn't comprehend what she just learned and continued to search the room for papers. She made a mental note to herself. She couldn't find her brother's Edward birth certificate and he, unlike the other siblings, shared the same last name with her.

"Mother," Momma shrieked, "I smell Mother."

Aunt Dorethea noticed it, too. The scent of lavender was everywhere, as if a gust of air had swept its way up the stairs, down the hall and right into the bedroom. Just then the mirror fell from the wall, shattering glass in all directions, but landing its frame flat on top of Mother's possessions.

"Mother, Mother," they screamed, flying down the steps and scaring everybody half to death.

"Mother's upstairs," they both insisted.

By then, the whole house was in turmoil. Guests started leaving in a hurry - Donald, Wayman, Darlene, Jessica and Marie wanted to go home, and Uncle Edward, Uncle Junior and Brother Vernard kept yelling at each other. Aunt Savannah was still telling her story about Mother sleeping with her boyfriend Joe, and Aunt Nita looked at all of them like they were crazy.

After Momma calmed down, Aunt Dorethea convinced her to go back upstairs and continue her search.

"Mother is trying to tell you something," she said. That's the only reason the dead come back and give you a sign."

Momma was scared, nervous, and wary of meeting Jessie Chapel as a spirit from the afterlife, but she did want to locate the papers. Reluctantly, she returned upstairs to the bedroom.

There was an eerie silence in Mother's bedroom. The scent of lavender was faint, but still enough to know that she had paid a visit. The shattered mirror distributed glass shards all over the bed, but mostly on top of one of Mother's favorite church pocketbooks.

Momma picked up the bag and shook away the sharp fragments of glass. She opened the bag to see what was inside. Nothing. She thought that, maybe, Mother wanted her to have the bag as a fine memento of her days as a refined church lady.

Momma shut the bag, and then she opened it again. She grabbed the bottom of the big purse and ripped out the lining. On both sides of the cream-colored cloth lining she found several stacks of twenty dollar bills. She was convinced that Mother wanted her, and only her, to have the money that was hidden inside.

The sound of loud voices and the crash of furniture forced Momma and Aunt Doreathea to return to the downstairs living room. They were fighting. Everybody. Edward and Junior had lost control. They were in a bare knuckles fist fight. Brother Vemard, who was good and drunk by now, started swinging in all directions. When Uncle Edward swung back, Donald and Wayman jumped in to protect their brother. Suddenly, Uncle Junior took Uncle Edward's side and started swinging at Donald and Wayman. Darlene, Jessica and Marie joined the fight. By the time Momma broke things up, the police were on their way. Momma told everybody to jump into the car for the ride back home.

Aunt Dorethea rushed to the door to say goodbye.

"Did you find it?" she wanted to know.

"No," Momma replied, disappointedly.

"What papers are you looking for?"

"The ones from the courthouse: when they charged Mother with prostitution and took Savannah, Junior and me away from her."

"Jesus, Lord have mercy…Grandmother Jessie…a prostitute?"

29

1968

It had been almost two years since Grandmother Jessie died, when they took her body to Eden and laid her to rest in an unmarked grave where she would spend eternity with Great Grandmother Pattie. Everybody remembered Mother, but nobody talked about her and the family had not gathered since the ruckus at her funeral.

I was still dancing, dating Butchy and thinking about graduating from high school. That's what Momma wanted for all of us, especially the girls. Things seemed to happen so rapidly. I couldn't remember whether the high school years were turning out to be the best or worst time of my life.

The nation was caught in the midst of the Civil Rights Movement. In '65, '66, and '67 we saw images of protest and social rebellions in the streets of major cities. In Los Angeles, Detroit and Newark Black folks had taken to the streets, demanding social change and social justice. Even in small towns, like Plainfield, New Jersey, folks were in the streets attacking businesses and the local police. Tensions between Blacks and whites were at an all time high. We were in the midst of a racial war and I knew Philadelphia would be next in line for a riot. I wanted to prepare myself to participate in the rebellion, assuming that it would probably happen in the streets of North Philly.

I watched Channel 6 everyday, waiting for it to happen.

Everything seemed wrong with the world. The war in Vietnam was on everybody's mind. Every day we would hear about the number of men who had died and folks said there were more Black men fighting on the front lines than white. They were drafting kids left and right, and we worried they would take my brother, Wayman, who graduated with the class of '67. We didn't have to worry about Donald.

We didn't see much of Donald anymore. During his second stint at the Youth Study Center, none of us were allowed to visit him. It wasn't that he couldn't have visitors, Momma wouldn't let us go. After his first stay, Momma warned Donald that if he ever went back, she would not travel up to the jail to visit. She was true to her word. Donald didn't come back home after that. He spent most of his time at Aunt Susan's house. Then we got a call one day. Donald was in the Army. And whatever problems he had, the Army would have to deal with him. Well…that didn't quite work out the way we hoped, either.

Donald made it out of basic training at Fort Bragg in North Carolina okay, but when they sent him to Thailand, something went wrong. According to my brother, who was always known for telling the tallest tales, he was in the middle of the marketplace playing his conga drums. The sun was shining brightly. Donald's eyes were covered with dark shades. In the midst of playing, the intensity of the heat caused his lenses to crack. The lenses on the right cracked into a positive symbol; the one on the left displayed the minus sign. The people in the marketplace thought it was a sign from God.

"Jesus, Jesus," they shouted. "Jesus!"

Donald continued to play. It was hot. The rays from the sun beamed down, covering his whole body. His hair, a golden blonde, framed his creamy tan face, giving him that holy look that we always recognized, and that's why we nicknamed him Jesus.

The police were alarmed by the growing crowd that continued to call out the name of Jesus. Finally, Donald was taken into custody and put in jail. However, that didn't stop the gathering crowd. They lined themselves up outside the jailhouse and continued to call for the appearance of the holy man. Somebody called the State Department and the State Department called Momma.

"Your son has caused a bit of disturbance in Thailand," the white man on the phone said, (Momma said she could tell by his voice that he was white) "and you need to bring him home as soon as possible."

"So...why you calling me?" Momma responded. And then she hung up the phone. Donald had been discharged, dishonorably, from the Army. The military was no longer responsible for him. Nobody could explain why he was still in Thailand. But none of that mattered. Momma couldn't afford to pay for him to come home. The State Department would have to take care of it.

We thought that we would never see Donald again. When he finally showed up, less than nine months after he enlisted and several weeks after the phone call, he said that the Army decided that they didn't need his services or special talents any more. He knew that we were in trouble and needed some help, but Donald took to the road and became a real traveling man: a road runner.

Momma never did go back to work at the Caldwell Dress Company. The welfare checks kept coining, but Momma kept talking about getting a job in an office or something like that. She wanted to study typing and shorthand to see if she could be a secretary.

Darlene and Wayman had real jobs, making about $1.25 an hour. It was a big boost to Momma 'cause anybody who had a job had to give up half of their pay. I think Darlene and Wayman were starting to get mad about it, but as long as they lived in Momma's house, there was nothing that they could do.

For the first time in memory, it was good to be a member of the Colored race. Everybody wanted to be Black, even the high yellow kids who always thought that light skin and straight hair were better than our tight, curly locks. Shouting "Black Power" was the rage of all the teenagers, and singing along with James Brown, "Say it Loud, I'm Black and I'm Proud," was the in thing, although most folks were just pretending. When Amy Mack showed up at the high school in a natural, the kids pointed her out, laughed and made fun behind her back. I thought she was brave, and beautiful, so I washed the heat out of my hair and showed up in an Afro that had not had the benefit of being shaped or trimmed. They laughed at me, too, and the folks on the block stopped saying that I was cute. But the folks at the dancing school, where I was deep in the throes of studying African dance, thought I had the look of an African Queen. I was cool and mature. They all encouraged me to leave my hair in its natural state. Sharon, Anita and Max all followed suit.

Dougie and I made peace and became close friends. No matter what his preferences were, he was still a member of the Crew. Dougie was harassed throughout his school years at Sayre and John Bartram High. Always the target of many taunts and jeers, I felt the need to defend him whenever I could. It's strange how you can love and hate a person at the same time. And Dougie finally confessed that most of the stories about him and the Crew being involved in unimaginable sexual activities were lies to make me jealous. I guess it made me feel better.

All of us in the class of '68 were stunned by the assassination of Martin Luther King. He was the leader of the Black race. We talked about it a lot and didn't know what was about to happen. I thought North Philadelphia was about to be on fire. Then, as we approached the prom and graduation season, we just forgot about it and went about our business like nothing had ever happened.

Jessica and Marie were no longer the baby girls that they used to be. Both of them were taller than me and I couldn't believe that I ended up being the short girl in the family. They were tall, thin and beautiful with store bought hair hanging down their backs. Lots of boys started to visit them, and Momma was always talking about getting a shotgun.

Finally, at last, we had a kitchen. We started to cook real meals again. The, stove, the sink, and the oven were simply beautiful. As it turned out, none of the girls, except maybe Darlene, spent too much time learning how to cook. We could boil eggs, scramble ground beef, and deep fry some chicken backs and necks, but that was about all. Daddy, Granny and Grandmother Jessie were all good cooks, but they didn't pass on any of their cooking secrets to us, or maybe we just weren't interested. And cleaning house was also one of our short suits. We certainly knew about the need for Black women to be skillful in cooking good meals and keeping a clean house, but we weren't trying to be domestics. However, we did know how to look fine.

We knew how to buy material on sale at the downtown Grant's Five and Ten Cents Store and make gorgeous, colorful outfits that no one else had. We knew how to paint our cheeks with a red rouge, color our lips a ruby red, and cover our eyelids with a powder blue. We knew how to accessorize with matching rings, earrings and bracelets from the John's Bargain stores. And we knew how to pull ourselves together, the best we knew how, and present ourselves to the world like we owned it. Grandmother Jessie, and Momma, they taught all of us girls how to do all that.

30

1969

I hadn't known him that long. Ronald Charles was his name. Following our first paid gig as professional dancers at the Imperial Ballroom on 60ᵗʰ Street, Sharon, Maxine and I went up to Germantown to crash a fraternity party. We didn't know much about the fraternity, Omega Psi Phi, and knew little of fraternity men. But we were certain that we could get into the party by flashing a little bit of flesh and using some sophisticated charm. Mini-skirts and halter tops were in vogue and all three of our dresses were twelve inches above the knee and four inches below the cheeks. And the older we got, the better we looked.

Sharon was the cute one, especially since she wasn't a hair over 4' 11". Her honey brown skin was smooth and pimple free, with dark brown eyes to match. The large, circular shaped black mole on the right side of her cheek was one of her most prominent features. The beauty mark drew everyone's attention. The short, form-fitting, thigh-clinging blue dress she wore that night was an eye-catcher, too.

Sharon may have been the cute one, but, without a shadow of a doubt, Maxine was the sexiest. Max was only a quarter inch taller than Sharon and built like a *Brick House*. She was superb at flashing her big brown eyes (which were framed by a heavy application of black mascara on her lashes), and speaking in a low, high-pitched, seductive voice. She wore her hair permed, in a short tapered cut, and always looked like she was about to come and get you. Hot pink was her color, and she wore it well.

Well...at least I was smart. That's what I often told myself to reaffirm my specialness. And I had proven that I was pretty smart by getting a full tuition scholarship to Cabrini College one year after graduating from high school in the top fifth of my class, even with all those dummy-down courses that I was forced to take. Sister Barbara, the Dean from the all white girls' Catholic college, saw me dancing my heart out in the local production of *Wake Up Man and Live*. I had finally made it in an off-Broadway type of production. She asked if I wanted to attend her college. Sounded good to me. I gave up my day job as numbers file clerk at the Lit Brothers Department Store and entered Cabrini as a freshman in the fall of 1969. It's not like I had more brains than Sharon and Max; I was smart for taking Cabrini College up on their offer.

That night I wore a strapless, lavender and pink chiffon dress that gathered above the chest and was held together by a piece of elastic I took out of a pair of Momma's old stretch pants. I made it especially for the occasion in less than one hour. The four yards of cloth with pink cotton liner twirled every time I made a move. It forced you to guess about the contours of my figure, but left little to the imagination. The three of us were a popular trio wherever we traveled, and charming our way into the party with a bunch of horny, sexually-charged fraternity boys would not be a problem.

It was Ronald who came to the door at the house on Price Street and asked us for three dollars apiece. I was the designated talker and explained that we didn't have any money, but we wanted to come to the party anyway. I had to talk fast, convincing him that we belonged inside. We told the cab driver, who was waiting at the curb, that we would collect the money for the fare from one of the party guests as soon as we got inside. We had no intention of paying him, either.

"You must think you're cute!" he responded in an arrogantly cocky manner.

"It never crossed my mind," I retorted with an equal dose of confidence and quick wit.

After several biting exchanges, Ronald finally relented and allowed us to enter the frat party, free of charge. I feasted my eyes on all the good-looking men in the room - every shade of the colored spectrum was present. The brothers were short and muscular, tall and thin, and soft and sinewy with small, medium and super-sized Afros. I wanted to wrap my arms around every single one of them. Rest assured, I was about to have a good time.

"Stay there," he hollered as I made my way through the crowded room trying to identify my first conquest.

"Just who did he think he was?" I thought to myself. Three dollars bought you a few seconds of my time, but no more. Ronald was already acting like he owned me.

"You Got me Going in Circles" was blaring on the stereophonic house speakers. Suddenly the mood had shifted from James Brown's funky version of *Cold Sweat* to the slow drag. Ronald wanted to grab me before anybody else had a chance, making certain that he was first to do the slow grind. It reminded me a little bit of the old antics of the Crew. If any other brothers were eyeing me, they never stood a chance. I was surrounded by his physical presence and captivated by his charm. It was a feeling of wonderment. I forgot about Sharon and Max. They had to fend for themselves.

The first time ever I saw your face...kissed your mouth ...and laid with you.

It was a quick courtship; just a few months before I finally gave in. The baby had visited me within hours of conception and I knew I was pregnant. With all my worldly hopes, dreams and aspirations, I was still too dumb and misinformed to know anything about birth control.

Now, I was a distressingly unsophisticated, pregnant teenager living on the 16th block of Chelten Avenue. I was totally unfamiliar with this new section of the city everyone called West Oak Lane. Black folks fleeing the slums of North and West Philadelphia started to take over this part of town in the mid 1960s. The houses in the neighborhood were quite nice. Stone facades, black wrought iron rails and ivy-laced lawns dotted the landscape in this upwardly mobile Black middle class neighborhood. We, on the other hand, were a little less fortunate.

My new home was a clean storefront that had been turned into an apartment. The spatial arrangements were awkwardly strange. Really, quite distressing! You could walk right off the street into the living room. There were no stairs or steps. The bedroom followed, then the kitchen and, finally, the bathroom backed up against the fire exit that was to be used only in the case of an emergency.

I hated the idea of entertaining. We didn't have any furniture in the front room and visitors had to travel through the bedroom to get to the kitchen. At least in that room you could take a seat. We borrowed a hand-me-down kitchen set from the basement of Ronald's parents. It was a light grey speckled table with four matching light blue vinyl chairs.

My world had been turned upside down. I was five months pregnant. The baby was due in November. I was clueless about every stage of the pregnancy and never bothered to tell Momma, Jessica or Marie about my condition. We never talked about sex. Hell, I never had a sex life to talk about. Momma warned us that we better not get pregnant, but she didn't tell us how to prevent it. And Darlene was long gone. She married some boy named John from South Philly. I was supposed to be the maid of honor at her wedding, but on the day of the ceremony she changed her mind. She married John in some judge's chambers and came back to the house for the reception, which really seemed more like a block party to me.

I had finally done it. I disgraced the family with my teenage pregnancy. Everyone always said that I was going to be trouble. I would be the one and, as Granny always said, "the proof is in the pudding." Miss Special K finally had something to be real special about.

Married and living on my own, I convinced myself that I had handled things the best way I knew how. I kept thinking about how I got to this point. What had gone wrong? Once I realized I was pregnant, I knew staying at home was not an option. Wayman, Jessica, Marie,

Alfred and Suzette were all still at home. There were too many mouths to feed. Momma's life was rough enough without me adding to her burden. She was struggling to make it on welfare. The checks continued to come every month, but it wasn't enough. After twenty years of working at the dress factory, Momma was resentful of her status as a welfare mother. She was always looking for work, although she stopped showing her union card. Besides, Momma always said, "If you get pregnant, you get out...don't think about coming back to stay!"

For a brief moment, I planned to run away by myself and get a cheap apartment in Camden, New Jersey. I could work, maybe as a waitress or salesgirl, until the baby was due, and then I would go on welfare until I got back on my feet. Camden, I heard tell, was right across the river. Lots of welfare people lived in Camden and I wouldn't be too far from home. But Ronald said that he would have none of that. He had been raised right by his mama, daddy and the Reverend Leon H. Sulllivan at Zion Baptist Church. Marriage was the responsible thing to do. And he was not about to shirk his responsibility. Yet, I was certain that I wasn't quite ready.

I was lonely and isolated in the new apartment. I didn't know anyone else who was pregnant. I was blazing a new path on my own. Sometimes I would walk up and down the street and go window shopping. Although I was nineteen, my youthful face belied my true age. Black and white women with saddened faces would stare at me, silently conveying the "you're a disgrace" message as they shook their heads in disbelief. I tried, albeit sheepishly, to flash my new diamond ring to show that I was married a lady. They never stayed around long enough to see it.

Bored and completely unoccupied, I started to watch soap operas. *Another World* with Miss Rachel was my favorite. All the drama surrounding the engagement of Steve and Alice when Rachel revealed that she was pregnant with Steve's baby was particularly titillating to me. It was pure, unadulterated scandal and I loved it. It was like having an out of body experience everyday at 3:00. For half an hour, I was a member of the small town community in Pine Valley, Somewhere, USA.

I heard the phone ring, but I didn't want to be interrupted. Watching *Another World* was the highlight of my day.

"Patricia?" I heard her question, "it's Momma."

I was somewhat surprised. Momma hadn't called much since I married Ronald. I waited until a month after the wedding to tell her I was pregnant. While the evidence was overwhelming, everyone was blind to my condition, or so they said. I hadn't known my husband that long, and I was skinnier than ever. I was so traumatized by the loss of my virginity, pregnancy, quick engagement and upcoming marriage that I started to lose rather than gain weight. Jessica said that I looked like one of the kids from Biafra that we would see on late night TV begging to be fed by the people in the free world. Rather than my trademark tight fitting mini-skirts and halter tops, I took to wearing unattractive, loose-fitting clothes and cried at the drop of a pin. It was the biggest secret. I didn't tell Deborah, Sharon, Anita or Maxine, and I didn't tell the Crew, although I think Butchy knew and he wasn't happy about it. And even though Momma made the wedding gown, she feigned total ignorance of my expectancy.

I announced my engagement, planned the wedding and moved out of the house within three months. When I finally told Momma that I was having a baby, she asked me why. Why did I march down the aisle, in a white wedding gown with tiny little pearls that she had sewn by hand on the bridal train, with four bridesmaids in pumpkin orange dresses and a flower girl? She hadn't talked to me since.

"Hi Momma," I responded enthusiastically. "I'm here watching Miss Rachel mess up everybody's life on *Another World*. Are you watching it, too?"

What was I thinking? Momma never called and certainly not in the middle of the day on a Friday afternoon. Something must be wrong.

"Your father is in Miseracordia Hospital, she said. "I think you should go see him."

"Why?" I questioned, irritable and inquisitive at the same time. "Why should I go see Daddy?"

I was puzzled. I hadn't seen my Daddy in months, or was it years? I didn't even invite him to the wedding. I did send an invitation to

Granny's house, with everybody's name on it: Rosa Reid, Lee Reid, and Curtis Reid. Daddy said it wasn't proper, so no one from Daddy's side of the family came to the church. Brother Vernard, looking frightfully nervous and stiff as a board in his black tuxedo with the ruffled white shirt, walked me down the aisle and gave me away…to Ronald. I felt no shame. After all, I didn't want Daddy to arrive at the church smelling like liquor, eyeing Momma up and down and getting ready to start some trouble.

"Your father is real sick and he's been asking to see you."

As she talked about my Daddy, there were feelings of warmth and concern in her voice that had been missing for years. Had she gone looking for love and found it in my daddy?

"How sick is he?" I demanded to know right away. "Is he going to die?" I inquired in a panic stricken voice. Morbidly fearful of death and dying, it was always the first option considered when confronted with any illness.

There was a brief moment of silence. "No," Momma said assuredly, "He's not going to die, but you should go and visit your father."

I dropped the receiver, hard. I sat there quietly, staring at the TV. How much of *Another World* had I missed?

I couldn't remember the last time I had a conversation with Daddy. We had drifted so far apart. Before he decided to leave, for good, I was angry that he stayed home for so long. Momma was so unhappy and she cried an awful lot. All of us kids sided with Momma. Daddy was the villain, the bad guy, a total fuck-up. He needed to go and we were happy when Daddy finally vacated the premises. As the years passed, I missed not having a father. But I never wanted Daddy to come back home. I hated what he represented: an unemployed, alcoholic, overweight mama's boy. Yes, a heavyweight. That's the image I now carried with me of my father.

I traveled by bus and subway back to West Philly to see Daddy at Miseracordia Hospital. I wore my white and green seersucker maternity dress with the checkered print pattern. I hated it. It was unattractive, unappealing and totally unfashionable. I couldn't wait to get my figure back after the baby was born. I wanted to wear mini-skirts, tight pants and a two piece bathing suit.

It was a two hour ride from West Oak Lane to West Philly. I thought an awful lot about how Daddy used to be before his life fell apart - taking me to the bar on holidays, bringing me presents from Casa Conti and giving me money to buy penny candy. How he still would call me Prima Donna even when Momma, threatening him with bodily harm, told him to stop. I was Daddy's favorite. I wondered if he missed me all the time that he was gone. He never called. He never visited. I guess not.

I was too scared to go through the front doors. I looked up at the giant building with the hard red brick surrounded by all those tiny little row houses and imagined that Daddy was somewhere in there, probably on the 13th floor. I paced anxiously in front of the hospital steps and walked around the block three times before I gathered enough courage to go in. I despised hospitals. I didn't like the hospital smell. Antiseptic. Mediciny. Clean, but not clean like Granny's Clorox.

Miseracordia was a Catholic hospital. Once you passed through the double doors you were transported to an unfamiliar place. I couldn't tell if the nurses were nuns or vice versa. They all seemed to be wearing white uniforms with habits. I struggled toward the information desk, inquired about where I could find my daddy and followed the instructions to the tee: *Walk down to your right, take the elevator to the fifth floor, make a right and walk all the way down the hall, pass Cardiac Care until you reach the end of the ward. You'll find him there.* Even the directions seemed frightening.

But seeing Daddy lying there in the hospital bed was unsettling. Tubes were running up his nose, around his arm and under the bed. And there was an awful stench about him. I wanted to run, turn right around and go back to the apartment on Chelten Avenue. I was overwhelmed with emotion, none of which I fully understood. There was instant guilt about the wedding, not really inviting him and letting brother Vernard walk me down the church aisle. And here I stood pregnant, the first one in the family. Did he know about my condition?

There were feelings of anger, too. After all, his illness was his own fault. He drank too much, ate too much, and just didn't care enough about himself to take care of his own body. I was searching for ways to justify the distance that I had put between me and my Daddy. Whatever had gone wrong, it wasn't my fault.

Daddy looked horrific. "*Like death warmed over,*" I thought to myself. How could I possibly know what death looked like? I had never seen a real dead person up close. But it was the only thought that came to mind as I took my first glimpse of Daddy. And that's what Granny used to say when anybody was in a degenerative state.

It was a dreadful sight. He tossed and turned as he struggled to make himself comfortable. It was difficult for him to move his body around in such a small bed. He looked like he was suffering. I sat down in the grey leather hospital chair next to his bed and attempted to compose myself before speaking.

My emotions raced from sorrow and self pity to frustration and rage. I was emotionally unstable and, unbeknownst to me at the time, had begun my rapidly spiraling descent into a deep depression. My life was in turmoil. Just at the moment when I thought my whole future was on track, I turned up as a pregnant nineteen year-old married woman. Did I know how to be a wife? A mother? A woman? I thought about my love for the theater, dancing and the performing arts and wondered if my fledgling career was already over. I missed Momma, Marie, Jessica, Wayman, Darlene, Donald, Alfred, Suzette and the Crew. Most days, I just wanted to go back home to Catherine Street.

My concentration was interrupted by the sudden appearance of a stellar-looking young brother who quickly glided into the room. It was the attending physician making his rounds. He stood there at my daddy's bedside - chocolate brown skin, chiseled features, medium-sized Afro and not a day over thirty. Gorgeous. I leaped to my feet and, with uncontrollable emotion, blurted out my most pressing concern.

"Is he going to die?"

My directness was unexpected. For a brief moment, the doctor appeared startled and hesitated before he responded.

"Are you a member of the family?" he asked, recovering quickly from his momentary hesitation.

"Yes. I'm his daughter," I uttered, trying to choke back the tears.

He smiled. "No," he confidently responded. "He's not going to die. But he has to stop drinking or it will kill him."

Those words were such a relief. The doctor continued to go about his business. He reviewed the charts, checked Daddy's pulse and pressure, and examined the skinny little white sheets spitting out of the ticker machine before he turned to leave the room. He had a curious look about him as he hurriedly brushed by me. Suddenly he turned about, gave me a quick glance and approached me as I stood waiting in the doorway.

"Are you seeing someone?"

"About what?" I snapped. What a stupid ass question, I thought to myself. Why was he questioning me? Was he trying to pick me up? Was he being fresh? What about my Daddy? Did he discover something new in the examination that was cause for worry?

He smiled, again. "You are pregnant, aren't you?" he gently questioned. "When is your baby due?"

"In November," I responded in a much calmer tone.

"You should check with your physician," he said. "I think you could put on a few pounds."

I was stunned. Totally embarrassed. Felt every bit like a complete asshole. Just how bad did I look? Jessica told me that I had the appearance of a starving child from Biafra, but I didn't realize that others would draw the same conclusion. I must've been a ghastly sight: five foot three, 102 pounds and five months pregnant. No wonder the doctor took notice. I would go stuff myself at Gino's Restaurant with cheeseburgers and French fries as soon as I left the hospital. But right now, I still had to deal with my daddy.

Nervously, I approached Daddy's bed. I wasn't certain that he recognized me.

"Daddy," I whispered quietly. "It's me. Patricia."

I repeated my name over and over again. There was a confused look on his face.

"Patricia...Daddy," I said again. "Patricia Ann. Prima Donna."

He rolled to his left side and looked at me in bewilderment. For several seconds he laid motionless staring at my face. He recognized my voice and, I'm certain, felt my presence. I was relieved, but still didn't know what to say or what to talk about. And I didn't want to touch him.

He looked disgusting.

"How are you doing, Daddy? How are you feeling?"

There was no response, just pain, misery and discomfort. That's all I could see in my father's face. He was trying to say something. I leaned forward, carefully concealing my protruding belly. He struggled to speak. I lowered my ear and leaned even closer to him.

"Of all of my children..."

His voice crackled. It was weak and void of the soft melodic tones that used to greet me when he came home from Casa Conti restaurant. His breathing was labored and the closer I got the more pungent the odor. The tubes in his nose hung over his face, making it difficult for him to continue. I could feel his anguish, his sense of urgency. He struggled to speak.

"Yes Daddy...Yes Daddy..."

"Of all my children..." he whispered, "I never thought that you would turn on me."

I never stopped crying, on the bus, the Market Street El, the subway, or as I walked the two blocks from the C bus to the walk-in apartment. I wept for two whole hours. I had been a terrible, terrible daughter. I neglected my father when he needed me the most. How was I going to repair the relationship? I didn't invite him to the wedding, didn't let him walk me down the aisle and didn't want him present at the reception. I was ashamed that he was my father. I didn't even have the nerve to tell him that I was pregnant with his first grandchild.

"Fix it. Fix it," that's what I thought to myself. "Whenever you have a problem, just fix it." That's what Grandmother Jessie used to say. If you were smart enough, and worked hard enough, you could fix anything. In the morning, I would begin the repair.

31

Mr. Chew Redux

"Patricia," she said without warning. "It's Momma. Your Daddy is dead."

There was an eerie, deadening silence. I could hear the slow and deliberate breathing, carefully measured inhales and exhales at the other end of the phone. Within a split second, the fondest memories of Daddy flooded my mind, soaking every available cell of my membrane. Just as suddenly, feelings of anger and rage captured my emotions. I was furious. I screamed back at Momma.

"You told me that he wasn't going to die. The doctor said he wasn't going to die. How did this happen?"

Whatever she said, it just didn't matter. I was in a state of shock. Total denial. This was all like a bad dream. It was not really happening. It was eight in the evening. I was home by myself when I got the news and ran back and forth in the three room apartment thinking out loud and talking to myself.

"Daddy's not really dead,' I screamed out loud. "He's only 42 years old. The doctor said that all he had to do was stop drinking. There must be some mistake. Just like that time they mixed me up in the hospital and gave me to the wrong mother. These hospitals don't really know what they're doing. Daddy's not dead and gone," I continued screaming in a delusional state. "After I get some rest, things will be better in the morning."

I remembered to call Ronald, who was working as a technician at the Philadelphia Electric Company. He called his dad, who quickly made his way over to the storefront apartment and waited with me until Ronald came home.

For several days I remained in a fog. Barely lucid. I couldn't, or wouldn't, talk to anybody. I grieved silently, then openly. I didn't know what to do. But one thing was for certain - a funeral was being planned and there was no way that I could avoid attending this one. Another body was on its way to Mr. Chew.

We all gathered at Momma's house. Everyone had on proper funeral clothes. Momma, Vernard, Donald, Wayman and Darlene wore black. Jessica and Marie wore white because they were still teenagers. I wore my much-hated white and green seersucker maternity dress because I was pregnant. Alfred and Suzette stayed home. I wondered who was babysitting this time.

A black limousine pulled up in front of the house. This was the second time the family would be taking a ride in a big limo; it would be my first. All the neighbors came out on the front porches and stared at us as we entered the car. Somber, wide-eyed, curious faces silently portrayed their sorrow, much like my own. As soon as the doors shut, Darlene and Donald started cracking Heavyweight jokes. I stared aimlessly out the window.

"Don't act like that!" Darlene shouted. "You know there ain't nothing wrong with you. We couldn't stand Heavyweight. That includes you. Ain't no use pretending now. Stop acting like Miss Special K."

I refused to respond. I wasn't going to talk to anybody. I dreaded this moment. I didn't want to go and see Daddy in a coffin for the last time and I found absolutely no solace in being with my sisters and brothers. Whatever people did at funerals, I was not going to do. I wasn't going to walk up to the coffin and look at the dead body. I wasn't going to kiss the corpse goodbye. And I wasn't going to scream, whoop and holler and fall out in the funeral parlor. I wanted to be dignified. I would carry myself like Grandmother Jessie. She was an elegant lady with class.

We all lined up in birth order and marched ourselves into Mr. Chew's. We seated ourselves on the first row: Momma first, then Vernard, Donald, Darlene, Wayman, me, Jessica and Marie. I remember sitting down, but little else. I quickly scanned the place – dark, velvet red curtains, chairs and a coffin. My eyes were fixated on the cardboard clock taped to the inside cover of the gray coffin. It was set at 12:52, the official time of death. It was the dumbest thing I ever saw. It reminded me of the pumpkins and Pilgrims we used to cut out and paste on colored cardboard at Harrity School. And the clock looked cheap. Real cheap.

I could see the body peeking out from the box. I saw Daddy's face, which looked much darker in death, and his jet black wavy hair which gave the appearance of being slicked down with Murray's grease. It would be the last time he had use for the orange can with the big black print. I still couldn't believe that it was true. People were talking, but I couldn't hear them. They walked back and forth from their seats to the coffin. But I refused to move. I sat there motionless, filled with empty sorrow, as if my soul was hollow.

Everybody tried to act proper. Donald and Darlene stopped cracking jokes and sat there, respectfully. Momma was trying to comfort everyone. Pop Pop wasn't saying much of anything. Aunt Susan, who was the only one of Daddy's sisters and brothers to come to the funeral, mourned and cried out loud. But Granny…she was the saddest of them all.

"My baby, my baby," she wailed. "Jesus, Lord…help me now," she cried out. "I can't take this pain and sorrow. Why my baby? Why my Curtis?"

When the undertaker instructed us to come and view the body for the last time, I refused to go. I sat there, alone, and cried.

We rose to follow the coffin to the hearse. I was trembling, shaking like a leaf. I held on to Wayman as we started to leave the funeral home. Jessica went straight to Momma.

"Patricia's not right," Jessica insisted. "I think she's having conniptions"

"Where's her husband?" Momma wanted to know.

"Nobody knows," Darlene said loud and sarcastically. "We haven't seen him and he wasn't at the funeral."

Momma was first to see Ronald approach as the processional made its way to the front door. He had just arrived. He explained that he stopped to get a haircut at the local barbershop and, because it was crowded, missed the whole thing.

Momma was steaming a little bit. She wanted to admonish him for not being there to provide support and comfort, but he was a new member to the family, and Momma didn't know him that well. In her view, he was a new husband who wasn't performing in his role very well.

"Patricia's at risk," she coldly stated. "I don't think she's going to make it. Take her home."

I sat in the car and watched as the black hearse, the flower car and the black limousine with everybody else in it but me headed west toward Eden where they last visited four years ago. That's when they left my Grandmother Jessie's body there in an unmarked grave, right on top of Great Grandmother Pattie. And now they would leave Daddy's dead body at Eden and drop him in an unmarked grave too. But there was one good thing about Daddy dying...we never had to worry about him again.

32

Tina Mina

"Ooh child, things are going to be easier.
Ooh child things'll be brighter."

The baby arrived, prematurely, two and a half months later. It was a girl: four pounds, eleven ounces, seventeen and a half inches long. I looked at her carefully when she came out. Nobody would be switching babies on me. We gave her a proper name, but because she was the tiniest baby I've ever seen, I silently began to call her Tina Mina. I sat around the hospital for four days watching the new mothers care for their infants. I didn't get to hold and feed my baby because she was too fragile. They placed her in an incubator and watched carefully over her for the first few days. I thought a great deal about how my life would be different and how Tina Mina would have a life unlike my own. A stable two-parent family, loving grandparents, and doting aunts and uncles awaited this new arrival. She was the first born grandchild on both sides of the family. Everyone would be as happy as me.

All the new mothers were wheeled to the front door with their babies in their arms as they departed the hospital. They didn't send a wheelchair for me. I walked to the front door and waited for Ronald to pick me up.

People called to offer congratulations and came by the house to see the new baby, but she wasn't there. It made for a few awkward moments. People laughed when I told them that it was a premature birth. "That's what all the girls say that have babies within nine months of their marriage," they teased. The hospital would keep her for twenty-three days until she finally weighed five pounds. When she hit that milestone, I carried her home.

I learned how to prepare formula, use thermometers and treat diaper rash. I bought new baby books to help guide me through the process. I was going to be a good mother, and thought all the new psychology books on childrearing would help. I would learn later that Dr. Spock never raised a Black child and his "talking therapy advice" did not apply to our children.

Just before Tina Mina turned five months, I decided to take her to see Granny. A wall of silence now stood between our family, Pop Pop and Granny. And all communication had ceased. Pop Pop was never close to us as children; he even had difficulty remembering our names. We hadn't seen Granny much after Daddy left us. When Daddy moved back to the basement, Granny stopped visiting. In fact, she never stepped foot inside our house again. Whatever we were feeling about Daddy's relationship to Granny and the effect of his premature demise, nobody was saying.

Winter was not quite through and spring had not yet arrived. It was still cold. I wrapped Tina Mina up in a pink snowsuit, tied a white bonnet on her head and covered her face with a hand crocheted, white lace blanket. I carried a pink and white baby bag on my right shoulder. I was happy to get back into my old clothes again and picked out the sharpest pants outfit in the closet. I wanted to look the way Granny remembered me: young, thin, pretty and innocent. We boarded the bus on Broad Street and headed toward West Philly.

I stood at the door shivering and clutching the baby as I waited for Granny to answer. I knew she had to be home because Granny never went anywhere. I was praying that she would answer soon because I needed to rest before heading back to West Oak Lane. I hoped that I didn't make this trip for nothing.

"Hi Granny," I shouted with enthusiasm when the door finally swung open.

"Oh my God, Patricia," she said with the broadest grin. "Your Granny's so happy to see you." Granny knew each and every one of her grandkids and I knew that her expressions of joy were genuine.

I hadn't been to the basement in years, but nothing had changed. The atmosphere stank, heavy with a damp musky smell of dirt floors and concrete walls without windows. All the furniture in the living room was a dingy grey, as if covered by soot from a coal burning stove. The tables, lamps and assorted curios were all junkyard variety antiques. The brown wooden box radio continued to work even though the burlap fiber which covered the speaker had shed its existence long ago. It was tuned to WHAT AM and Mary Mason was talking about some hot issue of importance to the city's Black community. An ancient TV box sat in the corner of the living room. It hadn't worked properly for years. The audio came through loud and clear, but there was no picture. All it was missing was a transistor tube, but Pop Pop decided that it didn't need to be repaired. It remained because it doubled as a table top and continued to fulfill its role as furniture. And there were plenty of black and white photos on top of the half-functioning TV set. Pictures of Daddy, Pop Pop, Suzanne, Uncle Herman, Cousin Richard and Jessica and me.

"I brought my baby by so you could get to see her," I said with a great amount of glee.

Granny quickly grabbed Tina Mina and held her closely in her arms. She sat on the dingy grey couch and carefully unwrapped the white crocheted blanket which covered the baby's face. Granny removed the white bonnet and expertly slipped her out of the pink snowsuit. She examined the baby closely, checking her hands, fingers and ears while gently brushing her straight black hair. I cautiously grabbed all of Tina Mina's belongings and placed them on top of my lap. I couldn't let them out of my sight. I had to make certain that we didn't take any critters home with us.

"Oh, the baby doesn't look like anybody in the family," Granny said lovingly. "She gonna have your color, but a little darker. Look here. See the ears and these knuckles?"

"Yes, Granny," I whispered uneasily as I took the baby out of her arms. My child wasn't about to be judged by the color test. Knowing how important the color thing is to Black folks, I wasn't surprised by Granny's comment. However, I was happy that the color thing was finally coming to an end. Everybody was talking about Black pride and Black power. People were giving up their processed hair and hot combs for afros. Black was in vogue. Everybody was saying, "The blacker the berry the sweeter the juice."

"Your Daddy was a beautiful corpse."

She caught me off guard. I didn't know what to say. Who in their right mind would comment on the beauty of a corpse? I stared at Granny and could see that she still had the death look all over her face. Granny grieved hard and it was difficult to watch her suffering. I guess nothing in life prepares you for the death of a child. And this was Granny's second loss. Maggie died in childbirth at age sixteen when they couldn't get a doctor to come to the house and the hospital would not take her in. She needed a c-section and they couldn't afford it. Now my Daddy, her baby boy, was gone, too. It had been seven months since he passed away, but she talked about his funeral like it was yesterday.

"Yes Granny, Daddy was a beautiful corpse," I said. I just repeated what she said. I didn't have anything else to add to the conversation. I couldn't wait to leave.

Jessica called me the following Saturday and told me that Granny was dead. She had died in her sleep in the big double bed that she sometimes shared with Pop Pop and sometimes with Daddy. She was a diabetic and, for whatever reason, stopped taking her medication.

The fighting started right away. Aunt Susan blamed Pop Pop. She insisted that a quick visit to the emergency room would have saved her life. Aunt Varnell and Uncle Lee (whom I never met) blamed Daddy. They insisted that Granny had grieved herself to death. She just couldn't bear to be without her baby, who not long ago had departed this earth. She couldn't cut him loose.

If there was a funeral and a burial service, I knew nothing about it. I was deep in depression. But I was fairly certain that they took her body to Mr. Chew's and then to Eden and left her there without a headstone or any mention of who she was in this life. That's what they did with everybody else. But for me, nothing much in life mattered anymore... except how I was gonna raise this child.

Grandmother Pattie wanted the best for Jessie; Jessie wanted the best for Momma; Momma wanted the best for me; and just like the three generations before me, I wanted nothing but the best for Tina Mina. She had been born to save my life.

33

Get a Grip!

Again, I felt the tight grip on my chest and lamented my growing breast size. I'm from a family of big-breasted women and I, unfortunately, was well on my way to joining the rest of the clan.

I cautiously applied my right foot to the brakes as I neared the end of the block. *"Exactly what did I expect to find: The Crew gathering on the street corner; little kids playing in front of the Lyons' house; or, Mr. Frazier, sitting on the porch in a white tee shirt with a can of Ballantine Beer in his hand?"* Catherine Street still looked the same, although the houses seemed smaller than ever. *Did all ten of us really live in that tiny little row house?* I had just passed the bar at the other end of the block. Kelly's was no longer the name, but the game remained the same. Local folks were still running in and out in the middle of the day trying to get a quick taste of something. The saloon business was thriving.

Sharon Baptist Church stood firmly on the northeast corner. I remember marching my pregnant self down the aisle in the white wedding gown that Momma made for me with the four bridesmaids in orange pumpkin gowns. The chicken and fish store survived too, along with the cleaners, but the drug store was no longer there. It had been converted to a nail salon - all Asian workers, all Black clientele. What an interesting twist.

For a brief moment, I slipped into a nostalgic trance, remembering life as it used to be. The memories of the good old days were fresh, but the era was long past gone. I added a good twenty minutes to my trip to Eden because I deviated from I-95 and jumped on the Skuylkill Expressway just to take a peek at life on the old block.

I rarely went back home, only for funerals. And it wasn't the mamas and papas of the Crew who were old and dropping dead like flies, or sick and in frail health. It was the members of the Crew who were the first to go.

Donny, Butchy and Bucky's youngest brother, died of a single gunshot wound to the chest before his seventeenth birthday. Lump was murdered (they say a $100.00 contract hit) when he was twenty-three. Denny died of A.I.D.S. just a few years back. Champ was in jail for life, fighting a daily battle to retain his manhood. Butchy had been married and divorced with three children of his own. His oldest son was in jail for murder. Butchy, too, spent some time in Graterford Prison shortly after I left the block, but for a much lesser crime. He was back home, living with mom and pop. A severe case of arthritis left him unable to work full-time. Putt Putt became a police officer and Dougie was a hairdresser. I did see Musk. He was as big as ever, at least 275 pounds. He was wandering around the block in a vacuous state looking for some adventure. I didn't stop and get out of the car. *"Would he still recognize me?"*

I continued straight on Catherine Street until I hit Cobbs Creek Parkway. I turned left to pick up Baltimore Pike and headed into Collingdale. All this time I thought that Eden was in Philadelphia. When I called Sharon for directions, I discovered that it was actually in Collingdale, Pennsylvania. Same difference. Collingdale is a small, little suburban town bordering Philadelphia on the west side. In the late 1960s, white folks from Philly started moving there to avoid integration with the Black folks. It was a good spot for white flight.

Eden wasn't hard to find. As I approached, I saw the tombstones shooting up from the ground. You could see the marble headstones from the left side of the road and giant miniature buildings that, I think, they call mausoleums. Some were large and magnificent looking; others were plain and simple. There were rows and rows of dead people that had been properly laid to rest. I felt a surge of guilt as I pulled into the front gates made of ornate, heavy wrought iron bars. That's when I noticed the sign: *Mount Zion Cemetery*. This, I was quickly informed, was not Eden.

"If you travel down a little further," the elderly white man told me, "you'll find Eden on this same side of the road. Just a little further down, keep on going till you see it."

Eden was less than a half mile down the road. When I pulled into the driveway, I knew this was the place where Black folks were buried. There were headstones and grave markers, but they looked nothing like the large, well maintained, neatly manicured plots at Mount Zion. The small, smoky gray, hut-looking structure to the right said "visitors." This was the place. I pulled the car off the road onto the dirt driveway and parked near the front door. I checked my makeup in the rear view window to see if I still looked decent. I took a couple of deep breaths, adjusted my tight undergarment and thought about composing myself before I walked through the door. This very image had played through my mind's eye a thousand times before this moment.

It was worse than I imagined. The room was dark, dank and distressing. It was poorly lit with zero ambiance. And a tall, small-framed, lanky-looking Black man in a dark gray or black work suit sat silently at the old commercial grade steel desk, just like the ones they used to have in all of the government's public offices twenty-five years ago. He was perfectly cast; he looked just like a character out of a Boris Karloff or Bela Lagosi movie. Vincent Price had to be lurking somewhere in the background.

"Can'I help yu," he mumbled, breaking the silence that stood between me, him and the gray walls.

"I'm trying to find some graves," I said, rather apologetically. My voice was weak, my speech slurred, like I had been intoxicated the night before. "I'm looking for my father and grandmothers," I added with a little more strength and certainty.

The caretaker jumped up from his desk and went to the one file cabinet that stood in the left-hand corner of the room. His energetic movements belied his ghastly appearance.

"What year?"

"Pardon?"

"What year? When they die?"

"One in 1959 and another in 1966," I loudly stated. "One in 1970 and another in 1971," I continued. He was making me nervous. This was only the first stage of the process and I was feeling unsure of myself.

"What's the name?" was his next question.

He reached into the top drawer and pulled out a black and white marble composition book, the same kind of books Momma used to buy, three for a dollar, at the John's Bargain Store on 52nd Street.

"What year?" he said again as he flipped through the pages looking for the names of the deceased.

I was stunned by their form of record keeping - black and white elementary school composition book. Didn't they know about computers? What if there was a fire? Or even a flood? Everything would be washed away, destroyed forever. I'd never find my relatives.

"Can you find them?" I blurted out anxiously.

"I can!" he said. "We knows where peoples is buried."

I sat there, patiently, hoping that sweat beads weren't about to pop up on my forehead. The room was hot and muggy, lacking the benefit of an air conditioner. I looked around a couple of times and imagined how bad this would be as a lasting memory of where you left your loved ones.

"One in Douglass," he mumbled, "the other in Letson Martin: Lots 1246 and 1378. Come, I'll show yu."

He closed the composition books (there were several by now) and carefully replaced them in the file cabinet. He walked slowly to the front door and pointed me in the direction of the Leston section and then to Douglass. *Was I supposed to find these graves by myself?*

I started walking in the direction of Douglass, which was closest to the caretaker's hut. I followed a winding path through the cemetery. He followed close behind. I looked to my right and left and thought about all the names I saw on the headstones. I didn't know any of them.

"Why you come?" he asked in an expressionless voice with the accent of the old south.

I hesitated, turned around and looked at him before I responded. He looked me dead in the eye. "Just something I needed to do," I uttered.

He steered me to the right and, eventually, on a path that required that we walk on top of the graves of the Colored dead.

"Right here," he said. "Right here!" He stopped in the middle of a rough patch of grass. A place where you could sit down and rest your feet for a minute as you viewed all the other gravesites.

"Right where?" I thought to myself. I was standing on top of a patch of freshly-mowed weeds and crabgrass. I saw nothing indicating that this was a gravesite and, more importantly, I sensed nothing. Didn't feel a damn thing. If this was the final resting place of my Daddy and Granny, their bones and spirits weren't talking to me today.

"How do you know they're there?" I questioned.

"We knows," he responded. "Yo daddy in there."

I looked down a couple of times, stared at the ground and walked around this fake gravesite. I wanted to do something, say a prayer, drop a tear or pour a libation. None of that seemed right at the time. And I wasn't about to act a fool in front of this stranger.

"You wanna see the other?" he interrupted, putting a temporary end to my confused state.

"Yes," I replied confidently. I felt much stronger now, and whatever fears I had about feeling the rising spirits of the dearly departed, reaching out from their graves, just to touch me, were greatly diminished.

We began walking toward the furthest edge of Eden. The cemetery was bordered by single homes with swing sets and above ground swimming pools in the backyards. Grandmother Jessie and Great Grandmother Pattie were there in Leston, closest to the people with the barbeque grills. While they were celebrating the summer, eating hot dogs, hamburgers and barbeque ribs, Grandmother Jessie and

Great Grandmother Pattie were lying there under freshly-mowed weeds and crabgrass waiting for someone to remember that they, too, had walked this Earth.

He said they were there, and I had to take his word for it. If no one had told me, I would have assumed it was a worthless section of land in an old colored cemetery on the outskirts of Philadelphia. I stood there for a few minutes, staring at the weeds and the crabgrass, trying to conjure up some emotion. I started to feel something. It was relief.

"Thank you," I said, "thank you very much." I turned on my heel and walked away.

He had stood there the whole while, watching me as I stared at the ground, quietly and respectfully. He looked me dead in the eye only once when he asked why I had come to Eden. He knew I had traveled far. My New Jersey license plates with tags that said "Afro-One" told him that.

I remained pensive on my way back, not knowing what to say or if a conversation of any kind was necessary. "*Thirty years*" is what I kept repeating to myself. *"It's been more than thirty years since anyone went to see about Daddy, Granny, Grandmother Jessie and Great Grandmother Pattie."*

"You gonna mark those graves?" he asked just as my Madza 929 came into view.

"Yes," I said with a tone of finality. "I'm gonna do just that."

34

Report From the Field

I stopped by Momma's first to tell her I had gone to Eden. Momma lived in a senior citizens complex in Mount Holly, New Jersey, close to me. Momma has MS. She has been confined to a wheelchair for twenty years, but she's still strong and fighting for the right to exist on her own terms. Momma was surprised that I went and equally curious about what I found. I tried to tell her everything, from beginning to end.

"Do you want go?" I asked rather excitedly.

"No," she responded matter of factly. "I don't wanna go there." And that's when she began to recall her memories of growing up in the North and the South, of living for a period of time without her mother and of all the struggles that separated her from her mother, and her from her daddy. I had heard some of this story before, but now, in the later years of her life, she was willing to fill in the details about the strange going-ons that were an integral part of her upbringing. It was the first time she admitted that Mother wanted all of her girls - Momma, Aunt Savannah, Aunt Dorethea and Aunt Nita - to follow in her footsteps, in a lifestyle she had been introduced to by Lester. He understood how good looks could be sold and bartered for cash and favors. It was their decision to do otherwise that began to split the family apart. Or maybe it was before that, when

Grandmother Jessie and Great Grandmother Pattie fought about the booze, the house, and the men who frequently came in and out. But maybe it started even earlier, when Grandmother Jessie, a rebellious teenager and fine young thing, plucked Lester from the altar just minutes before he was about to marry some other woman in Danville, Virginia, and ran off with him to Conshohocken, Pennsylvania.

Momma had other issues she was struggling with, especially about Brother Vernanrd. She never really had a relationship with his daddy, an older man that she met through all the strange going-ons at Mother's. And it was Mother who introduced Vernanrd to his lifestyle of drinking and bartending at such an early age. Momma was unhappy about that, too. Vernard was fascinated by the lifestyle and never gave much thought to doing anything else.

Momma talked about Daddy, too, about the years she spent with a mama's boy and how hard she tried to encourage her girls never to do the same. That was one thing that Mamma could brag about. All of the Reid kids survived. Jessica, Marie, Suzette, Darlene and I were all professional women with successful careers and with husbands who were not mama's boys. Vernard, Donald, Wayman and Al were still struggling to free themselves from demons; substance abuse of one form or another consumed their lives. We keep praying that one of them emerges at the top.

I rushed home and called Jessica. She wanted to hear about everything. That didn't surprise me because Jessica always responded to whatever you needed.

I called Darlene next. She laughed when I told her about my day trip to Eden and added, just before she hung up the phone, "Whatever floats your boat."

I had to remind myself that I was the strange one in the family and my quest to bring closure to the lives of my ancestors had great meaning to me, but no one else.

I couldn't wait to tell Bill when he got home (Ronald and I divorced after ten years of marriage. My only son and daughter represent the very best of our marriage). I knew Bill would listen attentively to anything that I said. We had only been married for eight years and the honeymoon was still on. And I talked on and on about my day at Eden.

Over the next several weeks I thought about what I was going to do and how I was going to do it. I wanted to be grand and put large marble headstones, like mini mausoleums, on each gravesite. When Sharon gave me the price list, I quickly dismissed that as a fantasy notion. Way out of my reach. I thought about asking the family if they all wanted to contribute. Fat chance. That would be like trying to squeeze blood from a turnip, as Granny used to say. This was not something that any of them was truly interested in. Smaller marble grave markers would have to do. At about 1,800.00 each, I should be able to afford to do this on my own.

I carefully planned an African ceremony, relying on all the knowledge I had collected over the years as a student of African and African American culture. I would dress in traditional clothing, drape my neck with a strip of Kente from my West African heritage, grab my cha umoja cup, a bottle of spirits and stand over the grave and offer a libation. I would invite the whole family and see if anybody showed up. I would order two grave markers:

CURTIS MACDONALD REID

SON

1927-1970

AND

ROSA HILL REID

MOTHER

1907 – 1971

DEAD BUT NOT GONE

JESSIE MAE CHAPEL

DAUGHTER

1904 – 1966

AND

PATTIE MARIE WRIGHT

MOTHER

1959

DEAD BUT NOT GONE

For me, this was almost over. I was glad that I got this far, even happier that I didn't kill myself when, just after Tina Mina was born, I was depressed out of my mind and felt that I could not live to face tomorrow. The more I talked about Jessie Chapel, Great Grandmother Pattie, Granny and Daddy, the more information was revealed about all the hidden secrets in our family life. I started to understand things I never understood before. And the more information I collected, the more certain I was that, one day, I would write a book about it.

It was the end of November, not yet cold enough to call the days winter. I had yet to order the headstones but I knew, eventually, I would. We had just left Darlene's for Thanksgiving dinner. It was done, as always, in the tradition of Grandmother Jessie: turkey, roast, chicken and salmon were surrounded by macaroni and cheese, cranberry sauce, mixed vegetables, candied yams, collard greens, string beans, brown rice, sweet potato pies, cakes, cookies and ice cream. Most of us were there: Momma, Aunt Nita, Darlene and John, Jessica and Ron, Marie and Arvid, me and Bill, Suzette, Al and a bunch of nieces and nephews. As always, we talked about the past, the good and the bad, and argued about the difference between the truth and a lie. I was unusually defensive because I made everybody uncomfortable with all the truths that I insisted were part of the family history. I had interviewed every elder in the family by then, and I had answers that no one else had. We, indeed, had a special history and a legacy... a tarnished legacy.

"Even if it is true," Marie shouted, "It would be too embarrassing to tell anybody. And who would want to read it?"

I left Darlene's home questioning my own motives. *"Why is the telling of this story so important to me? What could be gained by revealing my family's tarnished past? Was Marie right?"*

I was restless when I went to bed. I'm an incurable insomniac and sleep is always difficult to come by. I knew this night would be no exception. I was still hungry, but decided that it was too late to start eating again. Since I stopped eating meat, I never seemed to get that satiated feeling that comes along with wolfing down a plate of pork ribs, a Philly cheese steak, or a roast beef sandwich.

I wanted to scream when I saw her standing there in the corner, but I didn't feel frightened. I was just searching for my voice. She had on the same light-colored flowing dress that I remembered so well. Her hair was pulled closely to her head, I think, covered with a hair-net. She wore the same pair of oval-framed glasses that were always close by her bedside table. I knew I had to be dreaming, but I couldn't wake myself up. I was stuck between light sleep and bright conscious-ness, but my brain was functioning perfectly well. I was being visited by the dead and I didn't know what I was supposed to do. This was the third time in my life that I was standing face to face with a dead person.

First, Uncle Andrew scared me half to death when I was eight years old. He hadn't been dead for 24 hours before he decided to pay a visit from Deadland. Over time, the terror of that experience faded. I had convinced myself that all young children have nightmares, and it was really bad.

The second time was in 1983. I was just starting my fall semester at Stockton College and was enrolled in the doctoral program at the University of Pennsylvania at the same time. Money was tight and I didn't know where I would get the last few thousand dollars to pay my tuition bill. Having been a scholarship recipient all of my academic life, paying for tuition was news to me. Daddy came to me the day before Labor Day. I saw him lying there in his coffin with the cheap cardboard clock on top of the casket. There were three numbers posted on the front side of the coffin: 436. Daddy didn't move or speak from the box or anything crazy like that. He just laid there with his Murray-slick, wavy hair resting on the pillow, but his hands were placed close to the numbers. I was terrified when I awoke from that dream because Daddy had been dead for thirteen years and not once did he pay me a visit. In fact, I didn't think about Daddy at all.

I went to the family barbeque the next day and told everybody about what happened the night before.

"Play that number," they all shouted. "Play that number."

"They must be crazy," I thought to myself. I had a master's degree and was working on a doctorate from an Ivy League school. I was a college professor who knew something about the world. I didn't play numbers, and certainly not ones that came to you in dreams. Only root folks did that.

I went to school the next day and joked with my colleague, Bob Helsabeck, about the dream visit from my dead daddy and how my family encouraged me to play the numbers. He was a sociologist and, I think, I was giving him an example of Black folk ghetto culture.

The numbers, 436, came out that night. I, of course, didn't have a dime on it. I was "too smart" to act like I was the product of my people. I felt like an idiot. And I still owed a bunch of money to the University of Pennsylvania.

I told Momma that the number came out, and that I had not played it. She had strong words of advice: "The next time your father comes to you," she snapped, "you better listen." He never visited me again.

I was willing to listen this time because I knew that Grandmother Jessie wasn't standing there in the corner for nothing. I could smell the funk from the sweat dripping down from under my armpit and tried to remember if I had taken a shower before I went to bed. I hope she wasn't there trying to take me someplace. Maybe I should pray, call on Jesus or something like that. I stared at her for a few seconds longer, hoping that she would just fade away. But I wasn't afraid. She wasn't about to harm me.

Grandmother Jessie lifted her right arm, extended her hand and pointed her index finger at me. She was about to tell me something, in the same manner that she did when she gave us instructions on how to behave at Chapel's Luncheonette.

"Get it right," she said in a whisper. "Get it right."

I jumped out of the bed and stared at the corner one more time. I rubbed my eyes and started crying at the same time. She was gone. The only thing remaining was the scent of lavender.

35

Journey's End

Several years passed before I finally gathered up the courage, time and money needed to complete this journey. I called everyone in the family and told them that the headstones had been purchased and placed on the graves. I was planning a tribute to our ancestors and I wanted them to be there. I had to watch the Weather Channel four days prior to every Saturday in the fall in order to pick a day when I could guarantee that the sun would be shinning. The second Saturday in October was a promising day, and a celebration was being planned at Eden.

Darlene told me to pick her up at 10:30 at her home in Willingboro. She was in the midst of planning a wedding for her daughter, Khara, but "I wouldn't miss this for the world," she assured me. Years had passed since the difficult days of our childhood and Darlene and I were closer than ever. Aunt Nita said that she would meet us there. She wanted to be a part of any special tribute to Mother and Grandmother Pattie. Everyone else said that they were too busy, or that I haven't given them enough advance notice.

We drove straight to Eden. I knew exactly how to find my way there. The old gray looking building had a fresh coat of white paint. All the caretakers still looked a little bit strange to me. I had called in advance to tell them that I was coming, and they were waiting at the gate when I arrived. Now I was looking for six graves: Great Grandmother Pattie, Grandmother Jessie, Daddy, Granny, Wayman and Vernard.

Wayman, who was struggling to make it to the very end, died the day after my 50th birthday. It was a tragic bus accident on the SEPTA line, which had long ago replaced the old PTC. The shock and grief overwhelmed us all, never thinking that we would lose a sibling so early in life. It left a deep, penetrating hole in my heart that's been difficult to overcome.

We were still in deep mourning when Vernard left us two months later. The health clinic called Jessica to inform her that Vernard had missed two of his dialysis treatments. Vernard suffered for years from kidney failure and dialysis was keeping him alive. When Jessica and her husband Ron went to check on him, they found him dead, sitting in his black recliner in front of the television set with a bowl of popcorn. Who would be next to follow?

We stopped at the section named Douglass first. The beautiful headstone was there indicating, finally, that this was the resting place of Curtis M. Reid and Rosa Hill Reid. Wayman was in there, too. We had him cremated, his ashes interned with Daddy and Granny. He would have wanted it that way.

My Kente cloth hung loosely around my neck. I stood over the grave like I was endowed with some special ceremonial powers. I poured a libation (I brought a bottle of **Old Grand Dad** from home), said a brief prayer and placed flowers on the grave. Darlene and I talked about how important it was for us to be there and how this was a very precious moment. The caretaker just watched — silently wondering why I was pouring that goddamn good liquor on the ground.

Next, we drove over to Letson Martin to see Grandmother Jessie and Great Grandmother Pattie. The headstone was there; it, too, was beautiful. I poured some extra **Old Grand Dad** on the grave, (it was Grandmother Pattie's favorite), said a little prayer and placed the fresh flowers on the marble face. However, something didn't seem right. But, just like before, there was no sign from the ancestors.

When we finally arrived at the next section of Letson Martin to view the resting place of my dear brother Vernard, that's when it hit me, like a jolt from afar. I felt the power of the spirit, talking to me loud and clear. I looked at the stone. It said Vernard Vincent Chapel. And I knew he was not in there.

"He's not here," I shouted to the caretaker. "My brother is not here. My Grandmother Jessie and Great Grandmother Pattie are here, but Vernard is not!"

By this time, I was absolutely certain that Eden had mixed up the headstones. An argument ensued, with the caretaker insisting that the marking on the grave was correct. Aunt Nita had arrived by then and Darlene was explaining, "Patricia has gone ballistic. She says they marked the wrong graves...and I think she would know."

We compared notes, theirs in the black and white marble composition book, and me with my memory of small houses, swing sets, above-ground swimming pools and barbeques within viewing distance of my grandmothers' graves. Finally, they admitted that an error had occurred. They promised they would make the correction first thing Monday morning. Now I would have to go back, at least one more time, to see if they were true to their word.

36

Epilogue

Years of reflection helped me to understand the hidden meaning to our family life. Now, I'm absolutely certain that there's no such thing as being dead and gone. In fact, the dead influence the living, for we all carry within us powerful images, etched in our minds and in our hearts, of those who have left us behind. Understanding their life, struggles, fears and joys provides insight and guidance to those of us willing to learn from the epic memories of those who have passed on.

I am not the product of a stellar group of characters whose life stories provide examples of outstanding social achievements, high moral standards and endless gifts to the world. You will not find their names recorded in history as those whose life's work must be remembered, and family members do not always recall their names with fondness. Based on a simple accident of birth, some of us inherit wealth, status, privilege and bragging rights about the good deeds of our ancestors, others, like me, inherit a tarnished legacy that is, at times, difficult to embrace.

My search for the truth revealed a family history filled with scandal, betrayal, guilt, shame, struggle and doubt, coupled with all the social pressures and social consequences of being poor and Black in America. But I also found that silver lining: a persistent form of eternal optimism uncovered in the strengths, positive attitudes and good deeds of those who struggled to balance good and evil. This, too, is my legacy and it allows me to sing to the glory and praise of my ancestors. And as Daddy always used to say: "The truth will set you free!"

Great Grandmother Pattie may have buried five husbands, drank like a sailor and fought, often, with her daughter, Jessie, about her nontraditional lifestyle. But she also cared a great deal about improving the quality of living for her children and grandchildren, and the standards by which they would lead an exemplary life.

Grandmother Jessie was a pistol; there's no denying that. But she fought hard to get her children back once they were removed from her care. She took in children, who were not her blood, and raised them like they were her own. She set high standards for living and giving, and worshipped faithfully at the First African Baptist Church every Sunday. And above all, she was an entrepreneur - a Colored business woman who struggled to make it the best way she knew how.

Granny's life was so limited; a poor, southern rural woman who was destined to spend more than twenty-five years in a basement in the big city. And Lord knows, she probably loved my Daddy too much and turned him into a mama's boy. But Granny was always there when we needed her. She cooked the food, cleaned the house, sent us outside to play, cleaned and dressed properly, and taught us how to pray and stand reverent in the face of the Lord.

My Daddy stayed in trouble most of his life, and died way before this time. But not before giving the world eight offspring that, eventually, would make him proud. When the pressures of the world weighed heavy on his shoulders, Daddy would sing and dance to chase his woes away. He was creative in his approach to life, always ready to make something out of nothing. He passed his creative genes on to us. Suzette is the singer, Al is the musician and I'm the dancer.

It is difficult to accept the troubled paths that they chose, but easier to understand when viewed from the prism of Black life in

America. Race, class, gender, color, and poverty were the defining forces within and outside the community. Just learning to survive from day to day is, for many, life's greatest challenge. You're forced to "play the hand that you're dealt."

In appreciation of my worldly existence, I give respect and homage to all of my ancestors. I've accomplished what they could only dream about. And for this, I am most grateful. They deserved to be recognized and, in keeping with African traditions, we must continue to speak their names in order to keep their memories alive. I want the world to know that they were once here - free, wild, vibrant, colorful characters who learned how to make do. Marking their graves was an important first step. Not just for me, or members of my family, but for strangers, a mere passerby. A quick glimpse of the names on the grave markers would offer a brief remembrance of their existence.

We have gathered to celebrate the passing of our ancestors and the legacy that they left behind. It was the right thing to do. Marking their graves was the best way to let them know that we're all okay. We have apologized for the time it took for us to complete this task, and acknowledged that it was the many unresolved issues with the survivors that forced their memories into darkness. We tried to erase all the bad, but we also took away the good. Facing some of the most difficult obstacles in life, we found a way to reach for a higher plane. The power of the spirit rages within all of us and, as a family, we will remain strong for many generations to come.

I was born on Halloween. The day after my birth, the temperature soared to a record high, providing a brief respite from the cool chill of the fall season with a bright, warm sunny day. Momma was terrified for 24 hours when she realized that her baby had been switched with another. But I ended up in the right place, in the arms of a loving mother who would guide me through life.

On the day that Momma and Daddy took me home, Granny looked up to the sky in search of a sign. She was an old-fashioned,

EPILOGUE

root woman who placed her trust in her faith and the ways of the old world. She warned that I would be special, that it was important that Momma and Daddy learn to watch, carefully, over me. Granny was right. I am special...I am the link between the living and the dead.

... 249 ...

CPSIA information can be obtained
at www.ICGtesting.com
Printed in the USA
BVOW11s0426140517

484049BV00002BA/328/P